Dec 2023

The Schoolgirl, Her Teacher *and* His Wife

To my Beautiful
Sister
Enjoy!
Jo x

REBECCA
HAZEL

The Schoolgirl, Her Teacher *and* His Wife

VINTAGE BOOKS
Australia

VINTAGE

UK | USA | Canada | Ireland | Australia
India | New Zealand | South Africa | China

Vintage is part of the Penguin Random House group of companies
whose addresses can be found at global.penguinrandomhouse.com

First published by Vintage in 2023

Cover images © Michael Pole/www.southernstockimages.com (apple),
Shutterstock (background)
Cover design by Alex Ross © Penguin Random House Australia Pty Ltd
Internal design by Midland Typesetters, Australia
Typeset in 12/18 pt Adobe Garamond Pro by Midland Typesetters

Printed and bound in Australia by Griffin Press, an accredited
ISO AS/NZS 14001 Environmental Management Systems printer

A catalogue record for this
book is available from the
National Library of Australia

ISBN 978 0 14379 633 6

penguin.com.au

We at Penguin Random House Australia acknowledge that Aboriginal and Torres Strait Islander peoples are the Traditional Custodians and the first storytellers of the lands on which we live and work. We honour Aboriginal and Torres Strait Islander peoples' continuous connection to Country, waters, skies and communities. We celebrate Aboriginal and Torres Strait Islander stories, traditions and living cultures; and we pay our respects to Elders past and present.

Contents

Quotes from the transcript of the 2003 inquest into the death of Lynette Joy Dawson, V5795 40/03 RC–A1, 24–28 February 2003, have been edited to correct grammatical errors.

Timeline of events

26 March 1970	Lynette Simms and Chris Dawson marry.
9 July 1977	XD is born.
11 July 1979	YD is born.
1979	Chris begins working as a physical education teacher at Cromer High School.
1980	JC and Chris Dawson begin a sexual relationship while she is in Year 11.
October 1981	JC moves in with Chris and Lynette.
November 1981	Lynette learns about Chris and JC's relationship.

23 December 1981	Chris and JC leave Sydney, but turn around at the Queensland border, returning on Christmas Day.
2 January 1982	JC goes camping with her friends at South West Rocks.
8 January 1982	Lynette speaks to her mother, Helena Simms, on the phone at around 9 pm.
9 January 1982	Chris says he drops Lynette off at a bus stop in Mona Vale early in the morning. He then meets Helena at Northbridge Baths. While there, he says Lynette rings him and tells him she's going away.
10–15 January 1982	Chris drives to South West Rocks, collects JC and installs her at the Dawson family home in Bayview.
18 February 1982	Chris reports Lynette as a missing person at Mona Vale police station.
June 1983	Chris divorces Lynette.
15 January 1984	Chris and JC marry.
December 1984	Chris and JC move to Queensland.
8 January 1985	KD is born.
February 1985	A complaint to the New South Wales ombudsman leads to a review of Lynette's missing person file.

January 1990	JC leaves Chris and returns to Sydney with KD.
May 1990	JC goes to the police. An investigation begins.
1990	Police conduct a ground-penetrating radar search at Bayview. Nothing is found.
January 1991	Chris Dawson is questioned by police but the investigation ultimately leads to nothing.
July 1998	Detective Sergeant Damian Loone is given Lynette's missing person file.
January 2000	Damian Loone conducts a dig at Bayview. A pink cardigan is found.
February 2001	The first coronial inquest is held. Coroner Jan Stevenson refers the case to the Director of Public Prosecutions (DPP) with a recommendation that charges be laid. The DPP knocks it back, saying that there is not enough evidence.
February 2003	The second coronial inquest is held, lasting five days and calling on more than twenty witnesses. Coroner Carl Milovanovich's findings are the same as the first inquest and he refers the matter to the DPP. The DPP again elects not to lay charges.

2011	Damian Loone submits further evidence. The DPP again declines to proceed.
2015	New South Wales Police Force Unsolved Homicide Unit re-investigates.
April 2018	Detective Senior Constable Daniel Poole submits another brief to the DPP.
May 2018	*The Teacher's Pet* podcast is released, leading to renewed public interest in the case.
September 2018	Police carry out a new forensic dig at the former Dawson family home in Bayview. Nothing is found.
5 December 2018	Chris Dawson is charged with murder.
20 June 2019	Chris Dawson is charged with the historical sex offence of 'carnal knowledge by a teacher of girl between the ages of 10 and 17'.
15 July 2020	Chris Dawson's stay application is heard in the New South Wales Supreme Court.
9 May 2022	The murder trial begins.
30 August 2022	Chris Dawson is found guilty of the murder.
4 October 2022	Chris Dawson lodges a notice of intention to appeal his murder conviction.

2 December 2022	Chris Dawson is given a twenty-four-year sentence for the murder of his wife, Lynette.
29 May 2023	The carnal knowledge trial begins.
28 June 2023	Chris Dawson is found guilty of carnal knowledge.

Author's Note

WHEN I CONCEIVED OF WRITING THIS BOOK IN 2012, LYNETTE Dawson had been missing for thirty years. In the days after she disappeared, her faint presence hovered in her Bayview house for three days, until her husband moved a seventeen-year-old schoolgirl in, and Lynette was gone. Then the schoolgirl was sequestered in the house under Chris Dawson's controlling hand and she too faded from view. It seemed that anyone who could have helped these two women was bound in a conspiracy of silence, which flipped from one decade to the next. I wanted to tell their story.

I met the schoolgirl known as JC twenty-five years after Lynette disappeared. In unflinching detail she recounted the abuse that Chris Dawson inflicted on her and how he altered the direction of her life. She told me what she had witnessed in the eighteen months before Lynette disappeared and what happened afterwards.

In 2017 the journalist Hedley Thomas contacted me. I had only spoken to Hedley once, a few years earlier when I began the research for this book. We spoke and he told me then, 'It will be a great book.' He must have meant it because in 2017 he rang me to pitch an idea: he was going to make a podcast about Lynette's disappearance and he wanted me to join him. To say 'the rest is history' is an overused and sometimes misused expression, but *The Teacher's Pet* podcast did make history in Australia and around the world.

The book I started writing in 2012 has expanded twice, before finally being published in 2023 in this, its current form. In 2018 I included material about *The Teacher's Pet* podcast. On the eve of that version being published, in December 2018, Chris Dawson was unexpectedly, and remarkably, charged with Lynette's murder. My publisher immediately halted publication because the law of *sub judice* – Latin for 'under a judge' – prohibits the publication of material that might influence a matter before a court, especially a jury. The book has therefore expanded again, to cover Chris Dawson's murder trial in 2022 and the events leading up to it.

So what had changed – why was Chris Dawson charged with murder in 2018 and not in the thirty-six years after Lynette disappeared? How did the witnesses I spoke to some years before Chris Dawson was charged with murder stand up in court? Had 80 million downloads of *The Teacher's Pet* podcast forced the hand of police and the Director of Public Prosecutions (DPP), or had crucial new evidence been uncovered? I was still wrestling with these questions in the days after Dawson was arrested, when two detectives came to my house.

When the trial was over, I could compare what I had uncovered while writing this book with the evidence that was shared in the trial. Was the evidence in the trial any different to what was available in 1982 when Lynette disappeared?

This story began long before a podcast or a trial.

Prologue

I FIRST HEARD ABOUT LYNETTE DAWSON IN 2007, TWENTY-FIVE YEARS after she disappeared from her home on Sydney's Northern Beaches. I was working as a lawyer in a women's refuge, not far from where Lynette had lived in Bayview.

I would often drive to and from work the long way, following the road that tracked the jagged coastal ledge. On some days, big storms slammed massive swells of water onto the rock platforms. On others, the ocean was as calm as a bottle-green field. There were treats too – a pod of dolphins, a whale lolling close to shore or, further out, offering a farewelling spout of water as it headed north for winter. But at the refuge, 2 kilometres inland, there was no hint of the ocean. Dazed women arrived with their children, and in the communal kitchen and living spaces, they met and shared snippets of the ordeals that had brought them there. For the first couple of weeks they wouldn't venture out much, but eventually they'd find their way to the shopping centre, the park and the beach.

The staff didn't get out of the fibro cottage much either. The refuge consisted of two houses in a dull suburban street: one where the women slept, and the other – the fibro cottage – for the staff, where I shared an open-plan office in what would have once been someone's lounge room. We'd often sit together around the kitchen table and eat lunch. I liked sitting next to my colleague JC because she was smart and had a quick, dark sense of humour. I was in my early forties and, because I still had small children, I was always tired. JC was a year older than me but had a loose, jaunty manner, and when I was with her, I felt younger. One day, we were chatting about a trip to New York that I was planning.

'I bloody love that place,' she said. 'Nobody recognises me.'

'Are you famous?' I asked, jokingly.

'I'll tell you about it one day,' she said without humour, then abruptly pushed her chair back and walked off. In the days that followed, the conversation niggled at me.

A few weeks later, JC and I were in town for a meeting and afterwards we skived off to a café that made good coffee, something that wasn't easily found in the suburbs back then. At a little round table in the sun, and with some gentle probing, JC told me her story – or part of it.

'I married a man whose first wife had gone missing,' she began, and placed her cup heavily on the saucer. 'I moved into the house not long after. We got married a few years later.' Her voice turned hard, clipped. 'She's never been heard from since.'

As she spoke, she looked increasingly distressed. I saw a lot of distress at the refuge, but I couldn't get a read on what was going on with JC here. Did she still have strong feelings for this man? I knew that she was a single mother now, and I wondered if the divorce had been messy and painful. Was it this that had led her to work in a refuge?

'The police think that he killed her.'

We both fell silent. I felt the sun on my neck, tasted the bitterness of the coffee in my mouth. And when the shock of her words passed, I asked her his name.

'Chris Dawson,' she said flatly, like she was sick of saying it.

JC was seventeen when Chris Dawson's wife, Lynette, went missing in 1982, and she told me that within a few days of Lynette's disappearance Chris had moved her into his house with the Dawsons' two small children. Later, he and JC got married and had a daughter of their own. Then, after almost ten years, JC left Chris, taking only the little girl they'd had together.

Almost as an afterthought, she said, 'He was my teacher at school and whenever something like *this* comes up, they always drag me out as . . . I don't know.' She sounded frustrated, distressed too. 'I don't know what!'

What does she mean by *this*? I wondered. A teacher who lures a student into a relationship? A teacher who has a relationship with a student and whose wife disappears? JC shook her head, seemingly also confused by whatever *this* was, and why she was trapped by it.

'It's my life,' she said. 'It will never go away.'

I could see that she didn't want to talk anymore. We left soon after.

I came away confused, and with so many questions. It didn't make sense. How could Lynette Dawson just disappear? Wouldn't her family and friends have made a ruckus? What did the police do? What did the school do about a teacher having a sexual relationship with a student? And JC's parents? And how could the JC I knew have once been part of a story like this? What did JC think had happened to Lynette? And with her background, how could JC bring herself to be a resource worker in a women's refuge? Did working there remind her of the past? Or perhaps the tight security and practices at the refuge made her feel safe?

When I got home I googled Chris Dawson's name and dozens of articles came up – so many, in fact, that I couldn't understand how I'd missed the story over the years. At the time of Lynette's disappearance, Chris Dawson was a minor celebrity, having been a well-known rugby league player for the Newtown Jets, along with his identical twin, Paul. The two men were handsome and fit. And JC, his 'student lover', was always mentioned too. I began to read.

Many of the articles recycled the same two photos of Lynette and Chris. One was a black and white photo taken on their wedding day. Lynette is wearing a high-necked white dress with a daisy-chain headband and a long veil, and Chris has thick sideburns, and is in a slim-fitting suit with a ruffled shirt and a bow tie. He is leaning towards Lynette, and they look like an iconic 1970s Australian couple – happy, healthy, young and tanned.

In the other, they are sitting at the top of a football bleacher with one of their daughters. Chris is in shorts and a T-shirt and Lynette is wearing slacks and a jacket, with a scarf tied around her neck. Both parents are glancing down at their small daughter, who stands on Lynette's far side, not between them. They are both older than in their wedding photo, but there is something different about Lynette here – her hair is darker and shorter, and she's wearing large glasses. It's almost like motherhood has accelerated her maturity – has aged her – in a way that fatherhood doesn't seem to have affected Chris, who still looks fit, lean and handsome.

Many of the articles also featured a photo of JC when she was thirty-nine. In it, she is walking purposefully, wearing sunglasses and a bold pink blazer, and the wind is blowing her blonde hair back from her face as if to show off how beautiful she is. It's a powerful image. The sixteen-year-old schoolgirl who was groomed and abused by her teacher is gone and the mature woman is in charge now. There's a hint of arrogance to her as well, possibly because she's not looking directly at the camera. That frozen JC is nothing like the person I know.

The more articles I read, the more the same set of unsatisfying facts came up. It was clear that the police suspected Chris Dawson of killing his wife, and that JC's continued presence in his life was intricately connected with that suspicion. But if it was so clear, why wasn't he charged and tried? How was it possible that someone so strongly suspected of 'murder' hadn't been charged? Lynette's disappearance had attracted considerable attention, including two coronial inquests. Why had someone not been prosecuted? Could a murderer be living a pedestrian suburban life like the rest of us? Among us? Or had the police got it terribly wrong?

Back then, when JC first told me about this part of her life, I had three young children and a husband who travelled a lot. Those years were overly busy ones for me. Yet I kept thinking about Lynette: wondering about her life, her children's lives, imagining the sadness and complicated relationships that her disappearance must have left behind. One day, when my daughter was about two years old and I was bathing her, I suddenly became gripped with panic – she was the same age as Lynette's youngest daughter when Lynette went missing. As I knelt by the side of the bath, my daughter laughing as she splashed her fat hands on the water, it felt unbearable to imagine that I might never see her again. Even worse was the thought of her needing me and me not being there. There were other times with my children when I would think again of Lynette and remind myself not to take them for granted, not even on the bad days.

And I thought about JC's life, too. At work, I saw her a little differently, if only because I was looking for something that hinted at her past. I liked and respected her as much as ever, but it was as if a door had fallen open and she was the only person who could tell me what was on the other side. I kept looking to her for answers. Did she have trouble, as an adult and a mother, coming to terms with her relationship with her teacher-cum-husband? What did she tell her daughter about her father, knowing that as soon as she was old enough she would be able to read about him herself? Had JC's daughter stayed in touch with her father or her half-sisters? Did JC miss Lynette and Chris's girls? And how had Lynette's daughters fared, not knowing what had happened to their mother? And then losing JC too?

Some years later, when my children were at school and JC and I no longer worked together, I was still thinking about her. I often found myself tracing and retracing parts of her life as I tried to imagine what it must have felt like to have been involved with her school teacher, to have married him, then to have lived through everything that followed. Thoughts of Lynette were often with me, too. She was married with two children and she lived in a well-to-do, glamorous even, part of Sydney. She had a job, two brothers and a sister, and was close to her mother – from the outside she had a solid and safe middle-class life. If, in another universe, she had read about this happening to someone else, she probably would have thought, 'That could never happen to me, I have so many people who would come looking for me.' And yet, she vanished. She was just like me, and many women I knew, but a terrible thing happened to her, yet no one has been able to figure out precisely what.

My work at the refuge was connected with these worries. I could only remember one or two women who had arrived without their children, because in an unplanned moment they'd seen a chance to get out alive. They left because they wanted their children to have a mother, and once they were safely at the refuge, they frantically set about retrieving them. From the work I'd done as a lawyer in domestic violence, it was hard to believe that Lynette would have walked out on her two little girls, and even if she had, it was even more unlikely that no one would ever see or hear from her again. The law was mostly about paper trails, and I wondered where Lynette's ran out.

One day, I pulled out the file of newspaper articles I'd collected, and started writing. Since I was young, I've written as a way of making sense of things, usually on loose pieces of paper that I tear up and throw away as soon as I've finished. But I didn't discard what I wrote about Lynette and JC that day. I wanted to understand if Chris Dawson had anything to do with Lynette's disappearance. And why had JC's relationship with him continued to dominate her life?

In many of the articles I'd collected, Detective Sergeant Damian Loone of the New South Wales Police Force kept coming up. He'd already been investigating the case for ten years by the time I first heard from JC about Lynette's disappearance. It seemed that he couldn't turn away from it either. So I decided to try to find him.

Before I did, I wanted to read the transcript from the coronial inquest. There had been two inquests, one in 2001 and one in 2003. But only the 2003 inquest had called witnesses so it was this transcript that I wanted to get a copy of. I wanted to know what the witnesses had to say and to consider the evidence that the DPP had when he decided, twice, not to proceed with laying charges. And I didn't want to ask Detective Sergeant Loone questions I should have known the answers to.

I could have chosen to turn away from this dark story. It wasn't mine, after all. What exactly was I doing? Whatever had happened to Lynette Dawson all those years ago, her daughters, her family and her friends hadn't been able to turn away from it. And JC couldn't. So I decided not to either.

PART ONE

CHAPTER ONE

Damian Loone

THE NEW SOUTH WALES CORONERS COURT IN GLEBE, IN INNER-CITY Sydney, is a flat-roofed building that sits close to Parramatta Road. Those with the misfortune of having business there can often be seen smoking, or standing silently, on the narrow footpath outside, which is so close to the traffic that it's more like an extra lane. The building has been there for as long as I can remember. I used to pass it with my parents on our way in to the city and later, when I started work. In all those years, it seems that nothing about it has changed. I don't think it's even been given a fresh coat of paint.

The Coroners Court investigates 'reportable' deaths, which includes some 'natural' deaths, but also sudden deaths where the cause is unknown, or where the identity of the deceased is unknown, deaths in custody, and unnatural deaths from alcohol, drugs, suicide or homicide. Missing persons must also be reported to the Coroners Court when the police determine that the missing person is deceased. As part of the court's inquest, the coroner has the power to call witnesses to give evidence. When the investigation concludes, the coroner can make recommendations to improve public health and safety, or, if they believe an indictable offence might have been committed, they must suspend the inquest and refer the matter to the DPP with a recommendation that charges be laid. But it's the DPP alone that decides if there is enough evidence to get a conviction.

Lynette's disappearance has been the subject of not one but two inquests. The first one, in 2001, nineteen years after she went missing, was a paper committal. This means that the coroner read the police brief of evidence and was satisfied enough, without calling witnesses, to refer the file to the DPP with a recommendation that charges be laid. The coroner was named Jan Stevenson. To be a coroner, Jan would already have needed to be a magistrate (a judicial officer who determines matters in local courts). But the DPP declined to lay charges. Then, in 2003, a second inquest lasted five days and called on more than twenty witnesses. And it was the transcript from this inquest that I was trying to get my hands on.

I rang the Coroners Court and was advised to put my request in writing to the court registry. From there, we entered baseline rallies, with emails pinging back and forth without progress. Eventually, I received an email informing me that access to the transcript had been approved, subject to me paying an administrative fee. The next day I entered the grim, washed-out building that I'd passed so often before. At the glass-fronted registry counter I explained why I was there and the young man set about processing my payment.

I leaned on the counter and looked around. The bleak foyer had faded green carpet and exposed brick walls, and the furniture consisted of a row of plastic chairs bolted into a welded rod that ran underneath them. Compared to the family, district and supreme courts only a few kilometres away, it was a sorry and neglected building, inside and out.

'Here's your receipt,' the young man said chirpily. 'The file should be here tomorrow.'

Before I left, I slipped into one of the two courtrooms that the building housed. I bowed to the magistrate and a few people turned their heads to look at me. A young solicitor was on his feet. Beside him sat an older colleague, encouraging him as he tentatively asked a middle-aged man in the witness stand about the installation of fire safety equipment. The room was simply furnished, with pale bar tables, a wooden bench for the magistrate and plastic chairs in the gallery, where I sat down. The mood in the room was one of sombre boredom and after twenty minutes I left quietly, bowing again on the way out.

The following day I rang the registry and was told that the transcript was late and should be there the next day. But it wasn't there the next day or in the weeks to come. At first there was no explanation. Then I was told that they couldn't find the file, and then that the position of the person who retrieves the files was vacant, so there was no one to physically go and get it. I even fronted up at the counter a couple of times, hoping that my presence might inject some impetus, but still nothing happened.

So while I waited, I decided to contact Detective Sergeant Damian Loone. I'd read in one of the newspaper articles that he was based at The Rocks, so I rang the station. I expected that by now he would have moved on and hoped that they'd tell me where. But the young officer who answered the phone said, 'He's not here at the minute. Can I leave him a message?'

The following week, I caught the ferry from Manly to Circular Quay. It was a magnificent blue-sky day and as we chugged past the Heads, I played a game of picking the best secluded beach from the many dots of sand in Middle Harbour. I was annoyed that I hadn't been able to read the transcript of the inquest before meeting Damian, and I wondered if he was going to brush me off because I hadn't done my homework. I'd told him on the phone that I knew JC and that I was writing a book, which he seemed indifferent to.

In the thick crowd at the Quay, I glimpsed a blonde woman up ahead wearing sunglasses and carrying a black backpack. I only saw her for two or three seconds before she disappeared into the mass of commuters, but it was long enough for me to put the way she walked, and her hair, together. I zigzagged through the crowd, until it opened out into the park beside the Museum of Contemporary Art. I ran across the grass and up the sandstone steps to the cobbled streets of The Rocks, and when I caught up, I could see that it was JC.

I continued to follow her at a distance, spooked that I should see her there, on that day. I stopped in the middle of the footpath and the crowd streamed around me. Was she on her way to work? Or going to see Damian Loone too? But she continued up the hill past the police station without so much as a sideways glance – which made me think that she didn't even know that Damian was stationed there – and I watched until her blonde head disappeared. I steadied myself and decided to take this extraordinary coincidence as a good sign, an endorsement of what I had committed myself to.

It was a short, steep street, and I could see Damian Loone standing outside the station, smoking and talking to a man in a suit. I recognised him straightaway because his photo was often included in the articles I'd collected. He was wearing the blue police uniform and heavy black boots. I was wearing boots too, with a heel, but despite that, as I got close to him, I felt very small. I stood quietly and waited.

'Hi,' I said, when there was a break in the conversation. 'I'm Rebecca.'

Without even looking at me, he said, 'Wait inside. I'll be with you in a minute.'

I flushed with embarrassment. He'd seemed indifferent when we spoke by phone but his swift dismissal of me sent a different message. I felt that he'd very efficiently let me know that he wasn't going to do me any favours.

The station was in an old, cramped brown-brick building, with an arched wooden door. Inside, I sat in the small waiting room. A slim man in a grey suit stood with his hands on the open counter, talking with a female police officer about someone who had gone missing. She took notes in a spiral-bound notebook. The waiting room was so small that I felt uncomfortably close, almost part of their conversation.

'Are there any mental health issues?' the police officer asked him.

He began detailing a comprehensive list of his loved one's depressive episodes, medications and hospital stints. I watched as she wrote it all down in her police-issue pocket-sized notebook, wondering how many hundreds of them they must go through. Where did they keep them all? I could understand the little notebook when you were out and about, but here in the station? As I listened to the complicated case history, I was impressed by her respectful yet probing manner. She was caring but also straight-shooting, as if none of what she was hearing was unusual.

Just then, Damian strode through the arched front door and in one continuous movement managed to shake my hand and then punch a code into the keypad beside another door near the front counter.

'Follow me,' he said, without looking over his shoulder to see if I was. He led me through a maze of desks and cubicles, around an inconveniently placed stationery cabinet and printer, past a kitchenette squeezed into a tight corner, and up a flight of stairs, which I climbed with a little more ease than he did.

'You need to give the fags away,' I said, cheekily.

He let out a big, gravelly laugh. 'Barely in the door and you're having a go at me.'

There was hardly a sliver of natural light in the place, and although I sticky-beaked into each corridor and office we passed, I didn't see any glimpses of the harbour or the Opera House beyond. We reached a glass-fronted office with no windows, and Damian stood aside to let me in first. I felt that he was sizing me up, rather than being courteous. He motioned at me to take a seat on the other side of the desk, and then sat down in a big black chair. He leaned right back and stared down his nose at me.

'I was given Lynette Dawson's file in 1998,' he said, crossing his arms.

My pen lingered as I double-checked my calculation. That was sixteen years after Lynette had gone missing in 1982, and Damian's pause, I thought, was to let that sink in. By the time I came to be sitting in front of Damian, Lynette had been missing for more than thirty years.

'Well, you wouldn't call it a *file* . . . it was a piece of paper,' he continued distastefully, and rubbed his thumb and middle finger together, as if he were holding one flimsy piece of paper between them. I asked if he knew the original file number and after a few clicks on the computer he said, 'It was file number 07/29.'

It was still an open investigation, Damian explained, but I thought that his manner suggested that it wasn't as active as he might like. I should have asked him if that's what he meant but I was anxious to not criticise anyone at this early stage. Still, I thought then about the Coroners Court being unable to find Lynette's file, and an odd sensation came over me, as if I could see that Lynette had been disassembled into a file, and the file looked like all the others. How could they tell which one was hers?

Just then, the phone rang. 'Damian Loone,' he answered.

I looked around the room, following the etiquette of avoiding eye contact to signal that I wasn't listening to the conversation, when of course I was.

'I just want the texts that relate to the grooming,' he said, then hung up and looked at the desk briefly before directing his attention back to me. I could see he was trying to get back to where we'd been before the phone rang. I was too, but a dark beast had entered the room.

'Some job you've got here,' I said feebly, and he shrugged his shoulders.

'I can't believe they weren't knocking on doors,' he said, meaning the police. 'I see this all the time. People have a fight, one goes away to calm down. But they always come back. In 1991, Chris Dawson made his only statement to the police. He says that he dropped Lynette at the Mona Vale bus stop at 7 am on 9 January 1982. He said she was going to go shopping in Chatswood. He goes home, has breakfast with the children and then they all go to Northbridge Baths. That's the thing that raised my suspicions. Why wouldn't he drop her on the way?' He was staring at me, like he was expecting me to give him an answer. 'I don't know how well you know Sydney, but if I was going to Northbridge from the Northern Beaches, as he did later that morning, you go up over the Roseville Bridge and then out along Eastern Valley Way. You're virtually driving along the bottom of Chatswood then and there. Why wouldn't he just drop her on the way?'

In 1990, JC had spoken to the police about Chris and Lynette. 'But her interview wasn't in the file either,' Damian said, shaking his head in disbelief. He'd heard that a friend from his local surf club knew JC, so he got her number and asked her to come in for a chat. So, on 27 July 1998, only six days after Damian was given Lynette's missing person file, JC came in for an interview.

'I was investigating a missing person at that stage,' Damian said. 'After the information that I received from JC, it became clear to me that I'm looking at a homicide.'

I asked Damian if he ever suspected that JC might have had something to do with Lynette's disappearance. 'Absolutely not,' he said with certainty. 'She had everything to lose by coming to the police. She was a mature-age student then and her view was that she was highly suspicious. She just told us everything that happened.'

Three decades after Lynette went missing, and fifteen years after he was given her file, Damian was still speaking with energy and determination about the investigation. I asked what kept him going.

His face softened, his voice too. 'I have three sisters and I would leave no stone unturned if one of them went missing. I'd like to think the police would do that for me.'

Before I left I asked Damian for the address of the house in Bayview where the Dawsons had lived. 'Let me know what you think,' he said.

I wandered slowly back to the Quay and hopped on a ferry home. The harbour was as flat as an ice rink and the ferry seemed to glide its way back north. We were just past the Heads and only a few hundred metres from Manly Wharf when the engines suddenly cut out and squeals of delight erupted from one side of the boat. Everyone rushed over, causing the ferry to tilt precariously. Before us, a whale's barnacled head was gently breaking the water's surface. Phone cameras clicked furiously as the ferry drifted, letting the whale set its course around us.

When I got home, I wrote up my notes, sent another email to the Coroners Court, and then rode my bike in to Manly for a swim. As summer receded, the water was noticeably cooler each time I swam but that also meant it was clearer too. The ocean was almost as flat as the harbour had been, so I swam in the shallow water covering the rocks, my fingertips sometimes scraping their surface. Every now and then I hovered over a fish picking at some seagrass or darting in and out of a rock crevice, and when I started to feel cold, I swam hard over to Shelly Beach. On the swim back, I started thinking about going to have a look at the house in Bayview, and I knew the trip would be much better if I had JC with me, to tell me about the house and some of her memories of when she lived there.

I felt slightly sick. I knew the time had come to contact her and tell her what I was doing. There was a good chance that she'd be angry at me – very angry, because I knew that she was incensed every time a journalist asked her for a comment. She'd never spoken to any of them; she'd had enough of their lurid portrayals of her and she didn't trust them to do anything else. But I hoped that she would help me because the story of Lynette's disappearance was equally her story and I hoped that she might want to tell it her way.

CHAPTER TWO

Gilwinga Drive

ABOUT A WEEK LATER, I MADE THE DRIVE FROM THE NORTHERN Beaches to Northbridge, on Sydney's Upper North Shore. Just as Damian had said, I followed Warringah Road over the Roseville Bridge and then veered left onto Eastern Valley Way, at the bottom edge of Chatswood.

Chris Dawson had a summer job as a lifesaver at Northbridge Baths, where he was due at 9 am on 9 January 1982. Dropping Lynette off at the Chatswood shopping precinct on his way to the Baths would have taken an extra five minutes, and then Chris could have continued on to Northbridge, only a few minutes further along Eastern Valley Way. This would, in fact, have been far less effort than taking her to the bus stop at Mona Vale at 7 am. Their girls were four and two then, and the palaver of getting them into the car, driving Lynette to Mona Vale, going home, giving them breakfast, getting them ready for the day at Northbridge Baths and then back into the car would not have been insignificant. Any parent will recognise the difficulty of manoeuvring small children in and out of a car, especially for a man who'd left nearly all the childcare to his wife. What's more, in 1982, there was no direct bus from Mona Vale to Chatswood, so Lynette would have needed to change buses at Dee Why. Even with a good connection, the trip would have taken over an hour. Had they gone together in the car, Chris would have ended up dropping Lynette at Chatswood ten to fifteen minutes later than the bus would have gotten her there. And with most shops not opening until 9 am back then, there was no point in her arriving any earlier.

It wasn't until I did this dummy run that I remembered that many years ago, around 1997 or 1998, my husband worked in Chatswood and we used to go to a mechanic just off Eastern Valley Way. I'd drop my husband off at work, take the car to the mechanic, and then, with my first son still in a pram, I'd walk to the shopping centre while the car was being repaired. I was a few years behind Lynette, but I was struck by the ordinary coincidence. Even more surprising, though, was that although I'd been talking to Damian about Chatswood, I'd completely forgotten about the mechanic until I drove there. How were family and friends of Lynette's going to remember what had happened on 9 January 1982? Going to a mechanic and pushing a pram is so trivial, but her family and friends were being asked to remember similarly pedestrian details about a day that only became significant weeks or months, or decades, later.

I arrived and parked at the top of a steep driveway from which the water is completely hidden. Northbridge Baths is one of the many tidal pools that dot the Sydney Harbour foreshore – they are more low-key than the surf beaches, but just as beautiful. I walked carefully down the damp paved incline and could see a few houses nearby, camouflaged by the marshy bushland. The air was thick and moist, and the still water was cool and brackish; I knew from other harbour pools that I'd swum in that the water could be almost black after heavy rain had washed the topsoil down from the surrounding slopes.

The baths are enclosed by a netted boardwalk on three sides. This wooden perimeter exists not so much to mark out the pool as to keep the bull sharks out. The gate to the boardwalk was locked so I walked along the shore to the water's edge, where twigs and leaves floated in clumps. I sat down on a cold rock and wondered how such a beautiful and isolated place could be found in such a big city. I was seized by a strong urge to contact JC, so I reached for my phone and sent her a text message. It had been more than five years since we'd worked together and although we'd meant to stay in touch, time had slid by. I wasn't even sure if she still had the same phone number, but within a minute my phoned pinged. It was JC, and she said she'd love to meet for a coffee.

A few days later, I headed north to Dee Why Beach. The swimming area, park, playground and a string of cafés are all crammed into the beach's southern end and as I circled, looking for a parking spot, I could see JC, just as she'd said, waiting on the corner outside her favourite coffee shop.

When she saw me she stretched her arms out, smiling. 'Come here. Give me a big hug!' Sometimes she seemed petite or slight, like the day in the coffee shop when she told me about some of her history, and at other times, like today, she seemed strong, tall, happy, commanding – the JC that I knew best. It was good to see her again.

We took our coffees down to the beach and sat side by side, protected from the wind by the low wall built into the steep hill. We caught up on each other's lives, and I nervously waited for the right moment to tell her what I'd been doing and ask if she would help me. I was listening and responding to JC, all the while rehearsing what I was going to say. I felt like I was juggling four balls.

'I've decided to write a book,' I inelegantly blurted out. 'About Lynette Dawson. Well, about you and Lynette, and I was wondering if you would help?'

JC turned to face me. In the length of a pause, she seemed to be appraising me, looking at me from the inside out, as I felt Damian had done. Neither of them had time for a meddler.

'Absolutely,' she said, as if she were making a pledge.

I was so shocked that I asked her why – I seemed to be trying to talk her out of it while I was trying to talk her into it.

'Because it's the right thing to do. There's no way to avoid this,' she said. 'I always thought a book should be written about it. But I can't write a book, so this is perfect.'

I told her that I was trying to get my hands on the coronial transcript, that I'd already met Damian Loone, and that I was going to go and have a look at the Bayview house soon.

'Maybe you could come?' I asked gingerly.

'Love to,' she said, almost gleefully. I couldn't understand why she would be excited to be going back to Bayview, but I was very pleased. We chose a date and set a time.

A few weeks later, on a wintry July day, I followed the coastal road out of Manly. The plan was to pick JC up and then head towards Bayview. On the northern shoulder of Freshwater, the next beach north from Manly, the road sits high above rock platforms. The ocean was a dark churning mess all the way to the horizon, and when I reached Curl Curl the wind howled across the open scrub beside the lagoon, buffeting the car with sharp gusts.

As I drove down the street where JC lived, I could see her in a pink pea coat doing a little jig to keep warm, moving like a much younger woman.

'Hello!' we said, once she'd climbed into the car.

'Oh my goodness.' She moved her hands in front of the heating vent. 'That hot air is nice.'

'Love that pink coat,' I said, stealing a sideways glance at her.

'My sister bought it for me. I tell her that if she sees something that's a good price, just buy it for me.'

'Nice sister.'

'We're the same size, so it's perfect.'

As we drove by each beach, JC leaned forward, to look out at the stormy sea. We passed Long Reef, Collaroy, Narrabeen – each with its own character depending on which way the beach faced, and each with its own distinct sand, which changed colour from taupe to yellow and then mustard the further north we went. The sand became coarser too, as if the rocks hadn't long crumbled off the cliffs. When we got to Mona Vale, we turned west and headed inland to Bayview, a wealthy suburb at the foot of Pittwater, the magnificent drowned river valley 30 kilometres from the centre of Sydney.

In 1975, Lynette and Chris bought a block of land there big enough to build their dream home on. In Bayview, streets fan out and dead-end into difficult topography, which has protected it from overdevelopment but also left the suburb without a discernible centre or community. There are more bus services now, and a few shops, but most residents are still reliant on their cars to get around.

We eased around the curve of the bay. At the western end, JC directed me up a steep road that twisted and turned back on itself. Ferns and small trees hung from the rocky face of the escarpment, and houses projected at defiant angles. The Guringai people are the traditional owners of the land, and you can still see the whales and fish that they cut into the flat grey rocks.

We turned into Gilwinga Drive and stopped to look at a signpost at the top of the street.

> WARNING: ALL SUSPICIOUS PERSONS AND ACTIVITIES ARE IMMEDIATELY REPORTED TO OUR POLICE NEIGHBOURS ALERT AREA – WE LOOK OUT FOR EACH OTHER!

The threatening text was overlaid on a big eye with an exclamation mark. It reminded me of a Droog from *A Clockwork Orange*.

'How . . . bizarre,' I remarked.

'It's that kind of place,' JC shrugged. 'Strange things happen in this street.' None of this was news to her.

I got out and took a photo of the sign, then suddenly felt self-conscious, as if someone might be watching us and doing exactly what the sign said – ringing the police. Had the sign been put there because of Lynette?

We idled down Gilwinga Drive. Large houses sat on both sides of the street, some with tennis courts and multi-car garages.

'The street was more isolated then,' JC explained. 'All down here' – she pointed to the lower side of the street – 'was all bush.'

There were few streetlights, and at night I imagined that there would be a thick and sudden darkness at the bush line behind each house. Through the open window of the car, we heard the long note and snap of a whipbird's call shooting out of the stillness and across the eucalyptus vapour.

'This is it,' JC said, and I pulled over.

At the top of a steep driveway sat a ranch-style house made of brown and blond bricks. A large lawn and well-tended gardens separated the house from its neighbours, and at the back the encroaching scrub was so thick that only constant maintenance could have kept it at bay. I was surprised. When JC had told me all those years ago that she'd moved into the house after Lynette went missing, I had imagined a fibro or weatherboard cottage with a big yard and a swing set, not a semi-rural mansion.

JC also showed me where Chris's twin brother, Paul, and his wife, Marilyn, had once lived, 200 metres from Lynette and Chris's house. It didn't look as grand as Lynette and Chris's, although it was on flat ground, not perched at the top of a steep driveway. The plan had been for the twins and their wives to buy, build and sell and, with a nice profit, move to Queensland where their money would go further. It was a good plan: now the houses in the street sell for well over $2 million.

'It all seems like yesterday,' JC said quietly.

We looped around and parked on the low side of the street, looking up at the house again. From this angle, it seemed to float above the ridge, which was thick with gum trees and boulders, while the steep front yard had only a scattering of small trees, and rocks that looked like they had tumbled into place.

'Where do you think Lynette is?' I asked.

JC lifted her gaze up to the ridge and nodded her head. 'I think she's up there,' she said. 'It's so steep and wild out the back, you'd never be able to find her.'

We drove back towards the coast and stopped for lunch in Avalon. We chose a café with an open fire and leaned in close to talk. Suddenly, a well-dressed woman appeared in front of us.

'Excuse me,' she said, 'are you discussing a business plan?'

We looked up at her blankly.

'A venture together?' she suggested.

Before either of us could reply, she continued.

'I sense things,' she blurted out. 'Some people might say I'm psychic, but I've got this voice in my head. I get it from time to time.' She was galloping through her spiel, perhaps because she'd been stopped at this point before. 'I was just waiting for my coffee, and I know the voice won't stop until I tell you, whoever, what it is, what I'm hearing. I need to tell you' – she gestured towards us in turn – 'that whatever it is that you're working on, it's going to be very, very successful.'

The people at the table next to ours were listening. They looked from the woman back to us, back to the woman, shamelessly waiting for our reaction. When I looked at JC, she was smiling – beaming really.

'So, keep going,' the woman said, backing away. 'I don't want to interrupt. I just want to let you know.'

'This is fantastic, Rebecca! Just fantastic! KD doesn't want me doing this with you,' JC said, mentioning her daughter for the first time. 'She knows that it's bringing everything up again for me, and that it's going to upset me, but we both believe strongly in a spiritual side to life. Not religion,' she said, frowning. 'We are both very spiritual. I really believe in things like that.' She turned around to see if the woman was still there, but she'd gone. 'This is a great sign. KD's going to be stoked.'

JC had only touched upon KD briefly since we'd reconnected. She told me that she lived close by with her husband, and that they'd already bought their apartment. JC often went over and did the washing and helped in other ways, because they both worked full-time. It was clear that JC wanted KD to have more financial security than she'd had, and more love too. But this was the first time she'd connected KD to what we were doing. I didn't know if JC would ever fully bring KD into the picture and I'd also decided that I wouldn't ask JC about KD's relationship with her father and with her half-sisters, although I hoped that one day JC might tell me about this. So I didn't jump on the mention of KD's name because I felt that I needed to be invited. I couldn't see how it would work any other way.

'I went to a medium,' JC said, 'and through the medium, Dad told me that he wasn't a very good father but that he's going to make up for it. And he has. He died in 2010, and since he died he's been telling me it's all right to be me. My life has really moved on since then. I've done things that have made me happy. He's given me the confidence to do them.'

She sat smiling. The stranger at our table had confirmed that her father was watching out for her and that her future was going to be freed from the burdens of this past. I thought it was all snake oil and found it hard to share JC's enthusiasm.

Later that evening, I came across an article:

SHOCKED NEIGHBOURS PLAN CHRISTMAS GET-TOGETHER AFTER DEATHS OF RECLUSIVE COUPLE

Shocked neighbours of a couple whose bodies were found in their Northern Beaches mansion several weeks after they died are planning a Christmas gathering to get to know each other in the wake of the tragedy.

Anthony and Claudine Marland's badly decomposed bodies were found inside their home on leafy Gilwinga Drive in Bayview on December 7.[1]

I emailed it to JC. She replied quickly and said she already knew about this poor couple. She said she was still in touch with some people in the street and they'd mentioned it to her.

In the article, one of the neighbours said, 'People come up here [to Bayview] to be quiet and private, but that's no reason why we can't be on hand for each other if there's a problem.'

CHAPTER THREE

The Simms family

A COUPLE OF DAYS AFTER JC AND I WENT TO BAYVIEW, I RECEIVED A call from Damian Loone. 'Greg Simms rang me yesterday,' he said. Greg is Lynette's brother and I'd sent him an email a few days earlier. 'He wanted to know if you're okay to talk to. I told him you're okay.' Damian laughed. We'd come a long way. Greg, along with his sister Pat, were familiar to me from many of the articles about Lynette's disappearance. Greg was the family spokesman. Tall and stern-looking, he appeared strong enough to carry the greatest load. Pat wasn't often photographed but when she was, she was usually standing solemnly by his side.

Almost six months of emailing Greg slipped by without a face-to-face meeting, and it was apparent that it was Pat who was hesitating. There had been no sign of the inquest transcript during that time either. Then, just as I was about to suggest that Greg and I meet without Pat, he invited me to morning tea at her place, only a few minutes' drive from where I lived. So, on a November morning, I stood on her porch holding a Christmas panettone and I suddenly lost courage. What offering would be thanks enough for talking to me, a stranger, about her long-lost sister?

Small dogs barked furiously at my knock, and I could hear their claws skitter across floorboards. 'Come on,' I heard Pat say. 'Away from the door.'

She opened it. 'Rebecca,' she said. 'Come in.'

Pat was smiling, and reached one arm out towards me before the door was fully open. There was something so familiar in the gesture – I felt like I was visiting an aunt who I hadn't seen for a long time. I had to check my instinct to lean forward and kiss her on the cheek. Behind Pat, I could see Greg and his wife, Merilyn, straining to get a look at me.

We fixed tea and coffee, and Pat apologised for taking so long to organise the meeting – she'd been unwell, then away visiting her daughter, and then getting ready for Christmas. Merilyn arranged her homemade passionfruit slice on a plate and I blushed about the store-bought panettone, wishing that I'd baked something too. In the flesh, Greg's and Pat's similarities to Lynette were more striking, with their thick hair and open faces, but they were more broad-shouldered than I expected, taller too, and seemed to tower over Merilyn and me. They must be, I thought, descended from pioneering Scottish stock. They were both in their sixties.

'We're an ordinary family,' Pat said, as we sat down in the lounge room. 'Things like *this* don't happen to us.' She said *this* just as JC had, as if referring to something concrete but at the same time, not quite knowing what it was. Pat had the same look of worry that I'd seen in the photos of her in the newspaper.

Greg looked over at Pat from his spot on the couch by the window, quietly nodding. Thick bushes pushed against the glass of the front window, and bees were busily dipping in and out of them. Merilyn picked up the teapot and offered refills; and again, I felt like an intruder, wondering what I was doing there.

'We grew up in Clovelly,' Pat said, 'directly across the road from the beach. There were six of us crammed into a semi. I shared a bedroom with Lyn and the boys shared a room.'

There were four Simms children. Philip was the oldest, then Pat, Lynette and Greg. It was odd thinking of Greg as younger than Lynette. I had been thinking of Lynette as the baby, I realised, because she had stopped ageing in 1982. Frozen in time at thirty-three, she became the youngest sibling.

'Dad was in the navy and left to become a maths teacher. He walked to work at South Sydney Boys High. Mum swam every day,' Pat said proudly of her parents, Len and Helena. 'Mum was a typical housewife – everything was always neat and tidy!' She laughed, looking around at the books piled on tables, shoes bundled by the door.

I imagined that keeping a small, semi-detached house that contained a family of six in order would have been difficult. Although it didn't sound like they had very much to keep in order.

'Lyn was house-proud too,' Pat remembered. 'She had lots of hanging plants, all beautiful and green. The house was beautiful. [But] I do remember visiting Lyn one time' – Pat's voice became flat – 'on this visit, the plants were all dead. It was obvious things just weren't right.'

'Mum loved the water,' Greg said. 'And she loved nature. She was always at the beach with the kids and the grandkids.'

'Lyn was a really good swimmer. We all swam. Mum took us to swim at the Aquarium in Coogee, [she] was always there, walking along the edge of the pool encouraging us and barracking as loud as anything.' Pat looked over at Greg uncomfortably. 'Except for Greg.'

As the youngest, Greg was the outlier in the family. Ten years younger than Philip and four years younger than Lynette, his three older siblings had moved on from the Aquarium and mostly out of home by the time he was old enough to go, so he got involved with the surf club instead.

'Anyway, the surf club didn't admit women in those days,' Greg said, attempting, I thought, to ameliorate Pat's guilt. 'So, Pat and Lyn never had that option.'

In winter, they swam at Wylie's Baths, at the southern end of Coogee Beach. Pat recalled walking the 4-kilometre round trip 'even if it was raining'.

Greg moved forward with his hands clasped together. 'At some point, we did get a car, a Holden station wagon. Dad hit a tree in Centennial Park when a neighbour up the road was teaching him to drive it. I never saw it after that!' In any event, their mother, Helena, didn't drive, so everything was done on foot, or on the tram that stopped not far from the house. Lynette didn't drive either, but unlike Helena in Clovelly, there was no tram to Bayview. Helena was close to shops and was surrounded by friends, and the neighbourhood was full of kids. Once Lynette was home in Bayview, she only had a few neighbours and she was dependent on Chris to drive her places. At times, I think it would have been a lonely place.

Lynette and Chris started dating when they were about fifteen years old and still at school, Lynette at Sydney Girls High School, and Chris at Sydney Boys. Pat recalled that back then, the girls' uniform included a stiff hat, and on Lynette's first day, her hat had blown off and was run over by a car. 'We couldn't afford to replace it, so she had to wear this squashed hat with a tyre mark on it,' Pat said, with a big laugh.

The family all liked Chris. One day, Lynette asked Pat what she thought of Chris. 'I don't know why she'd care what I thought. I don't recall what I would have said but I do remember that he was quite charming. And he didn't drink or smoke! We all thought they were a good couple.'

Chris and his twin brother, Paul, were the youngest of five children. Handsome and athletic, they were the pride of the family and, like many twins, they were close. They went to university together and became physical education teachers, they played rugby for Easts Rugby Union Club and later, they changed codes and played first-grade rugby league for the Newtown Jets, where they developed a media profile.

After Lynette finished school, she worked in a bank for a while, but then decided she wanted to be a nurse.

'Lynette was a fantastic nurse,' Pat recalled, with pride.

'And,' Greg jumped in, 'when Dad developed diabetes, it was Lyn who diagnosed it.'

'When she went missing,' Pat continued, the energy gone from her voice, 'she'd been working in a childcare centre for a few years, because back then there had to be a nurse on staff. She loved it. If any of our kids were sick, she could whip out the medicine and have the child take it while the rest of us were still wondering how we were going to do it. She was so efficient.'

In 1970, after they'd been dating for six years, Lynette and Chris Dawson decided to get married. They were twenty-one. Pat was overseas but came home to be a bridesmaid and Greg, who was seventeen years old, had a suit made, which, I imagine, was quite a fancy and expensive thing to do then.

When they were first married, Lynette and Chris shared a house with Paul and his wife, Marilyn, and then, a few years later, they bought some land and built a house in Cromer, up on the ridge behind Dee Why Beach. Both Philip and Pat had moved to northern New South Wales by then, which left Greg as the only sibling still in Sydney. When Greg and Merilyn began dating, they spent a lot of time with Lynette and Chris. 'Lynette and I just clicked from the moment we met,' Merilyn said. The two couples were so close that when Greg and Merilyn decided to get married, Chris was Greg's best man.

Merilyn and Greg were sitting together on one couch and Pat sat opposite them on another. One of the dogs, a terrier, jumped up beside Pat and she stroked its head. I was perched between them, on the front edge of an easychair, but occasionally I sat back, and felt that the squashy old chair had swallowed me. They laughed easily when they talked about events from their childhoods and lives as young adults, in a way that only siblings do, but as they moved on to stories from their adult lives, the conversation slowed and at times they fell silent for reasons that weren't obvious to me but that I sensed were caused by private thoughts about Lynette, upon which I didn't want to intrude.

I asked them about Lynette as a mother.

'Lyn had very strong maternal instincts, but she wasn't falling pregnant,' Pat said with obvious strain, and then she sat back on the couch, unable to continue.

Merilyn picked up the conversation. 'They sought medical advice. There was some exploratory surgery and the news was not good.'

Then, around that time, Lynette and Chris bought the block of land in Bayview – 13 kilometres north of Cromer and even further away from Clovelly.

'We couldn't believe it,' Merilyn said. 'Why would they pay $32,000 for a block of land that was just bush and rock!' She and Greg were both laughing, at themselves, it seemed to me, thinking of how much those houses in Bayview were worth now. 'We just couldn't understand it then.'

They understood the Australian suburban dream of building your own place on a large block of land but they were incredulous that Lynette and Chris would pay so much for an undeveloped, and what they thought was useless, slice of bushland.

'Lynette threw herself into building her dream home. She made sure there was a spa for Chris because she knew he'd have aching joints when he was older, from all the rugby. She could just see how things would work,' Pat said. 'She could put a couple of sticks in a vase and make it look great! She was such a generous person. She put together a beautiful, beautiful home.'

'She'd entertain everybody,' Merilyn said. 'Dinner and barbeques, all at her place and often the Dawson and Simms families together.' And although Lynette lived on the other side of Sydney, she spoke to her mother every day by phone, sometimes several times a day. Pat and Greg didn't say this outright, but it was apparent that Lynette had assumed the mantle from her mother of passing news around the family and organising get-togethers.

'There was nothing that was too much trouble,' Greg said.

'Lyn was just overly generous,' Merilyn agreed, 'especially with the children. She'd buy one of the children four presents or more, when one would do. She was very like your mother in that way,' she said, nodding at Greg, who smiled back at her. 'When I was still a nervous first-time mum,' she continued, rolling her eyes to poke fun at her naivety, 'I mentioned to Lyn that I hadn't let [my son] Craig have an ice-cream yet. So, Lynette picked him up and put him in the high chair and gave him one. She was very cheeky.'

'I'll tell you how cheeky she was,' Greg said with a mischievous grin. 'When Merilyn and I started dating, she came to me one day and said, "I know a little hotel in Coogee if you need it!"'

And then, in the middle of building the new house, Lynette discovered she was pregnant. A happy marriage, a beautiful new home and the delight of an unexpected baby on the way. Lynette was elated.

'XD was born in July 1977,' Pat said. 'Lynette stopped working because she didn't want to miss a minute of the baby she thought she'd never have. You can't believe how happy she was two years later, when YD came along. I truly believe that she thought her life was perfect.'

A week or so later, I decided to visit the Simms family home in Clovelly. I'd grown up in north-west Sydney, not far from Parramatta, where summers were hot, and the coast was 25 kilometres away. The childhood by the beach that Greg and Pat had told me about was something that I would only have thought possible in a book, so I decided to go and have a look. I sent Greg an email asking for the address and he wrote straight back and said if it was all right by me, he and Merilyn would like to come along.

On the day of our trip, I swam early under deflated clouds that made the ocean flat and grey. Then I drove to meet Greg and Merilyn. They were driving down from Newcastle that morning and we arranged to meet at their son's place – the same son to whom Lynette gave an ice-cream thirty years ago. Greg knew his way around the eastern suburbs, so he drove, and I climbed in the back behind Merilyn.

On the way to Clovelly, they peppered me with questions. How many children did I have? How old were they? What did my husband do? Where did my kids go to school? I was conscious that day in the car that a true affection was developing between us. We were becoming friends, and I didn't want to let them down.

As we edged closer east, Greg and Merilyn talked excitedly, pointing out landmarks, laughing when they showed me the street they'd lived on when they were first married. Then, out of the dense suburbia, Coogee Beach and the ocean suddenly appeared. The grey clouds of early morning had burned off and the windscreen was filled with dark blue water, so stark against the pale clear sky.

'Wow,' I admired. We smiled and looked at each other as if we couldn't believe our luck.

First stop was a block of modern apartments, squeezed tight against the northern end of the beach.

'This was where the Aquarium used to be,' Greg said.

The Coogee Aquarium and Swimming Baths had had a 25-metre pool, a roller-skating rink, a toboggan (a Canadian toboggan, apparently), swings, a bandstand, an open-air bar and even a herd of donkeys. It had been there from 1887 until most of it collapsed during a big storm in 1984, and since then, the site has revolved through restaurants, bars and now, exclusive housing and a hip eatery.

'Bit different now,' Greg commented, as we sat looking up at the expensive apartments.

'Not only were there the pools inside – it actually was an aquarium,' Greg went on. 'There was a tiger shark on display there that had vomited up a human arm.'

James Smith was identified by a tattoo on the forearm. The grisly find, not surprisingly, was connected to 'crime figures' and made sensational headlines around Australia in the 1930s. Alex Castles, a law professor, wrote a book about it. A friend of mine used to give a copy to overseas visitors as a kind of scene-setter for Sydney – a boast, perhaps, of our hardy disposition: not even children were put off their swims by a shark and a vomited arm.

From the site of the Aquarium, we headed up the hill and followed the road's curve around the north headland to Clovelly Beach. We parked the car and stood behind a low white fence, looking down at the deep, narrow beach. The water was calm, rising and falling like a slow breath. A smattering of people lounged on the concrete platform in front of the surf club on the southern side, while a few swimmers did easy laps below them.

'See those trees over there?' Greg nodded over beyond the surf club. 'That's where we lived.'

We drove around to the other side of the bay and stopped at a little triangular park, no more than a patch of grass.

'That was our house,' Greg said, pointing across the grass. 'The street only had a few houses in it when we lived here, and the tram ran down to there.' He gestured up the street.

The once-white semi was about 10 metres wide. There was a low red-brick fence in front of the house and, down the side, a broken path led to the front door. I turned and looked out to sea. Apart from a few trees, the house had an unobstructed view of the ocean.

'Not much has changed,' Greg said, and turned to look out to sea too. He had his hands in his pockets and smiled as he surveyed the beauty of this spot.

I thought about my own small childhood house and imagined that life inside the Simms residence would have been similar – bunk beds squeezed into small bedrooms, all sharing one bathroom and only just enough money to feed the six of them. My thoughts then turned to Lynette's large house in Bayview. I wondered what her family had made of her moving on, and at such a young age, to what was a mansion in comparison.

'The kitchen,' Merilyn said, as if she had read my mind, 'well, it wasn't really a kitchen. A kitchenette, *maybe*. I don't know how your mother got six meals on the table when all she had was one small bench, a cook top and no oven.'

Greg's smiled broadened, remembering his mother, but perhaps also appreciating Merilyn's admiration of her. I remembered my pink-cheeked mother making dinner in our hot kitchen and then cleaning up alone for a long time afterwards, with no dishwasher to help.

'Lyn and Pat had some friends around the corner who had a TV and they'd go around there on Saturday nights to watch it,' Greg said. 'It wasn't until much later that we got one.'

In homes like theirs and mine, there weren't enough seats in the lounge room, so a few kids sprawled on the floor while the whole family watched the one television. Families were held tightly together, more connected, because there was nowhere else to go. Neighbours overheard arguments as well, and privacy meant something different then, more like minding your own business. But Lynette and Chris were baby boomers, and they had dreams of something bigger and better.

'Not many of the local kids came to our house,' Greg continued. 'I don't really know why.'

'Yes, you do,' Merilyn said, turning to look at him. 'They were scared of your father!'

I looked at Greg, expecting that he might deny it or not want it said in front of me, but he nodded calmly. 'Pa was a tough man. He had to be revered. He was the head of the household. He was a very controlling man,' he said, looking at his feet, and I thought I caught a glimpse of the boy he'd been when he lived there. 'Mum was very subservient, and placated him. We all knew not to make him angry, not to speak while the news was on.'

During our conversation at Pat's place, Greg had said that their father, Len, was a 'disciplinarian' and had in fact been head of truancy at South Sydney Boys. There was even a cartoon in the school magazine of him with a hungry grin on his face and a quivering cane behind his back. He was a big drinker and the kids at school had called him 'Schooner King'. But now, with those few sentences, Greg seemed to give voice to something bigger.

Perhaps it was for that moment that Greg and Merilyn had come, for something that had been unsaid for over thirty years to finally be said. Was it my presence, the presence of an outsider, that allowed Merilyn to say it?

'But,' Greg went on, 'of all the kids, Lynette was the one who would speak out the most. She was gamer. She was probably the most like him.'

Pat had also said that Lynette was 'stubborn' like their father, that she was strong and 'would stand up to a doctor at work if she thought the treatment was wrong'.

Strong and assertive was not how I'd imagined Lynette. But then again, standing in that little park and listening to Greg's reminiscences, I also now knew that growing up in the semi across the road from the beach was not the idyllic life I'd imagined. I reminded myself to be careful about making assumptions.

We stopped at a café at the bottom of the small gully that overlooks Clovelly Beach. We were sweaty; the heat had snuck up on us. We sat without talking for a while, drinking chilled water, and then over lunch we spoke about other things: Prince William and his wife Kate; the draw for the Rugby World Cup. Then, while we waited for our coffees, Greg returned abruptly to Lynette, his voice now filled with anger.

'Looking back, you can see that Chris Dawson was lazy. He only did the things that *he* wanted to do.'

'Lynette did everything in that house,' Merilyn agreed. 'Everything.'

'He wouldn't take the bins out at night. I remember Lyn wanted a branch cut off that was hanging over the driveway and she was always asking Chris to do it. One day, I was there, and I got sick of her asking him, so I drove back to Clovelly and got a bad old saw we had there and I drove back to Bayview and cut it down for her. He didn't care that I'd done that. Didn't seem to bother him,' Greg sneered. 'I used to do lots of little maintenance things for her that he just wouldn't do.'

Instead of lazy, I wondered if what Greg meant was that Chris was selfish. He often had a second job – as a lifesaver at Northbridge Baths, and with Paul as a model and garbageman. He trained hard, played professional rugby league, was a teacher. He seemed to have energy for the things that interested him.

Lyn had told Pat that any money from the second jobs was kept separate. 'It went into the "Twinnies' Account",' Pat had told me with obvious disapproval. 'Lyn told me that they [Chris and Paul] had money that was separate, you know, that their wives couldn't touch.'

Towards the end of 1981, Greg, who had joined the New South Wales Police Force in 1974, was transferred to Muswellbrook, a three-hour drive north-west of Sydney. When Merilyn was packing for the move, she came across some baby clothes that she'd borrowed from Lynette.

'I still had them, and there had been talk about Lyn and Chris having another child and I wanted to know what to do with the clothes.' So Merilyn rang Lynette. 'She told me then that things weren't going well. She said Chris hadn't been near her for weeks. She said she asked him if there was someone else and he had said no.'

Merilyn was uncomfortable telling me this – her voice dropped a register and quietened. It seemed like, all these years later, she was still worried about betraying Lynette's confidence.

On the way home, we were quieter than when we set out. It seemed that even the happier memories of Lynette were ultimately tarnished by her disappearance. Later, when I was driving back to my house alone, I realised that she had been missing for almost thirty-three years to the day of our outing to Clovelly – and that she'd been thirty-three when her family last saw her. She had now been missing for almost longer than her family had known her.

When I'd first met Pat and Greg, I wrote down in my notes, 'It's painful to witness the siblings' grief – it doesn't diminish.' Greg, who'd noticed that Chris wasn't taking care of his sister in the small ways he thought he should be, and Pat, who could see that the dead plants and changes in Lynette's housekeeping signalled that things weren't right. And the doubts that their sister had confided to Merilyn.

All these small things pointed to a 'rough patch' in the marriage, but nothing more. Certainly not to Lynette going missing. Nonetheless, they punish themselves for not intervening more forcefully, for not preventing whatever happened from happening. If they had done more, would Lynette have opened up to them? And if she had, would it have changed anything?

During our first meeting at Pat's house, I had asked them how often they thought about Lynette. Perhaps a couple of times a week, Merilyn said. And Pat told me that she didn't think about Lyn every day. 'But Greg does,' she said, nodding towards him, where he sat straight-backed and silent on the lounge.

'Greg has two photos above the computer,' Merilyn said. 'One is of Lyn holding XD and the other is of Lyn outside the house at Clovelly.'

Later, when I was emailing Greg, I pictured him looking up at the two photos of Lynette. I imagined him smiling at her, and then wondering where she is.

CHAPTER FOUR

An unhappy childhood

IN 1966, WHEN JC WAS TWO YEARS OLD, XC AND MMC MOVED WITH their three girls from South Coogee in Sydney's eastern suburbs, not far from where Lynette had grown up, to Wheeler Heights on the Northern Beaches. They were in search of a better life – one they couldn't afford in South Coogee. It was four years before Lynette and Chris would make a similar move, from the eastern suburbs to Cromer.

The streets of Wheeler Heights have wide nature strips and gullies of dry sclerophyll bush – eucalypts, wattle trees, banksia and pea flowers – that straddle the edge of an escarpment. The original 1950s and 1960s homes are modest, with trees that tower over their flat roofs. Originally lower-middle class, now Wheeler Heights would be considered middle class, with many of the smaller houses that had big yards replaced by big houses with small yards.

JC and I were on our way to see her childhood home. She'd surprised me again by wanting to come. When I asked for the address, she told me they lived on a corner block and used either street address. 'The postman knew us.'

In the car, JC told me again, 'KD doesn't want me doing this. My sisters don't either. They don't understand.'

I looked over at her to see if she was okay. 'I'm sorry to hear that,' I said. And I was, because I knew their disapproval would be hard on JC. I was nervous, too, that she might withdraw from me if her family relationships became too strained.

'That's it,' JC said.

I stopped the car and we wound the windows down.

'We're making a habit of this,' I said. 'Middle-aged pair caught prowling the streets – this time in Wheeler Heights!' Making a fist, I flicked my fingers out with each word as if I was reading a sensational newspaper headline. We laughed.

In JC's company, I felt carefree and often silly. When we worked together at the refuge, and now, spending so much time together, we laughed a lot, in a private way as if our shared humour was a secret. Or at least, that's how it was for me. Her playfulness hadn't changed after she'd initially told me about her past and it was still there now, even though we were dwelling on such difficult parts of her life. How could she have been through what she had and still have this lightness at the centre of herself? 'Resilient' has become a buzzword these days, but JC really was resilient, in ways I couldn't imagine.

'Not much has changed,' JC said, twisting to look out of the back window.

In 1966 her parents paid £16,000 for it. The house was uncannily like the one I'd grown up in: a simple weatherboard cottage on a corner block, which cost my parents about the same. I remembered running under the sprinkler's meagre fountain of water with my brother toddling behind me, his cloth nappy soaked and sliding down his chubby legs. My eyes suddenly filled with tears and I turned away, pretending to look at the houses on the other side of the street.

'MMC was very beautiful,' JC said, of her mother. 'MMC's father was handsome but her mother was very plain, so to produce a child of MMC's splendour was amazing.'

JC said her father married MMC because 'she was beautiful, outgoing and sporty' and he thought they'd make handsome children – and he was right. The four girls are handsome, but JC doesn't want attention.

'NC was always sick and at eighteen months she had heart surgery,' JC remembered, as we motored slowly around the corner to look at the front of the house. 'And because of that, her relationship with MMC was very different.'

JC was only four when NC was born, little more than a baby herself. She was desperate for her mother's love and attention, of which there seemed to be a finite supply. 'There was little left over,' she said. 'I felt lost.'

NC was often in hospital, and JC recalls visiting her one day. 'On the way in, I was bitten by a dog but nothing was done for me.' Later, riding her bike to school, she was hit by a car. JC can't remember if MMC was called to the school, but she does recall sitting for her high school placement tests that day. 'I arrived cut and in shock, but I was made to do the exams anyway. No one did anything. In high school I was put in the fourth out of eight classes and slowly clawed my way back up again over the years.'

Like Lynette's family in their small semi at Clovelly, and me out near Parramatta, JC and her sisters grew up outdoors. I'd recently decided that my own children should spend more time outside, remembering the mischief we got up to, but for JC, being forced outside felt like banishment.

'We always had to be outside. In the mornings, we would be really quiet playing with the Barbie dolls, trying not to wake MMC up because then we knew we'd be forced outside. No matter how cold or wet or unwell we were, we spent our days outside.'

And when they were inside? JC said that she and her sisters had to clean the house each day before they went to school, even though MMC didn't work. She felt that they were MMC's 'captives', with little control or say in their home life.

Cooking didn't interest MMC. Dinner was mostly cold meat and salads, occasionally bolognaise or stewed mince. Food seemed to be in short supply. JC recalled being so hungry one day that she stole some grapes and climbed up to the roof to eat them because she'd be in trouble if MMC saw her with food. Not surprisingly, JC isn't very interested in cooking either. 'Food's just a necessary thing,' she told me.

JC and two of her sisters did swimming squad training at Collaroy Rockpool, where, unlike the surf, the still water is freezing all year. JC liked their coach. 'He was a kind and generous man who took me under his wing because I was the youngest swimmer. I was only five! But he could also be tough too,' she said. One evening, JC and her sisters were skylarking and were late getting to the pool, so the coach sent them home.

'MMC was furious.' She tucked her chin in. 'We competed with each other. You were only safe if you sided with MMC. I might tell on one of my sisters, because if MMC was angry with one of them, it meant she wasn't angry with me that day. CC had a terrible time, probably because she was the eldest.'

But then again, JC remembers going to her grandparents' place one night. She was supposed to sleep over but she asked them to take her home. 'I'd have rather been at home than go out. I was afraid of my mother but I desperately wanted her to love me. I was very sensitive, and I think all these things affected me as a child. I went inward, and I think this made me more susceptible to events later in my life.'

We meandered around the back streets of Wheeler Heights, not saying much. Around one corner, the ocean was suddenly laid out, flat and wide.

'What a view,' I said.

'Magnificent. Every Sunday in summer we'd go to the beach – always Collaroy. I can remember sitting in the back of MMC's car with my sisters, listening to Petula Clark. MMC was happy. We'd meet up with other families and afterwards there'd be a barbeque. MMC would drink and often flirt with the other men and later, she and Dad would fight about it. Normally MMC was the aggressor, but on these occasions it was XC. I remember lying in bed listening to them shouting at one another, rehashing each other's behaviour. MMC was hitting Dad, I could hear her slapping and Dad was groaning from the impact as he defended himself. We girls would be in bed crying as we listened to them fight.'

If XC picked fights with MMC, why didn't he just leave the barbeques and take the family home?

'I don't know,' she said. I also wondered how the other women would have put up with MMC getting drunk and flirting with their husbands.

'When I was thirteen, I came home one day to find MMC having sex with my godfather. The bedroom door was open a little bit. I saw them. I don't know if MMC knows that I saw them,' she added, her voice rising with alarm. 'MMC also told us, several times, that she wished she'd married some other bloke. I don't know why she didn't,' she said bitterly.

MMC's wish to have married another man meant there would have been no JC or her sisters. It's hard to see how a child could have taken it any other way. All of it left her feeling unwanted and unsafe in her own home.

There were other nights when MMC would take herself off to Harbord Diggers, the mammoth club carved into the headland between Freshwater and South Curl Curl beaches, where she'd drink too much and be seen with other men.

'She got a reputation. She drank too much. Someone told me that she slept with an uncle of one of my sister's friends.' JC's voice was flat, her face strained. 'XC tried to stop her. He put a lock on the phone. So, he was a bit controlling. He was very moral. He was a Mason.'

'When I was in my twenties,' JC continued, the catalogue of unhappy memories pouring out, 'XC told me that he hit MMC once. He went to his parents' place and told his father what he'd done. His father told him, "Well, you can never do that again." And he didn't.'

I felt that we'd had enough for one day, so we headed home. As we turned into JC's oak-lined street, she recalled 'my mother' taking her to see a doctor one day. JC rarely claimed MMC as her mother, so it was noticeable that this small act of care fleetingly elevated her. I asked her why she nearly always called her mother by her first name. 'Because I no longer regard her as my mother,' she said with conviction. The writer Jeanette Winterson only refers to her mother as Mrs Winterson. When I got home, I took her memoir, *Why Be Happy When You Could Be Normal*, from the bookshelf. 'I can't remember a time,' Winterson wrote, 'when I wasn't setting my story against hers. It was my survival from the beginning.' Yet I worried that JC would be left with regrets when MMC died.

JC had been renovating her apartment – putting in a new kitchen, bathroom and laundry, and redoing the floorboards, so a few weeks after we visited her childhood home, I dropped by with takeaway coffees. When I arrived, the AFL was on the television.

'Who's playing?' I asked.

She laughed. 'I don't know. Remember?' JC didn't know anything about AFL but she'd told me that one day, she'd watched a grand final on television with her dad. They cheered and clapped, and it wasn't until the medal presentation that they realised they'd been watching the previous year's grand final.

JC proudly showed me the renovations. She'd lived in the same apartment for over twenty years and she'd never considered buying something bigger. She was happy with what had been enough for her and KD. We sat next to each other on the sofa and JC took some photo albums from a shelf. We drank our coffees as JC flipped the pages. Some of the photos were of her as a teenager, others from when she was much younger. Some of the faces I recognised, and there were others who I'd heard about. There was a photo of her at the beach with her parents. JC had told me so much about MMC but XC still seemed like a shadowy presence. I put my finger on his picture and I asked her more about him.

'He was quiet and sensitive, like me. He was a sales rep for Amoco [an oil company]. He worked long hours. When he was home, I always felt better. Always,' she said.

Every weekend he took the girls to their Saturday swim squad and afterwards they had ice-cream at Sam's Ice-cream at the beach. There were other times when JC would go alone with her father to get the car fixed. 'They were the happiest times of my life,' JC said.

It bothered me that JC only blamed her mother for her unhappy childhood, so I asked her gently if her father had known about MMC's mistreatment of her and her sisters. 'He never knew,' she said. 'He wasn't present. He played a lot of golf then. Sometimes all weekend it was only us four girls at the dinner table. It is interesting that none of us ever told Dad.'

She paused. 'There was a family down the street. They were normal,' she said. 'They knew that I didn't have a happy home. They had three boys and I was close to them. They were happy with one another, the boys played together. When they renovated their house, I must have been about twelve and I thought, I honestly thought they were going to adopt me.' JC flipped through a few more pages. She sighed. 'Dad said that he didn't know Mum was being abusive.'

Eventually, XC and MMC's marriage ran out of steam. Two days before Christmas in 1977, when JC was fourteen, her father sat her and NC down on the bed and told them that he was leaving. 'Years later, he told me that he'd been waiting for no-fault divorce to be introduced.' He wasn't alone. In 1975, the Whitlam government introduced no-fault divorce, which removed the need to identify and punish, either financially or with custody arrangements, the party who was responsible for the breakdown of the marriage. In 1974 there were 24,000 divorces in Australia and in 1976 this figure skyrocketed to 64,000.[2]

XC moved back to Rosebery, on the other side of Sydney, to live with his parents. MMC's drinking increased, and she became more depressed, her behaviour more erratic. Times were tough for the girls.

XC would come back to visit them, but: 'MMC didn't want us to see him. She was mean. She encouraged us to hide, to pretend there was no one home, so he would go away without seeing us.'

The house was sold, and MMC bought a two-bedroom apartment in Dee Why, but there was a six-month gap between when they had to move out of the house and when they could move into the apartment. So the girls had to split up.

'NC went with Mum, of course, CC with other family friends and BC was going to her friend VM. I was due to go with NC and MMC but VM's mum invited me to stay as well, so that's what I did. Eventually, all five of us moved into the apartment – on my birthday,' JC said, with an edge of bitterness. 'The five of us lived there for six to eight months.'

Around this time, CC's godfather, RN, came from Queensland for a visit and JC's father organised for everyone to have dinner at the local Chinese restaurant. They sat around a large round table – awkwardly, I imagine, with MMC and XC both there.

'MMC flirted with RN. Dad was horrified.' JC shifted on the couch to look at me. 'I think MMC did it out of spite. I can still picture the whole scene. MMC and RN, sitting opposite me, whispering and giggling together and deliberately looking over at Dad.' She shook her head. 'I will never forget the look on Dad's face.'

RN and MMC began seeing each other. CC had started uni by then and was living in Coogee with MMC's mother. In 1980, when JC was in Year 11 at Cromer High School, RN moved into the apartment. RN and MMC were in one room; the three girls were in bunk beds in the other. Later that year, MMC and RN were married. JC recalled with derision that MMC wore white.

In February 1981, BC moved out to go to university, leaving only JC and her sickly younger sister. With the flat less crowded, JC hoped that the pressure might ease but instead, life in the small apartment became even more intolerable. JC was kept awake by RN and MMC's drinking. RN was verbally abusive but he could be physically abusive as well, and there were times when JC had to intervene.

'RN was unpleasant. RN was a tiny man,' JC said sourly.

JC knew she was barely holding herself together. She was a bright and keen student, but she knew that her studies were suffering. 'I was exhausted,' she told me. 'I had too many problems at home. I couldn't think about anything, couldn't focus on anything.'

The year before, when JC was in Year 10, a new PE teacher named Chris Dawson had arrived at Cromer High. JC didn't have much to do with him that year, but in Year 11, she found herself in his PE class, receiving lots of attention.

By the end of the following year, she would be living with him.

CHAPTER FIVE

The missing person file

ON AN UNSEASONABLY COOL SUMMER MORNING, I HEADED SOUTH to meet Damian Loone for lunch in Kiama. I was surprised that he lived on the South Coast because I had imagined him as a gritty city cop through and through. Before I left, I rang the Coroners Court registry again, to see if there had been any progress on retrieving the inquest transcript. There hadn't. And I read an email from JC, turning down a request I had apologetically sent to her from Greg Simms, who was working with a television producer on a missing persons segment about Lynette. Greg was always looking for the next opportunity to publicise Lynette's disappearance, hopeful that, even after all this time, someone might come forward with new information. JC becomes fragile at each of these requests, and this one was no different. I understood JC's reluctance, yet when I wrote back to Greg, I felt that it was me who was letting him down.

By late morning, I had reached the southern edge of the city where it gives over, quite suddenly, to the Royal National Park. Two days earlier it had been 40 degrees, but as I descended the escarpment above Wollongong, mist drifted across the road and the temperature quickly dropped.

We were meeting at a hotel brasserie on a rise on the northern side of town. When I arrived, Damian was on the deck, leaning on the wooden rail with his back to me, looking out over Kiama. He was wearing a pale pink shirt, and beyond him I could see the harbour, the town and the green hills rolling off to the ocean. I went over to greet him.

'Hello, love,' he said, stubbing out his cigarette.

We went inside, placed our orders at the bar and took our drinks over to a table by the window.

He grew up in Avalon, a little further north of Bayview. His mother had raised five kids on her own – three girls, and Damian and his twin brother. 'I speak to my brother every other day. We still know what the other is thinking when we're together.' His dad walked out on the family when he was young. 'I assumed that he'd met another woman. Mum just said, "Your father's gone," and we never really asked more about it,' he said, without apparent rancour. 'Mum worked at Mona Vale Hospital. Raised us on her own. We just did what we had to.' Despite being abandoned, Damian thought he'd like to be a cinematographer, like his father. 'I gave it a go for a while but then decided to be a cop.'

'When I joined the police force, you had to be a certain height, be the right weight, have the right chest measurement.' Damian pulled his stomach in and pushed his chest out. 'I was a skinny bugger then, and had to put coins in my pockets to try and reach the weight. Mum got ill just weeks before I joined, and she died eleven weeks later. My father was supposed to come to the academy to see me pass out, but he never turned up. The next time I saw him was in St Vincent's hospice, a week before he died.'

After Damian graduated from the police academy in 1986, he was sent to Bourke. On the edge of the desert and 800 kilometres north-west of Sydney, it's not a place most people raised near the coast would happily call home.

'Nothing like here,' Damian said. 'I was a Northern Beaches boy. I'd never been beyond the Blue Mountains, but I loved it.'

As part of Bourke's community outreach program, Damian had a radio show called *Street Talk*. 'It started on a Thursday night but was moved to Monday morning. We had T-shirts that said, "*I Wake Up with Damian Loone!*"' he said, running his hand across his chest and laughing. 'It was fantastic. We started the Bourke Community Outback Trek. We'd travel around with a band. Some of the places we'd go, they'd never had a band in town before.'

After Bourke, Damian went to Coffs Harbour, then to Sydney, first to Ultimo and then Kings Cross, where he was part of the Major Crime Squad. From there, he was moved to Dee Why detectives – back on the Northern Beaches, where he began. 'It felt like an outpost after the Cross.'

The commander at Dee Why was a man named Paul Hulme, who was good friends with Sue Strath, a colleague of Lynette's from the childcare centre where she had worked. In the years since Lynette had gone missing, Sue had been protesting to Paul that the police should be doing more to find Lynette. In 1998 there was a state-wide missing persons review and there were two names on the Northern Beaches list. One was Trudie Adams, who, it turned out, had lived on the street in Avalon where Damian grew up. The other was Lynette Dawson. Paul Hulme gave Lynette's file to Damian, and then rang Sue Strath to tell her that Lynette's missing person file was active, sixteen years after she'd gone missing.

'I said to the other two cops on my team, "It's unlikely we'll arrest someone." They shrugged and said, "Oh well," as if it didn't matter.' Damian paused then, and his face became suddenly red. 'And that pissed me off.

'[In the file] there was one interview with Chris Dawson from 1991 at Surfers Paradise but it wasn't even transcribed. I was dumbfounded.'

I was unaware of a 1991 interview with Chris Dawson, and made a note to find out about it.

Damian continued. 'It's sixteen years later and I'm left with an inquiry with no records – no phone, bank . . . nothing.' He almost spat. 'I don't even know if those searches were done. Records only need to be legally kept for seven years, so I knew it was unlikely I'd be able to get them.'

Damian painstakingly transcribed the 1991 interview with Chris. 'It took me bloody hours. Stopping and starting the tape, typing it up with two fingers.' He splayed his hands and held them up. 'My instincts are never wrong. Even on an innocent person. People lie to me all the time and I get a gut feeling,' he said. 'Like that guy in Queensland. When I saw him talk, I thought, "He's killed her."'

I knew that he meant Gerard Baden-Clay, whose wife Allison had been found dead on a muddy bank under the Kholo Creek Bridge in Brisbane in April 2012, and was convicted of her murder in 2014.

The sleepy outpost in Dee Why had unexpectedly handed Damian something very interesting. He quickly came to the same conclusion as the detectives who had interviewed Chris Dawson in 1991: that Lynette Dawson's matter looked like a homicide. They'd asked Chris outright if he had killed Lynette. But why hadn't that interview been transcribed and signed? Why had they dropped what they clearly thought was a homicide investigation? And where had all that information gone? Why wasn't it in the file that Paul Hulme gave Damian? My list of questions just kept growing.

After such a long time, and with so little to go on, Damian knew that his chances of finding out what had happened to Lynette were very slim, but he didn't think that was a reason not to try. 'I'm not a typical cop,' he said. 'My mate said to me, "You play pool like you play chess." That's how I think.'

His hand rested on the rim of his glass, which he turned with delicate twists. 'I've done this for the family. They've put their trust in me. I'm a cop. I'm their lifeline.'

A stiff breeze had blown in, and down by the harbour the crowns of the Norfolk pines heaved from side to side. Knowing that Damian's father had abandoned his family, I wasn't surprised when he'd told me that he'd 'leave no stone unturned' if it was one of his sisters who'd disappeared. Damian had stepped into the role of taking care of his mother and sisters, and I couldn't help thinking that he'd extended those feelings, and now his duty as well, to Lynette.

'The other day I was coming home on the train and I knew within thirty seconds that I'd be throwing some young guys off,' he told me. 'They were hassling a young woman and I thought, "If that was my niece or daughter, I'd want someone to help." No one else intervened.' He had other stories like this, but even so, he said, 'My compassion isn't as much as it used to be. We see a lot of death. You block [out] a lot. I've been told I'm a hard prick. Once you cross a line with me, that's it.'

Damian completed his investigation into Lynette's disappearance in October 1999. This led to the first inquest in 2001, and a referral to the DPP recommending that a 'known person' had committed an indictable offence. But after nine months of reviewing the case, the DPP decided not to proceed. The DPP doesn't provide reasons for its decisions, which although not ideal, is understandable. The DPP has to be, and has to be seen to be, free of political and other pressures. If they provided detailed reasons, they would get bogged down arguing about the merits of every decision, rather than actually prosecuting matters.

But Damian kept working, continually frustrated that he was chasing down leads that most often went nowhere because by then, it had been over twenty years since Lynette's disappearance. Still, he gathered enough new evidence to warrant a second inquest two years after the first, in 2003. This time it would be a full inquest, meaning that witnesses would be called to give evidence.

By the time I left Kiama, a lingering pale sun was setting. I wondered if Damian had headed to the beach for a surf, where a week earlier, a shoal of sharks had been spotted swimming 50 metres from the shore. I turned the radio off and let the bends of the road carry me home.

'You look tired,' my husband said, when I finally came into the kitchen.

'I am.' And I put my arms around him and let my head rest on his chest.

I got undressed and stood under the shower until my limbs turned red. I felt exhausted. Why was I pushing into Lynette's and JC's lives? Now Damian's too? What was I doing? When I set out, I thought I'd be standing in the middle of a story, telling it as best I could, with a 360-degree account. But the view wasn't that clear. And if *I* was drained, how were JC, Pat, Greg and Damian feeling? I hadn't thought enough about how taxing this might be for them. What right did I have to ask anything more of them?

It was still early, but I just wanted to go to sleep. I went to the bedroom and sat down at my desk to turn off my computer. I was just about to close out of my email account when I noticed a new email, subject line: 'Coroner's Court'. I clicked it open, stomach churning. It was the approval I'd been sweating on – the inquest transcript was finally ready for me to inspect.

The next day, I was up early, all the doubts of yesterday forgotten. I had learned a fair bit by then about Lynette's disappearance, and about JC stepping into her life, but I couldn't wait to read the same material the coroner had heard in 2003, and the same material that the DPP had decided was insufficient grounds to prosecute.

At the court, I slid a copy of the email under the glass counter. It would be cheaper, the young man at the registry told me, if I purchased my own paper and did the photocopying myself – I think it was $1.10 per page if they photocopied it for me, which seemed to not so much reflect the value of their time as to discourage the whole exercise. So, I dashed across the street to Officeworks and returned clutching a ream of paper to my chest, and the same young man let me through the security door. I felt a silly frisson of excitement at being on the other side of the glass counter. He led me to a spare desk and I asked him to show me how to work the photocopier.

And it was at this point that he hesitated. 'I'd better just run this by my boss.'

Biting back my anger at yet another setback right on the cusp of finally getting my hands on the transcript, I tracked him as he manoeuvred around desks and filing cabinets, and then as he stood in a door frame, chatting to someone I couldn't see. When he returned, he seemed to be slumping a little more than before.

'Actually,' he said, pulling gently on his pale yellow tie and not looking at me, 'you're not allowed to photocopy it at all.'

I waited until he lifted his eyes and then I fixed him with a mean stare. 'You better get your boss out here.'

The boss was summoned and I took him through my communications and dealings with his staff over the last couple of months – the emails, the money paid, the receipt, the email I'd received only the day before, and the ream of paper that I'd been sent across the road to buy expressly for photocopying the file, which I was still holding to my chest. With each detail, he seemed to wince. When I finished, he exhaled loudly and looked at me with what I thought was his own sense of disappointment.

'Photocopy the transcript but not any of the correspondence,' he said.

I fed the almost 300 pages of the transcript through the photocopier, section by section. Around me, documents were piled on desks and on the floor as well, in cardboard storage boxes with file numbers and names, some which I recognised from newspaper reports, written on the side in black texta. Somewhere, there would be boxes of evidence that had been tendered at Lynette's inquest too. Where were they held? At so many turns it seemed that Lynette was lost – to her children, her family and friends, the police and then even here, in the archives of the Coroners Court. I felt that getting a copy of the transcript was a small victory for her, like it was proof that she mattered. I don't know how Pat and Greg, and Damian too, had endured through years of dead ends, and administrative indifference. Perhaps they don't know how they've done it either.

PART
TWO

CHAPTER SIX

The inquest begins

EVEN THOUGH I KNEW THAT COURTROOM PROCEEDINGS AREN'T anything like the high-drama jousts in *Law & Order*, I carried the transcript home from the Coroners Court excited that at last some pieces of the puzzle were going to come together. Sequestered in my bedroom that afternoon and evening, I read the transcript from cover to cover. The next day I read it through again.

I had initially wanted to read the transcript before meeting any of the witnesses so that I couldn't impose my impressions of them onto what I would find in the transcript. But, like most things, that's not the way it happened. Instead, I could match a face and a voice to nearly everyone. I tried to read the transcript as dispassionately as I could, but after a while I realised that I was sterilising the evidence too much, so I settled on imagining myself seated in the courtroom, looking at each person in the stand, and the coroner to their right.

The role of the Coroners Court is very different to civil and criminal courts. It has no power to find someone guilty of a crime, or to determine civil liability. Rather, the coroner's role is to determine what happened, and to make recommendations to the DPP, who will then decide if the matter is worth prosecuting. The latitude in the Coroners Court is unique.

The inquest opened on Monday 24 February 2003, and Damian Loone was the first witness. Looking at the date on the transcript, I realised that I had a six-week-old baby in February 2003 and would not have been paying attention to much else at the time. It made me think about Greg, Pat and Damian's dogged attempts to keep the case in the public eye. I had initially assumed that surely anyone who had information would have come forward by now, but then remembered that when JC and I had had our first conversations about it at the refuge, it had been almost twenty-five years since Lynette had disappeared, and I was only just hearing about it. Maybe there were others. Maybe there was still more to know.

The police prosecutor's name was Matthew Fordham. When Damian spoke to me about him, he called him Matty Fordham. 'Great bloke,' he'd said.

Matthew Fordham dealt with the mundane matter of handing up the paperwork – the brief of evidence and all the documents upon which his case would be built: marriage certificates, photographs, specialists' reports, items of clothing, aerial photographs, the names of the thirty-one witnesses who'd made statements, most of whom would be called on to give evidence. He also requested that the coroner make a non-publication order for those witnesses who did not wish to be identified in the media. Then he invited Damian to read his own statement.

Damian told the inquest that Chris and Paul Dawson had an 'abnormally close' relationship. He described their parallel lives that persisted into adulthood.

Chris and Paul's brother, Peter, is a solicitor, and he represented Chris. He's older than the twins and from the few photos I could find, he didn't particularly look like them, or at least, he wasn't as handsome. Damian, JC, Pat and Greg had each told me a little about him.

When Damian, in his statement, touched on the sensational sexual allegations against Chris and Paul, Peter objected on Paul's behalf.

'It has no relevance to this inquiry whatsoever.'

Matthew Fordham disagreed. The evidence 'goes to the heart of the motivation for Chris Dawson to leave his wife', he said. 'It goes to the heart of the proposition that there were marriage difficulties. It goes to the heart of the fact that the relationship between Christopher Dawson and Lynette Dawson was so strained that the events which are suspected of taking place could well have taken place, and for those reasons, sir, the evidence is pressed.'

The coroner presiding over the inquest was a magistrate named Carl Milovanovich. He asked Peter Dawson if he would like to be heard further. He replied, 'No, Your Worship,' giving the impression that had he argued more forcefully, the evidence would have been excluded.

Damian detailed other sexual misconduct. When Peter Dawson objected again, the coroner reminded him three times, and brusquely, that he had already objected and been overruled.

There was no dispute that Chris Dawson had had sex with JC but the other allegations regarding sexual activities with students weren't proven.

Damian continued reading his statement. In addition to his own investigation, he quoted from a 1985 report that was prepared following a review of the police response to Chris's 1982 missing person report.

> At 9.15 am on 18 February 1982 Christopher Michael Dawson of 2 Gilwinga Drive, Bayview reported to sergeant third class J Gibbons at the Mona Vale police station that his wife Lynette Joy Dawson born 25/9/48 was missing from her home since 15 January 1982. Mr Dawson informed sergeant Gibbons that he had dropped his wife off at 7am on 9 January at the shops in Mona Vale. Later that day she had contacted him by telephone at Northbridge by an STD call stating she wanted some time to sort things out and was on the Central Coast. His wife called him on 15/1/82 and stated that she needed more time to think. He has not heard of her since that date.

At the end of his statement, Damian told the inquest three times that Lynette had been murdered.

'I have a reasonable suspicion to suspect that Christopher Michael Dawson . . . may be involved in the commission of the class 1 offence of murder, contrary to section 18 of the *Crimes Act 1900*. I suspect that Christopher Dawson . . . murdered Lynette Dawson . . . together with the extraordinary situation of there not being any contact whatsoever with her mother, father, brothers, sister, friends and two very young daughters. It is extraordinary that we are asked to accept that despite not contacting any of those persons, she does in fact contact one person who she is in conflict with, being her husband Christopher Dawson. I believe that Lynette

Joy Dawson was murdered and her body disposed of between the hours of 9 pm Friday 8 January 1982 and 8 am 10 January 1982.'

After a short break, Peter Dawson began his cross-examination. From the outset, Peter Dawson questioned Damian relentlessly – that accuracy wasn't his strong suit, that he had decided too quickly that Lynette's missing person file was a homicide, that he had no experience investigating missing persons, even that Chatswood wasn't on the way to Northbridge Baths, where Chris had a holiday job. Then he moved on to the statement that Lynette's mother, Helena Simms, had given to Damian regarding the morning of Saturday, 9 January 1982. The plan was for Lynette and the girls to travel with Chris to Northbridge Baths. There, they were to meet Lynette's mother and spend the day together, swimming and having a picnic while Chris worked.

'In paragraph 6, you say that Mrs Simms indicates that Chris appeared in an agitated state when she arrived at the pool?'

'Yes.'

'The agitation was whether she'd heard from Lyn, isn't that correct?'

'Whether who had heard from Lyn?'

'Whether Chris had – sorry, Helena Simms had heard from Lyn Dawson?'

'No, Mrs Simms indicated that Christopher Dawson appeared in an agitated state when she arrived at the pool.'

'Are you suggesting that she doesn't say that he – in that agitated state – asked her if she'd heard from Lyn?'

'If Mrs Simms is in an agitated state?'

'No?'

'Could you repeat the questions, please?'

'I'll quote you precisely, it might make it easier. Didn't Helena Simms say [she] "was met by a very agitated Chris wanting to know if Lyn had contacted me"?'

'Well, that's what the statement says. She says she was met by Chris Dawson who appeared in an agitated state when she arrived at the pool.'

'What I suggested to you was that the agitation was due to the fact that he was anxious to find out whether she had heard from Lyn?'

'Why?'

'Sorry, is that your answer to the question, Detective?'

'Sir, I don't see where you're coming from with that question. It's only alleged after Mrs Simms arrives at the pool that Chris receives the [STD] telephone call.'

Peter Dawson seemed confused by the implications of Mrs Simms's statement, so Damian couldn't understand what he was driving at. If Lynette's mother noticed that Chris was agitated when she arrived at Northbridge Baths, before he allegedly received a telephone call from Lynette telling him she was going away, it begs the question, why? Chris knew that Lynette had gone shopping. It also leaves unanswered the question of how Lynette's mother could have heard from her. Helena was travelling from Clovelly to Northbridge by public transport, which would have taken some time. This was before the era of mobile phones, so there would have been no way for Helena to hear from Lynette. It's a very important piece of evidence. Sadly, Helena had died by the time of the second inquest, so Damian had to rely on the statement she had given some years before.

And I wonder who looked after Lynette and Chris's little girls until Helena arrived? The plan was that it would have been Lynette.

They were only two and four years old and still needing the watchful eyes of an adult, especially near water. Lynette was a dedicated mother, a nurse and a childcare worker and it's hard to imagine that she would leave the girls with Chris, while he was working and had to patrol the Baths and the large harbourside areas, because she had a sudden impulse to go shopping.

In other critical areas too, there is no evidence at all. For example, Chris Dawson says that he received an STD telephone call ('STD' meaning a call coming from outside the area, or a long-distance call) from Lynette later that Saturday morning and that she told him she was going away for a while to think about their marriage. In the 1980s, there were several beeps on the line when a long-distance call was received. He said that he was called to the office to take it, but Damian's theory is that that call never came, or, if it did, it was from someone else. One woman came forward after she'd read an article about Lynette in the newspaper. She'd worked in the office at Northbridge Baths, but she couldn't remember the call, or any STD call. I've asked JC if she rang the Baths that day. Chris had asked her to ring him every day and it's possible that because he was working that day, he gave her the number and asked her to ring him there. But JC can't recall doing that.

Peter Dawson continued. 'Don't tell me, Detective, that there weren't other ways of determining who worked at Northbridge pool?'

'Sir, there's no records – microfiche records – kept. I've made some inquiries, there is none kept.'

The testiness between them continues with little or no real value.

On the Friday before Lynette disappeared, she and Chris attended their first and only marriage counselling session. Peter

Dawson asked Damian if he had been able to find out where the appointment was.

'Well, if Mr Dawson had spoken to police and cooperated with our inquiries, we maybe [could have] looked at that information for him.'

'I see, it's all Mr Dawson's fault for not cooperating with you, is it, sir?'

'No, you are, because you instructed me not to speak to him.'

Peter Dawson questioned Damian about his theory that Lynette had never rung Northbridge Baths that day. 'You've got no evidence at all to dispute that, have you?'

'I do not, no. If Mr Dawson could have supplied me with the name of the pool attendant at the time or the girl working in the canteen where the phone call originated from, maybe it may have assisted me.'

'Did you submit those questions?'

'Sir, I'll put this to you again. You directed that no police were to speak to your brother.'

Damian referring to his cross-examiner's 'brother' lays bare the strangeness of Peter Dawson's role. Having representation at the inquest wasn't unusual, but choosing Peter was. It wasn't immediately clear that the Coroners Court was a jurisdiction Peter Dawson was familiar with, and it seemed odd to have him, Lynette's brother-in-law, cross-examining witnesses. Rather than providing assistance that might help determine what had happened to Lynette, Peter Dawson was cross-examining those witnesses who had come to the inquest to do just that. His efforts pitted the Dawson clan against Lynette. And Lynette had been a part of Peter Dawson's family – she had the same surname.

The antagonistic questioning could only go on for so long. When Peter Dawson asked Damian, 'In fact, didn't he [referring to a police officer] tell you that we volunteered every single possible assistance to help you find Lyn Dawson?' the coroner intervened.

'Mr Dawson, I've got to say something at this stage and it concerns me, I suppose, from this point of view, that you're a solicitor of the Supreme Court, yet you're asking questions about matters which are within your personal knowledge in relation to matters that you are putting to this witness. I don't really know whether . . . are you going to be called as a witness in these proceedings, are you going to give evidence?'

'That's a matter for Your Worship.'

'True, but do you feel comfortable, ethically . . .'

'Very comfortable, Your Worship.'

'I don't mind that either, providing you behave ethically correctly, and I don't think emotion should really take over your role as a solicitor, and I tend to detect that you are emotional in this matter and that may be clouding your judgement in relation to the manner in which you're conducting yourself in court and the way in which you're asking questions.'

'Not at all, Your Worship.'

'I expect 100 per cent professionalism . . .'

'Thank you.'

'If you can't do that because of your association with Chris or Paul Dawson then you should reconsider your position.'

'Thank you, Your Worship, for the advice.'

'It's not advice, you appear by leave.'

'Thank you, Your Worship. I believe, Your Worship, that the family has a right to be represented.'

'You appear by leave, the family certainly has a right to be represented—'

'Thank you, Your Worship. Does—'

'Please do not interrupt me when I'm talking to you. I'll give you the courtesy of listening when you speak, if you do the same to me. As a solicitor of the Supreme Court, you do not have a right of appearance before a coroner, you appear by leave, and I've granted you that leave and it will continue at my discretion.'

Carl Milovanovich chastising Peter Dawson makes for uncomfortable reading. Like all courts, the Coroners Court is overly busy, and Peter Dawson tested the coroner's patience. I could picture him in the small courtroom, with his back to the gallery, where those seated could hear every word but only see the coroner on the bench.

Carl Milovanovich has presided over many high-profile inquests. In the transcript, his respect and his compassion for each witness is evident. I still had some legal connections and managed to get his email address and I sent him a note. Although the Coroners Court is different to other courts, I still expected that, like most judges, he wouldn't talk to me. But he replied quickly: 'Give me a ring. You are welcome to come to our home.'

His invitation was spontaneous and warm, but I still felt that I was appearing before a judge, and I had to have my thinking straight. He lived not far from where I'd grown up in north-western Sydney, about 40 kilometres from Manly. Back when I was growing up, it had been semi-rural, but as I drove along a busy four-lane road, a thick urban sprawl had filled it all in. I had lots of questions about the inquest and I was nervous too, because I thought he might have a question for me – 'Why are you doing this?' – and I didn't feel that I had a convincing, or legitimate, answer yet. Most of the time, I did feel that I was doing something worthwhile, but occasionally I was full of doubt and worried that I was annoying, or even offending, Pat or Greg. Damian too. But having come this far, I had to keep going; they'd all given me so much, so I had to stick to my end of the bargain.

An hour after I'd set out, and with some anxiety as I followed new and large freeways across the city, I made a sharp right into a newish housing estate, where all the cars were garaged, leaving the smooth streets empty, and beside the houses, sprinklers were watering gum saplings.

I knocked gently on Carl Milovanovich's door.

'Rebecca!' He was as slim as a pin, wearing jeans, and not much taller than me. He looked fit, like he might be a marathon runner. 'Hope you found us without much trouble?'

'I went to school in Parramatta,' I said, 'so I know my way around a bit.'

Carl told me that he'd also gone to school in Parramatta. 'When I finished, I was given a scholarship to go to Armidale to study to be a teacher,' he said, as I followed him inside, 'but I wasn't ready to leave my family, so I took a position in the public service.'

I told Carl that I'd been shocked to learn that the first inquest into Lynette's disappearance hadn't happened until February 2001 – nineteen years after she had gone missing. It seemed a disturbingly long time.

'In 1982, the standard procedure was for something to not be done for years and years unless there was a reason to suspect something,' Carl said calmly, in contrast to my outrage. 'That Lynette Dawson's matter had taken so long wasn't unusual.'

When I later followed up with Damian, he told me the same thing. 'In the 1980s there was a manual reporting system – it was on cards. It wasn't until the early 1990s that the Computerised Operational Police System for missing persons came in. We relied a lot more on family then.'

'The only unusual thing was that there had already been an inquest,' Carl said, settling on the lounge. 'So, when it came back, I wanted to make sure that everything was done.

'Preparing for an inquest, a coroner reads the brief, directs police if there is more information to be collected. A good detective will come and meet the coroner quite a few times. They might tell the coroner what they need.' He paused until I looked up and made eye contact, telling me with that look that Damian was such a policeman. 'So, in Dawson, I applied to the Supreme Court for listening devices.'

That is, a listening device on Chris Dawson's telephone. A warrant for a telephone tap isn't easy to get. The Supreme Court must be satisfied that it will help the police investigate a suspected criminal offence and if the court is satisfied, the tap will only be given for a specific purpose and for a limited time period. Ultimately, Carl told me, the telephone taps 'yielded nothing'.

This relationship between the coroner, the police and the police prosecutor is another procedural anomaly of the Coroners Court. In other courts, judges remain at arm's length to protect their impartial role. In the coronial jurisdiction, the police and the police prosecutor consult the coroner to ensure they gather all the relevant and available evidence. So, when Peter Dawson cross-examined Damian he was, in part, also questioning Carl.

'Peter Dawson was a hopeless advocate,' Carl volunteered with surprising candour. 'From memory, I might have questioned him ethically if he could do it without feeling compromised. It would be like doing a frontal lobotomy on yourself.'

At the inquest, Peter Dawson continued challenging Damian on his theory that Chris had killed Lynette so that he could be with JC. He took Damian back to 23 December 1981, when Chris and JC had left Sydney and headed to Queensland to start a new life together. But before they'd even made it to the state border, they turned back because JC was homesick.

'In fact, Chris Dawson returned to his wife?' Peter Dawson asked Damian.

'Yes.'

'So I'm suggesting to you that he'd already left his wife and family so he showed that he was prepared to do that.'

He makes a fair point. We have to assume that if JC hadn't become homesick, they would have kept going and Chris would, in effect, have left everything else behind. But what is also true is that Chris only went back to Lynette because JC decided she couldn't go to Queensland and not because he realised he'd made a mistake.

It's a tough piece of evidence. It does show that Chris was prepared to forgo control of the family home and assets – which isn't to say that he would have ended up with nothing, although the court would have ruled in Lynette's favour – but it also shows him to be so cold-hearted that he was willing to leave his wife and children two days before Christmas. Worse, he left Lynette stranded at Warriewood with the children and the shopping, ringing the house from a public telephone trying to find him. She had to organise another lift home, where she found Chris's letter, telling her that he'd left. The note contained nothing about how Lynette and the girls would be provided for, nor any mention of when or how he would see his children. He had abandoned them. And while Lynette spent the next three days hoping that he would come back, the truth was that when Chris did come back, it was only because JC had had a change of heart. Given the state of their marriage and having made the break, it's hard to understand why he returned to the house at all. Perhaps, as Chris headed north, he had time to think about the financial difficulty of starting from scratch in Queensland. And could Peter Dawson understand the implications of Chris leaving the way he did and then coming back? Or was he blind to Chris's terrible behaviour because he was his brother?

On Friday, 8 January 1982, the day before Lynette went missing, she and Chris attended a marriage counselling appointment. They left the girls at the childcare centre while they were gone, and Lynette's colleagues say that when they came back to collect them, Lynette seemed happy. Peter Dawson questioned Damian about it.

'They attended a marriage counselling session?'

'Yes.'

'After which they left happy?'

'Yes.'

'I'm sorry, I'm having trouble finding the motive that you are suggesting, Detective?'

'Why would she leave if that was the scenario in which you've just agreed with me, if that was the scenario that Lynette Dawson . . . that they see a psychiatrist in relation to their marital problems and they both walk out of there and, in fact, Christopher Dawson says later in an interview with detectives in 1991 [it] was the first time in six months, they walked out holding hands and he had wished, and if I could find the paragraph, that things were going – and he says, this is on 15 January 1991 when he's interviewed by detectives from the Homicide Squad, if you'd like to hear me out, sir, I'll give you the answer—'

'I'm agreeing with you?'

Damian then quotes from Chris Dawson's 1991 interview.

'"I remember walking out of there for the first time in six months and holding hands and thinking that our marriage was going to, sort of, that our problems were going to be resolved and things were going to work out." It defies logic that if – on the eve of her disappearance she's happy in her marriage, she goes missing the next day.'

Rather than presenting a narrative that is plausibly supported by the evidence, Peter Dawson seems to ping-pong from one idea to the next. But here, he can't seem to understand what Damian is saying. So, rather than actually challenging Damian, he continues to press him, until Damian explodes in frustration.

'Why would she leave if that was the scenario?!'

In the same interview, Chris told the police that 'after the marriage guidance, for a few days, Lyn seemed disturbed by the results of that'. This is interesting, in light of his previous statement that Lynette was happy after the counselling session. It's also curious that several people gave evidence that Lynette and Chris attended marriage counselling on Friday 8 January and she disappeared the next day, not 'a few days' later.

Chris claimed that Lynette had used her bank card twice in the week after she went missing, the first time on 12 January 1982, and then again, a few days later. Damian had told me that, in his view, Chris had concocted the bank card use to support the idea that Lynette was still alive after the morning of 9 January 1982, when he said he last saw her. But at the inquest Damian's evidence about the bank card was contradictory.

Initially, when he'd read his report to the court at the outset of the inquest, he'd said, 'There were two bank card transactions on Lynette Dawson's account at the Warriewood Square shopping centre in 1982 subsequent to her disappearance. It is felt that if Lynette Dawson's bank card was fraudulently used, then it is likely it was used by another female in order to suggest Lynette Dawson was alive and well.' A few pages later he included part of the 1985 report that had been composed following a complaint to the ombudsman about the police's missing person investigation. 'To assist the court in relation to some important information contained in the file, I will transcribe this report . . . as follows: "A check of his wife's bank card revealed that she had operated it at Warriewood on 12 January 1982."'

At both mentions, Damian appears to accept that the bank-card transactions took place. Later, when Peter Dawson questioned Damian about the bank card, he again appears to accept that it was used.

'There were two bank card transactions on Lyn Dawson's account?'

'Yes.'

'You have resolved that those transactions are not genuine, is that right?'

'I said it's likely it was used by another female, then it would be fraudulent.'

'In fact you asked Marilyn Dawson outright?'

'Yes, I did.'

'When you interviewed her and she denied using the bank card?'

'Yes, that's right.'

And further on: 'In fact, you've got no evidence whatsoever that anyone other than Lyn Dawson signed that bank card?'

'That's right.'

'And if in fact Lyn Dawson signed the bank card, Detective, she was alive after 9 January 1982, wasn't she?'

'[Bank card charges] weren't always processed on the day or the week and often enough from my own personal experience that you may get a bank card statement two weeks after with a wrong date on it, when it was processed by the batch through the bank,' explained Damian. 'It may be another date. It doesn't mean to say that on that day you purchased something, it may be the date that it was batched through the bank.'

'So what you're suggesting now is that not some other female signed the bank card but the bank card was used on a different date?

'It could be both, it could be both. I am not sure, I don't know.'

'The only thing you've suggested so far, Detective, is that another female signed it?'

'Yes.'

Later, Peter Dawson questioned Damian further about the bank card, this time referring to the report that had been prepared in 1985, following the complaint to the ombudsman.

'"A check on his wife's bank card revealed she had operated it at Warriewood on 12 January 1982."'

'Yes.'

'Not that it was processed that day but she had operated it on that day?'

'Well, it's a report saying a check on his wife's bank card revealed she had operated it at Warriewood on 12 January 1982. Yes, that's right.'

'And if in fact that's the case, Lyn Dawson operated it on 12 January 1982, she was alive well after she left Chris Dawson on the morning of 9 January 1982?'

'Well, I disagree, sir, it's a report from an inspector referring to the inadequate investigation and he says – he does say here in the report, a check on [Chris Dawson's] wife's bank card revealed she had operated it at Warriewood on 12 January 1982.'

'That's fairly clear though, isn't it?'

'But I can't confirm that with the inspector, if where he is saying that she operated it, where he got that information from. Did he personally know? I wouldn't imagine so. He's been told that.'

'Detective, isn't this the case, if in fact Lyn Dawson operated her bank card on 12 January 1982, your allegation that Chris murdered her on the night of 9 January 1982 is incorrect?'

'I cannot say that it was Lyn Dawson who operated the card on 12 January 1982.'

'The question was, if Lyn Dawson operated it on 12 January 1982, she could not have been murdered on the night of 9 January 1982, could she?'

'That's right.'

'And you have no evidence that it was *not* Lyn Dawson who operated the bank account – the bank card on 12 January 1982?'

'That's right.'

Why didn't he nail the view that he had expressed to me, that the bank card transactions were never made? Why hadn't Matthew Fordham elicited that information from Damian? Fortunately, in his final submissions, Matthew Fordham clarified the point. 'The closest we get to locating her [Lynette] are the bank card transactions which were allegedly processed on 12 and 26 January 1982 . . . I note that the bank card statements have never been produced by Chris Dawson.'

CHAPTER SEVEN

Physical evidence

PETER DAWSON ALSO BROUGHT DAMIAN'S ATTENTION TO THE DIGS that were carried out under the paved area around the swimming pool at Chris and Lynette's house.

'But in any event you've now had two digs at the property?' Peter Dawson asked.

'Yes.'

'And ground-penetrating radar?'

'Yes.'

'Cadaver dogs?'

'Yes.'

'And the only item of interest whatsoever you found is a cardigan?'

'Yes.'

When the inquest opened, the cardigan, along with the brief and other reports, was tendered into evidence. Exhibit #6, 'Items of Clothing Found Around the Swimming Pool', would have been handed up in a marked plastic bag, the panels of fine-knit fabric dirty and pale. Greg Simms told me that he and Pat had wanted to be present at the digs, but they weren't allowed. However, in 2013, *Wanted* – a television program about cold cases – ran a segment about Lynette, which included footage of the 2000 dig around the swimming pool. I pulled the episode up on YouTube.

'We are attempting this morning to dig with the possibility of a body being found in this area,' Damian says directly to the camera, as he stands beside the pool. He's wearing jeans and a blue T-shirt and looks younger, of course, although heavier than he is now. A white wrought-iron fence frames the swimming pool and, elevated behind it, a garden bed of thick greenery pushes against a wide verandah.

Two policemen in navy trousers and short-sleeved shirts walk slowly around the pool, looking, it seems, for the best place to start digging. The camera zooms in on a mallet that's breaking the pavers, and I flinch with each blow. It then cuts to a man in white overalls, with 'Police Rescue Service' across his shoulders, standing a foot deep in a rectangular cut of clay. He bends over and, from the clay, picks out a faded, dirty pink cardigan, which he gently spreads on the ground.

'And we did find a cardigan buried in the ground,' Damian says to camera, in his suit, back in the office. The footage then cuts to the cardigan splayed on the clayish soil by the man in the white overalls. Damian's voice again: 'A female cardigan. And the cardigan was in five pieces.'

The camera cuts again to a woman delicately holding a dirty cloth panel, turning it over to show the front and the back. She holds the panel up to her chest, to show where it would have fitted as the front left part of the cardigan. She isn't identified, but I know she is Denise Donlon, the forensic archaeologist who'd assisted Damian at the dig. I was so absorbed by what she was doing that I completely missed what Damian was saying, until I replayed the video. 'And there were some cut marks.'

I rewound the footage and watched it again. Denise tentatively holds the cardigan and turns it front and back for the camera. This time, I noticed the straight and deliberate cuts. Instead of really seeing what was in front of me, I was thinking about how hard it must have been for Pat and Greg while the dig was happening, anxiously waiting for Damian to call, all the while imagining what was going on; and later, the trauma of seeing the ferocious mallet and shovel footage. It wasn't hard to imagine my distress, if they'd been digging for my sister. I paused the video and rested my head on the back of the chair, wondering what the discovery really meant. I wasn't given access to the exhibits so I couldn't read Denise Donlon's report, which was handed up to the court and entered in the transcript as an analyst's certificate, so later that night, I sent her an email, asking if I could chat to her about the dig. The next day, she replied.

'I'm sorry but I don't give interviews about my forensic work.'

Denise's work needed to be kept 'clean', and any compromise risked potential contamination of the evidence. It's easy to imagine a cross-examiner inferring that her opinion of the cardigan could have been influenced by a meeting with someone like me and by what we might have discussed. I imagine that Damian hadn't allowed Greg and Pat to be present at the digs for the same reason – because he had to protect his work from any suggestion that he'd been influenced by their presence. As best he could, he also had to put his personal feelings aside.

A few days after watching the *Wanted* episode, I met Damian for a coffee. Outside the police station, I almost felt as if I was waiting for a friend. Damian appeared, and I followed him across the street – the traffic slowing to let a cop go through, with me tucked in his slipstream – and into a café with a sandstone courtyard.

'I've been as sick as a dog,' he told me, as soon as we'd ordered. 'Shocking flu, off for two weeks.' I could see that he'd lost weight, although his cheeks looked rosy and healthy.

'Did you have someone to look after you?' I asked.

'Nah. *Had* someone,' he chuckled, 'but that's over.'

The conversation came to Lynette, and I asked him about the cardigan.

'There were sixteen cuts in the cardigan made by a sharp object, perhaps a knife,' he said. 'And the cuts suggested a pattern consistent with classic defence wounds.'

Defence wounds, he told me, might be cuts on the outside of the arms if they were being held up to protect the face. 'And don't forget, Chris and Lynette bought the block of land when it was rock and bush,' he said, 'so the jumper has to be Lyn's.' It's likely that the cardigan was Lynette's but there's no way of proving it. It could easily have been left by someone who'd been over at the Dawsons' for a barbeque.

Pat had told me that there was an empty juice-box with a use-by date of 1982 found near the cardigan. 'In the same hole at the same depth of three feet,' she said. The significance of this detail, which Pat had pressed on me as a prosaic piece of carbon dating, now found its place.

'Peter Gunn was my crime scene officer,' Damian said. 'He examined the cardigan and found DNA, most likely blood.'

Damian fixed me again with his steely stare, which I was coping with better, but I nonetheless felt my blood pressure rise. 'The tests showed signs of mitochondrial DNA, and Peter, who was excellent, suggested I take it to a lab in Texas that does mitochondrial analysis.'

Mitochondrial DNA, I found out, is inside every cell and is inherited only from the mother, so testing can prove, for example, that two individuals have the same mother. If the Texas lab detected mitochondrial DNA, it could be compared to Pat and Greg's mitochondrial DNA, and if it matched, then the DNA on the cardigan would most likely be Lynette's. It's of course possible that it might be someone else's DNA, someone else close to Lynette. But it could be a strong piece of evidence. It was an expensive analysis and after years of lobbying, Damian was able to take the cardigan to Texas.

The *Daily Telegraph* published an article about it in May 2009.[4] There's a photo of Damian, his hands deep in the pockets of his black suit, and the photographer has shot him from below, so he appears to be looming across the page, like a gritty film noir detective. A sub-editor's gauche headline, 'Relentless Cop's DNA Quest in Cardigan Killer Case', feels like another slight that Greg and Pat have had to endure in their efforts to find Lynette.

> When Sydney Detective Sergeant Damian Loone boarded a Qantas plane bound for the United States he had more than just a wallet and newspaper in his hand luggage.
>
> Inside his case was a hoard of DNA samples – 15 swabs taken from the mouths of family members of missing Australians plus

specimens of unidentified bones and tissue collected by NSW police.

But more importantly to him, was a very delicate pale pink cardigan believed to be owned by missing Northern Beaches woman Lynette Dawson.

'It was never out of my sight,' Sgt Loone told the *Daily Telegraph* yesterday.

'Wherever it went, I went.'

And further down, Greg is quoted: 'If it comes back with DNA it just means everything to us.'

In another article in the *Daily Telegraph*,[5] Chris Dawson is quoted as saying, 'Of course they're going to find DNA on it. My DNA on her cardigan doesn't mean anything. I'll give them my DNA, I'm more than happy to discuss this with my lawyers and the police.' Had Chris just confirmed that the cardigan was Lynette's and that his DNA would be on it?

The Texas lab did find DNA but, despite the technology, couldn't detect any mitochondrial DNA.

'Blood degrades very quickly,' Damian told me, with understated disappointment.

At the inquest, Peter Dawson asked Damian, 'And no evidence at all as to who that cardigan belonged to?'

'No.'

Pat had told me, 'They found Lynette's top in the backyard.' But no one could produce a photo of her wearing it or positively say they remembered her wearing a pink cardigan. Nothing else – the digs, the dogs, mallets, star pickets, the scientific tests – supported

Damian's theory that Lynette was murdered and then buried at the Bayview property.

Peter Dawson could have left matters there. But instead, he opened a bizarre line of questioning.

'Isn't Task Force Fenwick looking into the disappearance of Newcastle women in the seventies, eighties and nineties? Did you investigate any of the suggestions that Ivan Milat was in that area at the time?'

'It's like saying how long is a piece of string, Mr Dawson,' Damian replied. 'I could go on here for days and days and days and I'll keep doing it.'

'Exactly, Detective, but what I'm suggesting to you is that you've made a lot of efforts in one direction but no efforts to actually locate Lyn Dawson.'

'Sir, when I do an investigation it is part of my plan as a detective that I have a management in which way I do my investigation, because at the end of the long day it is the [. . .] taxpayers' money that is paying for this and I am not going to go out willy-nilly because something might be something. I have nothing to lead me in that area and I have to discount it. There is nothing to suggest that Mr Milat was in Bayview on 9 or 10 January. He may [have been], I don't know that. No one knows that.'

Damian's frustration is palpable. It's hard to know if Peter Dawson was attempting to do more than insinuate that Damian's investigation was deficient. With the bank card evidence, Peter Dawson was trying to show that the transactions were proof of life, but when he raised the Ivan Milat angle, he was suggesting that Lynette was murdered. Lacking real conviction about this suggestion, he soon took Damian back to where he began – claiming that the Dawson family had offered every assistance, and Damian was to blame for not enlisting that assistance.

'But you can't say you didn't have assistance if you hadn't asked for it, can you?'

'Mr Dawson, you are aware that you've sent faxes to the Dee Why detectives' office where I was not allowed to go anywhere near your brother Christopher Dawson.'

At this point, the coroner interjected.

'Mr Dawson, this line of cross-examination is not particularly assisting me. If you somehow feel that you or your clients haven't been given the opportunity to assist police, I'm quite happy for them to walk through the back door now and have an interview with the detective straightaway.'

Peter Dawson pressed on. 'Do you have one scrap of evidence that Paul Dawson assisted Chris Dawson to kill Lyn Dawson?'

'If I had,' Damian replied, 'we wouldn't be in a coronial inquest, we'd be at the Supreme Court.'

During those crucial eleven hours, from Friday night to Saturday morning, Paul says that he was holidaying with his family at Munmorah Park on the Central Coast, which is about a two-hour drive north of Sydney. Lake Munmorah is unremarkable, and is surrounded by dry scrub, but it's close to some beautiful beaches. Damian questioned Paul about that holiday, when he interviewed him in 1999.

'When had you gone on holiday, say, in relation to that Saturday, the 9th of January?'

'I think we were gone a week or so, so it would have been a matter of days. We went to Lake Munmorah so we probably would only have stayed with the three kids, we probably only stayed a week all together, so, school holidays, probably a Wednesday to a Wednesday, I think, I'm, again, Marilyn might remember, I don't know.'

'Right. So, if Saturday was the 9th of January, the Wednesday before would be the 6th of January, and just in approximate terms you're looking from the 6th to the 13th you were away?'

'I think so, yeah.'

'Have you done research into the behaviour of identical twins?' Peter then asked Damian.

'Yes.'

'And you know the statistics and availability of identical twins?'

'I am one,' Damian said.

It's also possible that Lynette's body wasn't disposed of on the Friday night, but later. But it's all conjecture.

The coroner tried to wrap things up. 'Mr Dawson, look, I'm sorry but I'm going to have to draw the line here . . . unless there are further questions of relevance, please sit down.'

But Peter Dawson didn't sit down, and after a short recess, he said, 'Would Your Worship note my objection to what I regard as Your Worship gagging my line of cross-examination?'

The coroner exploded. 'You can't *object*, Mr Dawson! This is my inquiry.' When Peter Dawson persisted, he dealt him a swift lesson in practice and procedure.

'This is not a criminal court where anyone is charged with any crime. It is an investigation into the disappearance . . . if you're going to suggest something to the detective that you feel needs to be investigated or something new that we haven't looked at that might assist me, or that we can look at, I'm happy to hear, but if you're simply going to attack the officer on his investigation, it is not assisting me.'

Then, nearing the end of his cross-examination, Peter Dawson tried to wrong-foot Damian with statistics. He told Damian that around 8000 people go missing every year, of which 99.6 per cent are located quickly, leaving thirty-two persons unaccounted for in New South Wales every year.

'But of course, what that means, Detective, is that thirty-two persons a year are not located, is that right?'

'If my mathematics is correct, probably, yes.'

The coroner interjected. 'We know all these statistics, Mr Dawson. We also know the statistic that most of those people who are not located are subject to homicide.'

Dawson paused. 'I'm sorry, Your Worship, I don't know that.'

'Well, I do, that's why I'm the coroner.'

CHAPTER EIGHT

The star witness

ON THE THIRD DAY OF THE INQUEST, THE WITNESS EVERYONE WAS waiting for took the stand. JC was thirty-nine in 2003, and she was attractive and self-assured – so utterly different to the elfin fifteen-year-old she'd been when Chris Dawson arrived at Cromer High. JC is a great communicator – she's confident, intelligent and capable. She has a psychology degree, and can offer insight into other people's behaviour, as well as her own. But she is equally fragile and when she falters, her composure completely collapses.

I pictured that small courtroom. There would have been few empty seats when JC was called to the witness stand. I could see her striding firmly across the room, avoiding eye contact.

Matthew Fordham took JC briskly through the circumstances of her life at the time Lynette went missing: the crowded apartment, her absent father, MMC and RN's drinking and violence, the generally abusive environment at home, her loneliness, her vulnerability.

'Were there incidents of violence towards yourself from [RN]?'

'When I . . . when I stepped in, in front of my mother, when he was attacking her, yes.'

She told the inquest what happened after Chris Dawson arrived at Cromer High as a PE teacher.

'He told me that the year before, when I was in Year 10 and he was a new teacher to the school, that he noticed me in the play-ground and said that he wanted to get to know me better and, so he deliberately took that class.'

'And throughout the Year 11 class in 1980, could you describe his behaviour towards you?'

'He was very attentive.'

'Was there any particular instance that stands out in your mind as demonstrating that attentiveness?'

'He would brush past me in the classroom, he would direct his attention towards me, fairly obviously, I thought.'

'Did he ever write you notes or anything like that?'

'Yes, he left numerous notes in my bag every single day, but there was more later on.'

'What sort of notes did he leave in your schoolbag?'

'That he loved me, that he needed me, that, you know, I was really important to him.'

'When you were in Year 11 did you come to be in contact with Chris Dawson away from school?'

'Yes. I can't remember days but a friend of mine and I used to play tennis, and Chris and his wife were invited to play tennis at the school with us. I don't know who instigated it, but that's how it happened and then I was asked to babysit for Chris and Lyn.'

'At the time that you came into contact with Chris and Lyn, at this time, what were the circumstances like at your home with RN?'

'It was very abusive and very uncomfortable for everyone.'

'And at the time that you came into contact with Mr Dawson and his wife, what was your opinion of Chris Dawson?'

'I went to him for help. He saved me in lots of ways from what was happening in my own home.'

Even though JC had told me everything, I still found reading about her abuse in the transcript upsetting. Peter Dawson didn't raise any objections, because the facts – that JC was from an abusive home and then was abused by the teacher she turned to for help – were accepted. 'Agreed facts', they call them in litigation. I kept thinking back to my own schooling and wondering if the same wilful blindness by teachers and administrators could have occurred. But the real question took me a little longer to formulate: could the same thing have even *happened* at my school?

From time to time, I would drive past Cromer High and I'd always slow down to have a good look. I'd always liked the campus's brutalist architecture, with a smattering of ghostly gums and square concrete buildings that looked like gigantic blocks, cutting sharp lines against a blue sky. Then, one day, I noticed a banner tied to the powder-coated aluminium fence advertising an open night. I rang JC from the car and asked if she'd like to go with me.

'You bet I would,' she answered.

It was raining when I picked JC up for the open night. We parked a discreet distance from the school and made up a story about why we were there, just in case we were asked, just in case we looked suspicious. We were looking at the school with my children in mind; she had come along as a friend.

'It looks exactly the same,' JC remarked, as we made our way through the front gates and into a courtyard. She pointed to a short flight of stairs. 'I punched a girl over there.'

'Why?' I asked, frowning at her.

'Because my friends dared me to. She turned around and we had a fistfight. That's peer pressure for you.'

My only experience of a public high school was the one I used to walk through every day on my way home from primary school. Through a cloud of smoking teenagers, there was talk about drugs and someone 'getting their head bashed in' by a fellow student. It was a fearsome thoroughfare for a shy eleven-year-old, and I was relieved when my parents sent me to the Catholic girls' school in Parramatta instead.

We took the stairs up to the library, which was split-level, a common feature in buildings of the time. As we turned to leave, JC whispered, 'Do you remember that woman over there?'

'No,' I said blankly, looking at an attractive woman with her teenage son.

'She was at the refuge.' She looked no different to any other mother who was there that night and I wondered if that was because she now had a life free of violence or because, like many other women, she was able to disguise that she lives in fear.

A little further on, we came upon a sign, which JC read aloud with mock pride. '"Respect, Responsibility, Achievement, Integrity." They're talking about the teachers, not the students.'

We guffawed like schoolgirls.

We went back down to the quadrangle and JC showed me the science labs and the area outside where they left their schoolbags while they were in class.

'That's where he put notes in my bag,' she said. 'He knew my bag. It was one that I wanted, and he bought it for me.'

Later, JC showed me some of the cards from Chris that she has saved. They are puerile. There are a few that are obviously part of a set, that have a cartoon of a baby, wearing only a nappy, with the words 'I Wuv You' – something tweens might give to each other. There are cards wishing JC a happy sixteenth and seventeenth birthday.

We stepped inside the gym and I looked over at JC, searching, I suppose, for a reaction, but she only looked quietly pleased to be there. We stood at the back and listened to a band with a girl, still in her school uniform, singing out front. The crowd was a mix of students sitting on the ground in twos and threes, and mums and dads, smiling and moving to the music. We left as they were finishing and behind us, loud hooting and whistling erupted.

'They were good,' I said.

'In Year 7, I was very good at music,' JC said, proudly. 'I played the trumpet. I couldn't read music but they never detected that. I just played by ear.'

Back in the quadrangle and a little further along from the gym, JC stopped. 'This is it,' she said, pointing to a door. 'This is the PE staffroom.'

There were no windows looking into the room, just the door. 'Really? It looks like a broom closet.'

'It's quite big actually,' JC said. 'There were four teachers in there. And a shower.'

Someone put me in touch with a student who'd been at Cromer High at the same time as JC and Chris. He sent me an email and asked that he not be identified.

> It was no secret that Chris and JC were involved somehow. As young kids we knew it was wrong or weird but not really knowing . . . I'd see JC seek Chris out at lunchtime, visiting his office. Seemed to be a daily ritual of her standing at the door to the small PE office every lunch hour chatting with Chris. I remember [teacher X] shared the same little PE office space as Chris, seemed to be the only person in the whole school who was outraged by it all. I guess [teacher X] was in there listening to it all.

On the night we visited the school, JC had been upbeat. I think I felt more outraged, as if I was visiting a historical site and trying to imagine the awful things that had happened there. But she was slow to burn, and wasn't angry until a few weeks later. She recalled that in the PE staffroom one day, she and Chris told another teacher about their relationship. 'Stunned' was how she described that teacher's reaction. Then, in Year 12, the same teacher asked some students who they were taking to the formal and JC 'famously' announced that she was going with 'Mr Dawson'.

How did all of this go unchecked, or sufficiently unchecked that more wasn't done? Everyone seemed to know that Chris and JC were involved and every student in that class knew, as well as the teacher, that JC was going to the formal with Mr Dawson. Would I have gone home and told my parents about this startling piece of news? Some of the teachers must have seen something – some certainly knew something – but little was done.

JC told the inquest that not too long after she and her friend had started playing tennis with the new PE teacher and his wife, she was babysitting for the Dawsons regularly. There were no buses from Bayview late at night, so Chris would drive her home afterwards. Then she began staying overnight in the spare bedroom to save Chris the drive. Soon, she was staying the whole weekend, even when Chris and Lynette weren't going out.

Around that time, Chris started giving JC driving lessons. Matthew Fordham directed JC to one particular driving lesson, when they'd parked by the beach. Chris confessed his feelings for JC and then kissed her. Not long after that, towards the end of 1980, Chris took her to his parents' place in Maroubra.

'That was the first time we had sexual intercourse, any sort of intimate behaviour like that,' she told the inquest. 'I was sixteen.'

When JC gave this evidence at the inquest I wondered if she'd tried to detach from her feelings, from what she was recounting. She was going to be in the witness stand for a long time and sticking to facts might have been the only way she could get through it. Sometimes, it made her appear harsh.

Damian had stressed the closeness of the twins, and JC gave examples to the inquest as well.

'They lived within metres of one another, they spent every waking [minute together] – they went to school together, they had the same bottle of Coke every day together, they had – Paul had girlfriends, young girlfriends at the same time. I saw them with him.'

She told the inquest that Chris and Paul would sometimes turn up to where she and her underage girlfriends would go drinking on a Friday night, as if seducing JC was also a joint enterprise.

'He [Chris] isolated me from my friends and he talked about himself, about his football prowess and you know, trying to impress me, as I saw it.'

Matthew Fordham asked JC more.

'Before December 1981, before you went up to, or tried to go to Queensland with Chris, did you have much contact with Paul Dawson?'

'Yes, I . . . I'd spent a fair bit of time with him.'

'You mentioned the University of New England, that was the university where Chris and Paul were both studying by correspondence, is that correct?'

'Yes.'

'And is it the case that part of that degree involved a residential school?'

'Yes.'

'And do you remember how long before Lyn went missing that the residential school took place?'

'I remember the trees were dropping their leaves, so that's autumn, isn't it?'

'Do you know how long that residential school was for?'

'It was a week.'

'And you mention that you went up with Chris?'

'Yes.'

'And another girl went up with Paul?'

'Yes.'

'Do you know if Marilyn was aware that the other girl had gone up with Paul?'

'No, I don't know.'

'Did it appear to you that yourself and the other girl were both there in secret?'

'Yes.'

Piece by piece, Matthew Fordham was building a picture that suggested that the Dawson twins engaged in disturbing behaviour and thought the rules didn't apply to them. And in some ways, they didn't.

From 1969 to 1975, the ABC ran a social affairs television series called *Chequerboard*. Some of the topics were challenging for the time – an episode about a homosexual couple who 'came out'; a personal portrait of a Vietnamese refugee; and, in 1975, an episode about twins, which featured Chris and Paul Dawson. They were twenty-seven years old then, and at the height of their athletic abilities. There's footage of them running around a field, passing a football, lifting weights, coaching schoolboys. They are trim and handsome, thoughtful but not boastful. Paul is the well-mannered spokesman, Chris the much shyer twin. Sitting side by side before a studio audience, they present as the most wholesome, well-bred men you'd ever hope to meet.

They recalled that when they were nine or ten years old, they went shopping separately only to find, when they got home, that they had both purchased the same shirts; and like many twins, they invented their own language. 'We had our own language and we had to go to sort of speech therapy at five to seven years of age to learn how to speak properly,' Paul said. 'We could understand each other and as far as we were concerned it was good enough.'

Asked if their parents ever separated them, Chris said, 'Mum went to the fete and Paul decided to go to the fete with Mum and

I went to the pictures with Dad and we both had miserable times, vowing that we'd never, sort of, go our separate ways again. So most of the time it was to our own choice – the only choice – that we should stay together rather than be forced to separate.'

The reporter, Robin Hughes, then asks, 'There's a lot of controversy about how to bring up children who are twins, and some people are against their being brought up as twins and think that their individuality should be emphasised, and there are others who like the idea of twins being brought up very much as a unit. Now, how were you treated, how did your parents bring you up?'

'We were treated as a unit but I think our own individuality still developed,' Paul replied. 'It's a very hard relationship to explain to anyone that's not a twin . . . it's not like a husband and wife relationship, it's not a brother–brother, so just normal brother–brother relationship, it's something apart from all those.'

It's a jumbled answer, possibly because it's not clear to them how to define their relationship.

One day, when JC and I were walking across the rock ledge that jutted out above the ocean pool at Dee Why, we sat on a bench that was only a few feet back from where the ledge fell away to a rocky platform, 10 metres below. I knew enough about the sexual allegations against Chris from reading the transcript, so I'd decided not to ask JC anything more. This suited me; I don't want to talk about anyone's sex life. But she continued, as if telling me this were no different to anything else she'd told me about.

We stood up to head back, and only a metre behind us, a young couple stood, looking out to sea. They must have heard us. What had they made of two middle-aged women sitting on a bench, shouting into the ocean breeze about their sex lives? It probably worried me more than JC. She'd lost her privacy years ago, when she gave evidence at the inquest and saw it gobbled up by the media both at the time and since. Perhaps she didn't care about strangers; I imagine it would be more embarrassing for her friends and workmates to know, or even the guy at the corner café where JC is such a regular that when she walks in he asks, 'A JC?'

JC was just seventeen when Lyn disappeared. Chris had been manipulating her for nearly two years – she was sixteen years old when he zeroed in on her and at thirty-two years old he was twice her age – and she couldn't have fully understood the implications of what she was doing. Chris had groomed JC into a place she shouldn't have been, and the power balance was still set at teacher–student.

'It wasn't an equal relationship. He had Paul for his adult relationship,' JC told me. 'What he needed from me was a slave and someone to make him feel like he was king of the world. I was a trophy.'

JC held nothing back when she told me about these events, although sometimes it felt like she underplayed them to the point where she seemed more like an eyewitness than a participant. I wondered if she did this partly to distance herself from them, and partly because she didn't want to be dismissed for sounding melodramatic.

JC and Chris's relationship continued into 1981 as she was going into her final year of school. Her friend MC was concerned that she was spending a lot of time in the PE staffroom and asked JC about it. They're still good friends, so I gave her a call and she invited me over.

MC lives in a quiet street that runs along Narrabeen Lake. The edge of the road runs off into a grassy verge and at the back of the houses, tall reeds mark the waterline. A bitterly cold wind was blowing from the south when I visited, and from where we sat at the back of the house, we watched the water being blown into sharp brown peaks.

'I could see,' MC said, 'we all could, that JC was going to the PE staffroom a lot. She told me that he was helping her with her problems at home. I knew there were a lot of issues going on at home. I didn't like going to her place because her mother was cold and mean and I think by this time RN had moved in as well.'

'One day I went to the apartment in Dee Why. I wanted to talk to her to see if she really was all right about being involved with Chris. She was only sixteen. But she ran away from me. She didn't want to talk about it.'

Then one day at school, Chris called MC into his office. 'He told me I was being a bad friend to JC. He accused me of spreading rumours. My mother thought it was odd that he had called me [in] but she didn't do anything, didn't go and see him or say anything to the school.' I looked up from my note-taking and MC and I shared a look – two mothers, registering alarm. 'It was different then,' she said. 'Parents stood back a lot more. My mother even remembers that Chris gave me a tennis racquet to appease me in some way.'

After they finished Year 12, MC heard that Lynette had gone missing and that JC had moved into the house. 'We kept asking her out, but she wouldn't come, so eventually we just stopped asking. We lost touch and I really only saw her again when she came back to Sydney with KD.'

Later, when I told JC what MC had said, she was upset. 'I wasn't *allowed* to associate with anyone. He even discouraged me from seeing my family.'

MC looks back with dismay. 'The culture at the school was terrible. Teachers were buying alcohol for students, smoking dope with them after school. We all knew another girl was seeing one of the teachers. I can't understand why the headmaster didn't do more at the time. Why didn't the police step in?' She paused. 'It's horrifying. My daughter is sixteen. I sent my kids to private schools because of what had gone on at Cromer.'

Not long after my visit, an article appeared in the *Sydney Morning Herald*, about the sentencing of another Cromer High teacher over abuses during that same period.[7]

> Peter Wayne Scott committed 14 child sex offences in the early to mid-1980s while working as an art teacher at Cromer High School on the Northern Beaches.
>
> Scott used his position to groom, drug and then sexually abuse teenage boys from the school, molesting and assaulting them in classrooms and storerooms during school hours or after school in his panel van and at his beachfront home.
>
> It was only years later that the students, then grown men, felt capable of coming forward to police to talk about what had happened to them years before.
>
> 'The offender was an educated and mature-aged man who embarked on a course of criminality and by his actions exploited and indecently assaulted the victims for his own purposes,' Judge Sarah Huggett told the Downing Centre District Court in sentencing Scott.
>
> 'These acts were carried out by a teacher who adults trusted and who students thought was "cool and nice".'

At home, things continued to deteriorate for JC. RN and MMC were drinking and fighting more. One night, when RN and MMC were having a particularly ugly dispute, JC stepped between them. RN then turned on JC, and pushed her and struck her. And it was after this, JC told the inquest, that, 'I was forced to leave my home.'

The longer and sadder story was that her father came up from Blakehurst, 50 kilometres away on the southern side of Sydney, where he was living with his new wife, Norma. He took her to Chatswood police station where she reported the assault. But JC didn't want the police to charge her mother's husband, because then she would have had to testify against him. It is a common feature of domestic violence: the victim is reluctant to proceed with charges against their abuser because they feel responsible for the inevitable breakdown of family relationships that will follow. Faced with this reality, many victims prefer to do nothing. XC wanted JC to come and live with him and Norma in their two-bedroom apartment, but she only had a few months of school left and wanted to see out the year with her friends at Cromer High.

'MMC never asked me to come back. She chose RN over me.' Tears filled JC's eyes. 'Who would've thought that she would take him back in preference to her own daughter?'

So Chris invited JC to move in with him and Lynette while she finished her HSC. JC told her parents and asked for their permission. 'MMC never cared about my relationship with him. She said nothing.' But her father showed some concern. 'Before I moved into their house, Dad did ring Lyn to talk to her about it. I think he just asked her if it was okay. She would have told him all the right things,' JC said. She frowned. 'How could Mum and Dad let me go and sleep at a teacher's house anyway?'

JC believes that Lynette wouldn't have objected to Chris's proposal because, in her view, Lynette generally did what Chris wanted. And although JC and Lynette didn't speak directly about JC's home life, she assumed that Chris had told her about some of it, to justify why she was already staying over on weekends. So JC moved into Gilwinga Drive permanently In October 1981, a few months before Lynette would disappear.

'Lynette told me once that they'd had other babysitters who were immaculate,' JC told me one day, 'but she said she didn't feel threatened by me because I would come out all dishevelled and not trying to impress her husband.' The terrible irony of this aside, the implication, of course, was that other babysitters had.

Why didn't Chris move out with JC? Perhaps he thought word would spread and he'd be sacked. Perhaps he worried that Lynette, or one of her friends or family, would phone the school. He could have put JC in a flat on her own, but having JC move in with the entire family made it appear respectable, admirable even – like it had been Chris and Lynette's decision to take her in. Most likely, it was just easier, and cheaper, to have JC move in with them. It also gave Chris control over JC – he took her to school where he kept an eye on her and then he brought her home. Then what? Where did he think all of this was going?

At the inquest, Matthew Fordham asked JC about moving in with the Dawsons.

'In the months before the end of 1981, at the time when you were still living in the home with Chris and Lyn, firstly, what was Lyn's behaviour like around Chris?'

'She loved him. It was very loving and she behaved as though there were nothing wrong with their relationship.'

He then asked JC about Lynette's alcohol consumption.

'At the time you were living in the home as the babysitter, did you ever see Lyn drinking alcohol?'

'Only when Chris made it for her, because she didn't drink as a rule.'

'Can you tell me about those times?'

'At night, sometimes if he wanted to be alone with me, he knew that the easiest way to get Lyn to go to sleep was to give her a drink and she went to sleep after he gave her alcohol.'

'Do you know whether anything was put in those drinks—'

'No.'

'Apart from alcohol?'

'I don't know.'

'Did Lyn ever ask for Chris to go and make her a drink?'

'I don't remember her asking for a drink.'

'When Chris brought drinks to Lyn did he have one himself?'

'No.'

'Did he ever give you one?'

'No.'

'What was the effect on Lyn?'

'She went to sleep.'

Lynette's mother, Helena, had died by the time of the second inquest, but she had given Damian a statement before the first one in 2001. In it, she told him that she rang Lynette on the night of

Friday 8 January 1982 to confirm their plans to meet at Northbridge Baths the next morning. On the phone, Helena thought that Lynette sounded groggy, which was unusual because she knew Lynette wasn't a big drinker.

I'd heard about the phone call from Pat and Greg and, later, Pat emailed me about it.

> When Mum rang Lyn, approximately 8.30 pm on the Friday night, as you know it was to confirm arrangements about meeting Lyn on the Saturday at Northbridge pool. During that call Lyn made no mention of any intention to go to the shops before going to the pool.
>
> I think we have mentioned that Chris answered my mother's phone call and was very reluctant to put Lyn on, and only did so at Mum's insistence. When Lyn came to the phone her voice was slurred. Mum said, 'Lyn, you sound sozzled.' Lyn's reply: 'My husband has just made me a lovely drink.'

It is distressing that Lynette's behaviour towards Chris was still characterised as 'very loving' when Chris was treating her appallingly. In this same part of JC's testimony, she also detailed some of the cruelties she witnessed while she lived with Chris and Lynette.

'In the last few months that Lyn was still around, how did Chris behave towards her?'

'He was very cold and he used to sing songs to her that had double meanings.'

'When you say they had double meanings, what were the meanings that you could glean from them?'

'That he didn't care about her, that, you know, she was physically unattractive or—'

'You mentioned in your interview that you believed that the songs were used to terrorise Lyn. What do you mean by terrorise?'

'Just digging away at her, you know, singing songs that were hurtful, just to wear her down and upset her.'

'How did Lyn react when that was happening?'

'I must admit that I wasn't looking for her reactions because I wasn't sensitive to what she was going through, obviously.'

'Was there another occasion when Lyn caught yourself and Chris in a particular position that gave rise to some further conversation with her?'

'One incident only and that was in the presence of both his daughters and we were playing this game he called "Stacks on the Mill" and I was sitting on his lap and she walked in after work.'

'The game "Stacks on the Mill", can you describe that to us?'

'It was just someone sitting on someone's lap, as I saw it.'

'When Lyn came in and saw you playing this game with Chris, what happened as a result of that?'

'She confronted him and we were standing in a triangle and she was talking to him. You know, "What are you doing?" and he was saying, "Nothing, nothing's going on."'

'How did Lyn sound?'

'She was angry.'

JC now thinks that Chris was trying to push Lynette to the point where she'd ask for a divorce. 'He was a coward. He wanted her to look like the baddie.' At the time, JC didn't give the bullying much thought. Although she didn't join in, she acquiesced, which she knows amounts to the same thing. Over lunch one day, I asked her if she believes it was this incident of the children's game, of all things, that confirmed to Lynette what was going on. She put her cutlery down and pushed her hair behind each ear without lifting her eyes.

'Lynette Dawson showed me more kindness than my own mother had ever shown me,' she said. Her mouth was drawn down as if she were trying to not cry.

I reached across the table and let my hand rest on top of hers.

'Sometimes I feel that it's all my fault,' she said.

Just then, a friend of mine walked into the restaurant and came over to say hello. JC pulled her shoulders back and smiled when I introduced them. She gave nothing away.

At the inquest, Pat, Greg and Merilyn were distressed to learn of Chris's other cruelties to Lynette, in addition to the ones JC had already told them about, and they blamed themselves for not seeing what was going on. Pat recalled being at Lynette's house one evening when Chris and JC returned from a driving lesson. Lynette told Pat that in the evening she'd often be bathing the girls while Chris and JC relaxed. Or in the kitchen cooking dinner while 'Chris and JC would be with the girls "playing happy families". Those were her words,' Pat said. She berates herself about missing these small signs or not sensing that Lynette might be trying to tell her something bigger. Perhaps Lynette felt unable to fully express her fears. Perhaps she was hoping that Pat might ask her the right questions. Perhaps.

After these gruelling sessions, I had imagined Pat, Greg and Merilyn huddled on the footpath outside the building in Glebe, or pressed together in the small foyer, but Carl Milovanovich told me that the inquest was held at Westmead Coroners Court, a few minutes west of Parramatta, in a 'lovely sandstone cottage'. In late February 2003, when the inquest began, it was the end of a hot summer. By the end of the week, those travelling from the Northern Beaches each day must have been exhausted by the commute and the heat. Still, at least at Westmead there was space to move away from the building, and each other, and there were also some counselling rooms inside where JC or Lynette's family could find some privacy.

Although Lynette didn't tell her family about what she feared was going on with Chris, she was more open with her work friends. Anna Grantham, who worked at the childcare centre, told the inquest more.

'She would tell me different stories about how one day she had gone home and it was school holidays and she left JC and the husband at home and for some reason she had a premonition to go home and she did, at lunchtime, and when she came back to work she was very sad, and she actually said that on the line, on the clothesline there was JC's . . . the bottom part of the bikini, and her husband's trunks and she was sure that they had – they had swum together and that's all I remember of that.

'There was also an occasion when she came to work and she was actually very sad and she said, "Last night I was cooking dinner when JC and Chris were sitting watching TV and they were both next to each other on the chair and I'm not sure whether it was him or her that they actually put the chair next to each other and they were holding hands." And I remember saying to her, "Lyn, you better watch it, you know, it doesn't sound that good." She said,

"Oh no, not my Chris. I don't think it will ever happen, you know, that he goes off with her or anything."

'Another occasion was when there was something at school, at night-time, perhaps [. . .] a party at the school. She actually went to the toilet and she said that as she was walking through the playground one of the teachers approached her and she said, "Lyn, do you know that your husband is having an affair with JC?"'

Anna Grantham was a close friend of Lynette and she and Pat have stayed in touch over the years. It was hard to get in contact with her, and when we finally spoke on the phone, she said, with obvious displeasure, 'I've been a bit surprised that you hadn't been in touch,' which I understood to mean that Lynette meant a lot to her.

Anna lives on the Ingleside escarpment above Narrabeen, about a twenty-minute drive from Lynette's home in Bayview. We sat in the kitchen at the back of the house, where the land dropped away steeply. The house was propped up on stilts, which made it sit among the treetops of the angophoras and eucalypts. Anna had laid out a tablecloth and put out dips and crackers.

'I worked at the childcare centre for eleven years and I had already been there for a few years when Lynette began. I worked in the same room as Lyn and we became friends right away; we clicked, and I got really good vibes from her. I thought she would stay forever because she was so warm and affectionate.' Anna's face was heavy with sadness. 'Please. Eat,' she said, pushing a plate towards me.

I wasn't hungry, but I tried to nibble a few things because I knew she'd prepared the food, not so much for me but for Lynette.

'Lynette talked about Chris and the children – what beautiful girls they were. She adored him and the kids. She was a very good wife and mother,' she said. 'The last time I saw Lyn was just before Christmas. Then, or maybe just a bit before, she told me that Chris wasn't as nice as when they were first married. She said she didn't look like when she got married. She thought that she was fat,' Anna said, her voice hard with disapproval. 'When I saw her before Christmas, she told me that there were mirrors on the doors in the bedroom and she hated seeing herself in them when she got out of bed.'

Anna recalled what she'd said at the inquest about Chris and JC sitting together. 'My Chris, he's not like that,' Lynette had told Anna when she pressed her about it. But if Lynette really wasn't worried about Chris and JC, why would she tell Anna? Anna must have been thinking the same thing.

'I thought maybe she didn't want to say the truth,' she said.

In the months before January 1982, 'Lyn started looking pensive and tired at work, like she had taken something. Sometimes she looked drugged' – Anna paused to look me in the eye – 'but I definitely did not think she had drink or drug problems. A couple of times I said, "You all right, Lyn?"'

At the inquest, Anna said, 'As much as she was a very easygoing and very happy person, she was always sort of in a bit of a trance I think.' But she again stopped short of saying that Lynette looked drugged. I also wondered if Anna might have absorbed a detail of JC's evidence, about Chris giving Lynette a drink. I wondered if she'd accidentally picked it up – it's easily done when you've got several views of the same events. And said so many times, over so many years.

As a gift, Lynette had given Anna a blue oven mitt with a wooden ring on the end, and a heart-shaped photo frame. Anna brought the photo frame out from the bedroom and collected the oven mitt from the kitchen. She sat down at the table and held them, not passing them to me. A few years after Lynette went missing, she took the picture frame to a clairvoyant. 'When she held the photo frame, she said, "Oh my goodness, there is something not very good brewing here. I see two people at the edge of the water. They are hand in hand, friendly. Then I can see they are arguing. He's pushing her into the water and he's holding her down by the shoulders." She told me Lynette was gone. Sometimes I see someone from behind and I think, "My god."' Anna put her head in her hands and sobbed.

I gently lowered my pen and notebook onto the table. Outside the air was still. When Anna stopped crying, we sat comfortably in silence. Of all the people I'd spoken to, Anna wore her grief most visibly and I liked that she didn't apologise for that. As we said goodbye, she said, 'Lynette was carrying a big load. She had the veil up.'

Towards the end of 1981, JC and Chris drove to a hotel somewhere in Sydney, JC told the inquest.

'We drove to the – I remember driving there and worrying that other people would see me and he got out of the car and went up these stairs to the hotel and then came back. I don't know how long it was, but it wasn't very long, and I was looking around and he came back and he said to me, "I went inside to get a hit man to kill Lyn but I decided I couldn't do it because innocent people would be killed."'

'At the time this was happening, was there anybody else inside the car?' Matthew Fordham asked.

'No.'

'At the time that Chris said those words to you, what did you think was going to happen to Lyn?'

'Well, I thought that he wouldn't do anything because he said so. I believed him.'

'Did he say it in a way which would suggest to you that he was joking?'

'No.'

'You said you believed him. Did you believe that he was capable of such a thing?'

'I think I dismissed it instantly because he said he wasn't – he wouldn't do it. I thought what a great guy because he was worried about innocent people.'

'Do you remember what you were wearing on that occasion?'

'I think I was wearing my school uniform.'

Hearing this for the first time, Lynette's work colleagues later told me that they sat stunned. Pat, Greg and Merilyn already knew about this incident because around the same time that JC spoke to the detectives at Chatswood in 1990, she decided to reach out to Lynette's family, especially to her mother, Helena.

In 1990, when they were living on the Gold Coast, JC finally left Chris. She and KD packed the car and drove to Sydney. She arrived with limited options and turned to Barb Kilpatrick, who was running the refuge where JC and I met, many years later. Pam Eckford was a counsellor at the refuge and although JC and KD didn't stay there, Pam began helping JC. She told the inquest that her first impressions of JC were of 'a very nervous young woman, very unsure. Just didn't know what was happening. Very, very, very frightened young woman.'

After a few months, JC told Pam that she'd like to speak to Lynette's mother. 'I told her that I could organise that,' Pam told me by phone from Queensland, where she now lives. She set about tracking down Helena's phone number. 'So, I rang Helena.'

Helena took Pam's call, but told her she wasn't sure about meeting JC and said she'd have to speak to Greg and Pat. They all felt unable to face JC, except Merilyn, who rang Pam to say that she would meet her. In the inquest, Pam said she'd made a note that she spoke with Merilyn around 28 March 1990. Greg and Merilyn were living in Newcastle by then but Pam's mother lived at Point Clare, on the Central Coast, about halfway between Sydney and Newcastle, so it was decided that they would meet there.

Merilyn is a fantastic woman. She's caring and gregarious, but she's also tough enough to step into the ring in such troubled circumstances. One day, when I visited Greg and Merilyn at home, I was nursing a swimmer's shoulder, and throughout our conversation that day, she could see that I was in pain. Then, a day or so later, she and Greg rang me, concerned to have seen me in such discomfort. Greg had told me several times that Merilyn is his 'rock'.

On the drive to meet Merilyn, JC was scared. 'I imagined they would hate me and blame me. I blame me.' Greg and Merilyn were anxious too. Greg planned to wait outside but as Merilyn opened the car door, he suddenly decided to go with her.

The meeting lasted over four hours. JC told Greg, Merilyn and Pam Eckford what she knew and what she had seen, including about the night Chris had told her he tried to get a hit man to kill Lynette.

'I watched the blood drain from Greg's face,' Pam told me.

'Merilyn was terrific, but Greg looked like he was having a nervous breakdown. Maybe he was.'

JC also learned things at the meeting. She had been away camping at South West Rocks for the week surrounding Lynette's disappearance, and so some details about that time were news to her. She didn't know about the plan for Lynette and the girls to meet up with Helena at Northbridge Baths or that when Lynette spoke to Helena the night before she sounded 'sozzled' because Chris had made her a drink. And she didn't know that Chris had said that Lynette had rung the Baths to tell him that she had decided to suddenly go away. I assumed that JC would have known those things, but why would she? She could only have known if Chris had told her. Or Paul and Marilyn, and that was unlikely. Having delivered such harrowing news, JC was shocked by Greg and Merilyn's kindness. When they said goodbye, they hugged each other in what JC felt was shared grief.

Merilyn and Greg carried the startling information from their meeting to the family. Pat had trouble absorbing it. 'You can't believe any of it could have happened,' she told me, her voice still strained with disbelief. They kept much of what JC had said about the hit man from Helena, not wanting to add to her pain, but it all came out after the first inquest, and Helena was knocked sideways again.

JC can't remember what the hotel looked like, or where Chris had driven that day, except that it was on the other side of Sydney, which she was unfamiliar with back then. Damian has tried to jog her memory, but the only real detail she can recall is that the hotel had a flight of stairs up the middle to the entrance, and scaffolding, suggesting renovations were underway.

'I think it was the [Newtown] Jets Club,' Damian told me. 'Back then it had long wide steps leading up to the door, which is what JC remembers.'

When Peter Dawson cross-examined JC about the 'hit man', he asked her why she hadn't told anyone about it until after she left Chris in 1990.

'Because it didn't have any impact on me at the time.'

'In fact, you completely disregarded it, didn't you?'

'Yes, I did.'

'You just didn't believe it was possible?'

'He told me he wasn't going to do it, so I didn't have to think anything more about it.'

'In fact, there isn't any evidence that he did do it, is there?'

'Only from what I've said because I was there.'

Peter Dawson continued to press JC about this sensational allegation because there is only JC's word.

'You said earlier that you knew – you were afraid that someone would see you?'

'Yes.'

'You went for driving lessons every Friday night?'

'No, it wasn't Friday nights, it was during the week.'

'So you were used to being in the car with Chris?'

'Yes.'

'Why would you be afraid that someone would see you?'

'Because the driving lessons were by consent from my parents and driving in the car ordinarily was not.'

I had heard tape recordings of JC's interviews with Damian, and in them, her answers are short and sharp, and I can hear that same hardness in her voice, as she gives this, and other, evidence at the inquest. Defensiveness can be a sign that a witness doesn't want to answer a question because their answer would be a lie, but I know that's not what JC is doing. Her defensive tone is frustration at being asked to give a reasonable explanation for events that are almost unbelievable, but are nonetheless true.

When Pat gave evidence, she had something to say about this too. She told the inquest that she was unhappy with the first statement she gave to Damian in 1998.

'I heard for the first time the allegations of the many abuses Lyn had suffered. These revelations were so shocking to be confronted with, and by the time I was interviewed [the next day] I was quite distressed.' Pat's husband was also chronically ill.

So at the second inquest the coroner gave her permission to read from prepared notes because otherwise, she was afraid she might 'forget something'. When she came to what she called the 'hit man incident', Peter Dawson objected but the coroner allowed it. 'This is the only forum in which Lynette Joy Dawson has a voice . . . that's through her family and the people who cared about her who have an opportunity to be able to speak on her behalf . . . whether it's admissible in criminal proceedings is not the issue.'

Peter Dawson objected again and was again overruled. He tried one more time to prevent Pat from giving testimony about the 'hit man', suggesting concern for Lynette and Chris's daughters.

'Your Worship might bear in mind that I also represent Lyn Dawson's daughters and that perhaps they don't want this said.'

The coroner was angry.

'Well, they can sit outside if they find anything uncomfortable, Mr Dawson, just like Christopher and Paul aren't here either, are they?'

'Your Worship continues to comment on that, thank you.'

'I'm entitled to.'

'Yes, Your Worship.'

'And I will continue to comment about it.'

'Thank you, Your Worship.'

I had assumed that Chris and Paul had attended the inquest, and that the Simms and Dawson families sat corralled on either side of the courtroom, almost like they might have been at Lynette and Chris's wedding, but the coroner had just revealed that Chris and Paul weren't there. Then, when I read this exchange between Peter and the coroner, it took me a moment to realise that XD and YD didn't go either. What Peter Dawson had meant was that the girls might read it in the newspaper. And the coroner's angry retort that 'they can sit outside . . . like Christopher and Paul' was a swipe at Lynette's husband and brother-in-law. None of the extended Dawson family came to the inquest, even though they'd known Lynette since she and Chris began dating as teenagers in the mid-1960s. For seventeen years, she had had Christmases, weddings, birthdays, christenings, dinners, cups of tea, afternoon swims, barbeques with the Dawsons – and many of them at her house – but the only Dawson present at Lynette's inquest was Peter, who was there cross-examining her family and friends. JC later confirmed this. She also told me that KD, who was eighteen then, didn't go.

I was surprised, too, that Lynette's daughters weren't there. Damian had told me that when he took over Lynette's file in 1998, Chris wouldn't let him speak to XD and YD, even though at that point they would have been nineteen and twenty years old. But by the time of the second inquest, they were twenty-three and twenty-five, and with that extra maturity, I would have thought that they would want to be there, if only to learn one small thing about what had happened to the mother they barely knew.

Yet I could also understand the bind they were in. They might have felt disloyal to their father by attending the inquest, in light of the evidence about his conduct. And, having lost so much already, I could understand why they wouldn't want to risk losing their father as well.

As for Peter's request that they be protected from what would be printed in the papers, he made no concessions himself during his own cross-examination of others. The coroner's job was to ascertain facts and, through that process, give some answers and comfort to the families of those who have gone missing. He wasn't interested in protecting those who weren't prepared to come to the inquest, to tell the inquest what they knew, or to show their respect.

Back in court, Pat read her notes about the hit man.

'This is part of my letter to the DPP. Referring to a statement by JC where she recalled being driven by Chris Dawson to a hotel where he told her under no circumstances to get out of the car, he was going to see a hit man. Questioned about this by police, Dawson's comment was to the effect, "How would I know how to find a hit man?" Chris Dawson played first grade for Newtown during the 1970s. Paul Hayward also played first grade for Newtown around the same time. He was arrested in Thailand in 1978 with William Sinclair and Warren Fellows for trafficking heroin. In the book *Kingdom of Illusions: The William Sinclair Story* . . . Paul Hayward's association with Arthur Neddy Smith is referred to . . . Hayward and Smith were relatives of a kind, for their respective de facto wives were sisters . . . What seemed a total improbability becomes not so improbable.'

Pat gave me her copy of *Kingdom of Illusions*, with its black cover and yellowed pages; yet another ill-fitting piece in the puzzle. Criminal figure Arthur 'Neddy' Smith dealt heroin and committed armed robberies around Sydney for thirty years, starting in the 1960s, often in the company of Roger Rogerson, the notoriously corrupt policeman. Smith was convicted of murder in 1990 and sent to Long Bay Correctional Centre in Sydney's south-east. While Smith was at Long Bay, he was found guilty of a second murder and was transferred to Lithgow Correctional Centre, in the coal mining town on the other side of the Blue Mountains. There, Smith developed Parkinson's disease and as his health deteriorated, he was shuttled back and forth between Lithgow and Sydney for medical care. He eventually died in Long Bay jail in 2021.

In 2010, Pat wrote him a letter.

28th September 2010

Dear Mr Smith,

I am writing to you in the hope that you can help me. I would appreciate if you could take the time to read my letter.

I have heard that you are unwell, I believe suffering from Parkinson's disease and I'm very sorry about that. As two of my aunts had Parkinson's I have seen what a hellish disease it is and how truly bad it is to live with; seems it is enduring rather than living.

> What I hope you will find within yourself to do is to write (or if you are unable to do that because of your illness someone could do it for you) to say you had family and social connections to Paul Hayward. That is all I need, and I cannot tell you how much we would appreciate it if you could do that.
>
> I'll give you the reason for my strange request. I have read the book, *Kingdom of Illusions: The William Sinclair Story* in which as you may know you are mentioned often. The book mentions what seems to be a close association with Paul Hayward; both by family and socially. All I need, and I hope you will do this for me, is to verify this for me – that you knew Paul Hayward.
>
> My sister's husband, Christopher Dawson, played 1st grade rugby league with Paul Hayward for the Newtown Jets. My sister, Lynette Dawson, went missing in January 1982 at a time when her husband, a school teacher, was having an affair with one of his students. Within days of my sister's disappearance he had moved this girl into my sister's home. Lyn had two young daughters, 4 years old and 2 years old and was totally devoted to them.
>
> . . . In evidence, the girl claimed Dawson and she had driven to a hotel and Dawson had gone inside he said to speak to a hit man. He came out and said 'I couldn't do it because . . .'

Pat has lost the rest of her copy of the letter. In an email, she told me that she'd sent the letter 'with trepidation, I didn't want him to think I was accusing him of being involved in Lyn's murder. I found it very difficult to write to such a person, but would have regretted it if I had left such a stone unturned.'

She received an undated reply from the regional superintendent of Long Bay jail.

Dear Ms Jenkins

Re: Letter sent to inmate Arthur 'Neddy' Smith

I refer to your correspondence dated 28th September 2010 requesting an attached letter be given to inmate Smith asking for information on a possible association with another person Paul Hayward.

I apologise for the late response however I advise that while I appreciate what you and your family are trying to achieve, a decision has been made not to allow inmate Smith to receive the letter. I have included the correspondence you sent with this letter.

Yours sincerely,
[. . .]
Regional Superintendent
Metropolitan Region

Why was Pat's correspondence returned to her? Was I boxing at shadows now?

Around October or November 1981, Chris needed nose surgery. While he was in hospital, Lynette spoke to him by phone. JC was annoyed that she couldn't do the same, so one day she went to see him.

'I was sitting on the edge of his bed and I was wiping his nose – it would have been just after our high school formal. Just as I was doing that, Lynette's mother arrived and saw us. I went to work at Coles that night and Paul picked me up and took me home.' JC exhaled loudly. 'But Lynette was waiting for me. She said, "You've been taking liberties with my husband."'

JC told the inquest: 'I waited for her to go to bed. It was 10 o'clock by the time I got home anyway, just about, and I snuck out of the house and walked up the road and I don't know how it happened that Paul was up the road, up the top of the street, and he lived further down, and he was there, and I went to stay with them.'

JC stayed in Paul and Marilyn's study, which was attached to the master bedroom, and sometimes she saw Lynette come down to ask for a lift somewhere because she couldn't drive. It was November, and JC's HSC exams were upon her when Paul and Marilyn told her that their children were anxious that Santa wouldn't come if JC was staying with them, and that they wanted to conceal her from them. The more likely explanation, of course, was that Lynette knew that her brother-in-law and his wife were housing her husband's 'lover' and was angry and hurt. I imagine that Chris then told Lynette that JC was no longer living with Paul and Marilyn, and to persist with that lie, he needed to make sure that Paul and Marilyn's children didn't tell Lynette that JC was still living with them.

'I had to leave the house before the kids woke up and I could come back in when they'd left for school,' JC told me, as we sat near the beach one day with takeaway coffees. It was too cool for swimming, but a group of children were chasing waves. As each wave came in, they ran away squealing.

'I left via Paul and Marilyn's ensuite. In the afternoon, I had to leave before the kids came home and I hung around in the bush and would come back after they'd gone to bed.'

Each step of JC's story seemed more unbelievable than the one before, yet she frequently spoke with a kind of detached bemusement. Beside her, I often sat quietly, gazing into the distance. Looking back, I think at certain points I was in shock, or preoccupied at least, as I tried to imagine her life. How could these things have occurred? Chris must have still been driving Lynette and the girls around. But how did JC get to school and back each day? How did she get her homework done? The psychological toll must have been enormous – thrown out of her mother's house, thrown out of Chris and Lynette's house, ejected from Paul and Marilyn's house to linger in the bush, pretending that she didn't exist.

I remembered that on the day we'd visited Gilwinga Drive, JC had pointed out a spot in the bush, down the hill from Paul and Marilyn's place.

'That's where I used to go,' she'd said. 'It was peaceful.'

I'd taken it to mean that she'd spent a little time there, enjoying the quietness; it was only now that I understood that it was where she waited in the morning, and then again at night, until she could return to the house. Later, I imagined JC's comings and goings from the house to the bush and back again as a Molière parlour farce, with doors opening and closing, and collisions avoided by seconds. Then, I was surprised at how quickly I had converted the tragic situation to comedy, or at least something more palatable, just as JC had. We adapt as we need to.

CHAPTER NINE

Escape to Queensland

IN NOVEMBER 1981, CHRIS PUT A DEPOSIT ON A RENTED FLAT IN MANLY. There were flowers in a vase on the table when he took JC to look at it. But they never moved in. Instead, two days before Christmas, they packed Chris's brown Toyota Corona, which was identical to Paul's, and headed to Queensland to start a new life together. JC showed me a photo that Chris had taken of her looking relaxed, standing beside the packed car in front of the house at Bayview just as they were about to set off. It seems an odd time to take a photo. Behind the car is the house where Chris had left his wife and children with no more than a note to let them know that he'd gone. I wondered whether Chris told Paul about their plan – JC doesn't know, but considers it likely – and whether Paul had then had to pretend to Lynette that he didn't know where Chris had gone.

The drive up was hot. The car didn't have air-conditioning, so they drove with the windows down, and even now JC can recall the smell of the northern New South Wales countryside. 'On the way up, I got hives; I felt sick,' JC told me, her voice rushed and pitched higher than usual as she remembered this event, three decades on. Then, not far from the border, she told Chris she wanted to go home. 'So, we turned around and came back.'

When Matthew Fordham asked her about this at the inquest, JC said, 'I was absolutely stressed about leaving my family.'

What did JC mean when she said 'leaving my family'? Was it the same feeling she'd had when she stayed with her grandparents and then inexplicably wanted to go back home to the mother who shunned her? Perhaps the reality of what they were doing only hit her the further away they went. I asked her what upset her so much about leaving.

'I didn't want to leave my friends and my sisters.'

And when she said that she wanted to go home, where was that? Back to Paul and Marilyn's? To one of her sisters' places? Two of them had already moved out of home – one lived on the other side of town where she'd started university, and the other was sharing an apartment with a friend in Neutral Bay. Or back to MMC and RN's, where her youngest sister was still living?

Lynette didn't tell her family that JC had gone with Chris. Perhaps because Chris hadn't mentioned JC in his note, or perhaps Lynette deliberately kept that detail from her family. In court, Pat told the inquest about Lynette's distress when Chris abandoned her and the girls just before Christmas:

> I spoke to Lyn two and a half weeks before her disappearance during the time Chris had left. She was terribly upset that she and the girls had been left without warning just before Christmas.

She said she waited outside her workplace for an hour with all the shopping. When Chris didn't arrive to pick her up she phoned his brother Paul to see if he was there. She found the note Chris had left when she got home. The way the note was worded she didn't know if Chris was coming back at all. Apart from not knowing if he would return the only other thing I remember Lyn telling me of the contents of the note was, 'Don't paint too black a picture of me to the girls.' She said when she put the girls to bed that night she told them their father had had to go away on a holiday suddenly and she gave them both a kiss from him. Lyn spoke of Chris's anger with her all the time. She used the words to describe his glaring at her, his black eyes flashing. She said she had gone up to give him a hug one day and he just pushed her away. Another time she wanted to ask him what sort of day he had had but he gave her such a dirty look she didn't ask. I could hear voices in the background during one conversation. Lyn said that Joan and Sid Dawson, Chris's parents, had come over to give their support. She had little money and the girls to look after. She could not drive, had no transport and to get to public transport was some distance away. She spoke to these worries. Her friend Robyn had come over to help her put up the Christmas tree for the girls. Lyn had promised the girls a cubby house for Christmas and she was upset as she didn't want to disappoint them. She didn't know how she was going to get it. It had been organised but she had no transport. She didn't think she had enough money to pay for it or if she could spare the money if she had to support the girls, I'm to [sic] sure which one it was. I said to her, 'How about you and the girls come up here for Christmas.' We were living on the mid-north coast. She said she couldn't come as she didn't have enough money.

I said, 'I'll send some money down to you.' She said she couldn't come anyway as she couldn't risk losing her job which she needed and liked. She only had the time off over Christmas or until the new year, I can't remember which it was. The third thing she said for not being able to come up was that she wanted to be there in case Chris came back. She said all the tension in the house had gone now that Chris was out of the house. One of the last things she said to me was, 'Everyone sees Chris one way but there is a dark side to him that nobody knows,' and that's all I can remember of those conversations.

When Chris and JC arrived back in Sydney on Christmas Day, they went straight to Paul and Marilyn's place. It must have been very early because JC told the inquest that they 'snuck in and hid in their wardrobe, when their children came in for Christmas'.

'How long did you stay in the wardrobe?'

'Until Paul and Marilyn left the room to go out and open presents with their children.'

'How long did you stay inside Paul and Marilyn's house that day?'

'We slept there all day.'

'After you'd woken later in the day, what did you do then?'

'We went to the Forest High School where we stayed the night in the gym.'

'What was the connection with Forest High School?'

'Paul was a teacher there so he had the keys.'

Why didn't they just go to a hotel for the night? Chris was a grown man in his thirties, and a father, but was behaving like a teenager who shoves his half-dressed girlfriend in the wardrobe when he hears his parents come home early from a night out.

From the wardrobe, they heard Lynette and the girls arrive to get a lift with Paul and Marilyn to Christmas lunch at Chris and Paul's parents' place. Chris's car couldn't have been parked at Paul's house because Lynette would have seen it, but JC can't remember where it was. Perhaps they'd hidden it in Paul's garage. Had Chris let his parents know that he wouldn't be at lunch? Had Lynette and the girls hoped that he might turn up there? Something must have been said over lunch about Chris's absence. And, knowing what they knew, how could Paul and Marilyn sit at the table with Lynette? Peter Dawson might well have been at the Christmas lunch too. Did Paul or Marilyn tell him where Chris was? Did Peter know about Chris and JC hiding in the wardrobe? Or was JC giving evidence about it the first he heard of it?

When Chris was interviewed by detectives in 1991, they asked him about the failed dash to Queensland.

'And what day did you come up to Queensland?'

'Just prior to Christmas, and returned, it was just after Christmas, it was only two or three days.'

'Did you stay at your brother Paul's place when you returned to Sydney?'

'My children were with him, no, I didn't, I got back, by memory I went to my place, my place was just up the road from his . . .'

Chris gives two different answers here. He tells the detectives that his children were with Paul, which he is certain about because he was hiding in the wardrobe with JC and heard them arrive. But when he says that he went 'to my place', his answer shifts, and he adds 'by memory' – an idiomatic expression that may alter the meaning to, 'I'm lying and that's why my memory isn't very good.'

Damian had asked Paul in 1999 about his recollections of Chris and JC returning on Christmas Day. Interestingly, he used the same expression.

'And do you remember what, when he came back down from Queensland, what period of time?'

'No. No.'

'Do you recall that, when he returned, was he with JC then?'

'I think he came by himself. From memory.'

'Does this trigger anything in your memory about Chris and JC returning from Queensland and arriving at your home on Christmas Day, 1981. Does that ring any bells?'

'Yes, it does. No, was JC there, I can't remember JC. Marilyn might remember.'

'Right.'

'I know I spoke . . . they did arrive back, I think. Because Lyn was . . . we had the family at our place. I know I was speaking, I'd spoken, I spoke to Lyn that day about it. She wasn't . . . she was very calm. I remember I had a bit of a cry about . . . upset about . . . this was the first time that we hadn't had the family together, and I hadn't been together with Chris, for that many years, well, you know, it was the first Christmas we'd been apart. She was very calm, but we . . . we sort of had a talk together. And now, wait a minute. I . . . I don't think I saw Chris, I think he rang me, didn't he? I . . . I can't remember. Either I saw him or he rang me, and said he was back from his holiday and . . .'

'This was Christmas Day, was it?'

'I'm pretty sure, I think it was. It was . . . it was one day when Lyn was at our place, so probably Christmas Day sounds fair.'

'Do you have any recollection of Chris and JC staying the night on Christmas Day . . .'

'Yeah.'

'At [. . .] Forest High School?'

'No.'

'In the gym?'

'No.'

Paul recalls talking to Lynette on Christmas Day and that she was calm, but *he* cried because it would be the first Christmas that he and Chris had been apart, which wasn't right, because Chris and JC were at his house. It's hard to accept that he'd forgotten that Chris and JC were hiding in his wardrobe, but he does remember Lyn being calm and him crying. Then, he suddenly does remember that Chris and JC stayed somewhere on Christmas night but that it wasn't in the Forest High School gym.

In 1999, at the same time that Paul spoke to the police, Marilyn was also interviewed by Damian. Marilyn's interview has a spontaneous crack of truth about it. She gallops through her responses, giving the impression that she's earnest, although quite naive.

'Were you aware – you've mentioned earlier that you were aware – that Chris and JC went up to Queensland together?'

'I know that because they were at my house on Christmas morning.'

'Having returned?'

'Having returned, and they wanted to spend the day in my house.'

And further on: 'Was your husband, Paul, aware of Chris and JC arriving home as well?'

'He should be.'

'Would it surprise you if he can't recall that?'

'It would because he would, no, because he would be protecting his brother but I remember the day vividly, because I then had to go pick up his, Chris's, wife and take her to my mother-in-law's for Christmas lunch. Now, that's a pretty big ask to have Chris arrive in, and be in my room, my bedroom, on Christmas Day and for me to go then with my family and pick up Chris's wife and take them to Nan and Pop's for the day, that's something that's not easy to do, that means you're hiding Chris's whereabouts from his wife and from his mother and father . . . It was a dreadful day. It was a terrible position to be in.'

It's interesting that Marilyn says that she picked Lynette and the girls up, whereas JC recalls being in Paul and Marilyn's wardrobe and hearing Lynette and the girls arrive. It's possible that Lynette and her girls came down early to open Christmas presents and then went home to get ready for lunch. It's a conflicting piece of the story that can possibly never be ironed out.

When the interview concluded, Marilyn was asked, 'If required, would you attend any legal hearing in relation to giving evidence about Lyn's disappearance?'

'Of course I would, I'd have to.'

'Okay.'

'I wouldn't want to incriminate my brother-in-law, though.'

On one hand, Marilyn seems unaware of the gravity of the events she is being asked about, then suddenly, she tells Damian that she wouldn't want to 'incriminate my brother-in-law'. Perhaps that possibility only dawned on her as she was being questioned. Or only after Damian asked her to give evidence.

In the inquest, Greg, Pat and Merilyn struggled with what they were hearing. They had thought that Paul, Marilyn, Chris and Lynette were a tight and supportive group. Lynette and Chris had even lived with Paul and Marilyn for almost a year after they were married, and Lynette was a dependable wife and sister-in-law, but all three betrayed her.

'The general picture we saw of Chris and Lyn was of a very happy family,' Greg told me with an anguish that seemed to be not only about how Lynette had been treated, but also about his own perceived failings. He had been close to Lynette and Chris and felt that if anyone should have seen anything, it should have been him.

On Boxing Day, after they had spent the night in the Forest High gym, JC was exhausted and fed up and she told Chris she wanted to end the relationship.

Matthew Fordham asked JC about that. 'What was his demeanour when you told him that?'

'He threw my bags out of the car.'

'Did Chris take you back to your mother's house [. . .]?'

'Yes.'

'Did you stay for very long at that address?'

'No.'

'What was the reason for that?'

'I walked in the door with all my possessions in garbage bags. My mother said to me, "You can stay, but only if you live under RN's rules." I knew that, given the circumstances, where I'd had to leave because of him, then that was not possible.'

JC was more dejected when she told me about going back to MMC's place. 'After two hours I realised I couldn't be there. The last time I'd seen RN he was beating MMC. All that came back to me once I got there and I just realised I couldn't stay.'

In the stand, Matthew Fordham asked JC where she had gone.

'I rang Chris Dawson and asked him to come and get me.'

'Did he take you somewhere?'

'Yes he did.'

'Whereabouts did he take you?'

'He took me to my sister [CC's] place at Neutral Bay.'

'Did you stay there very long?'

'About a week.'

'During that time did you have any further contact with Chris Dawson?'

'Yes, every day.'

'What sort of contact was that?'

'There were phone calls and he came to the place as well.'

'At Neutral Bay?'

'Yes.'

'At the times, during the period of time when you were speaking to him, what were the conversations about?'

'About staying together, you know, keeping the relationship going.'

'What was Chris's intention?'

'To keep me.'

'What was your intention in relation to the relationship?'

'I wanted to stay away.'

'Did your opinion of the relationship change during that period?'

'It was – I wanted to end it. I'd had quite enough, it was very hard.'

'Did Chris's point of view about the relationship, did that change at all?'

'I think he was more intense about keeping it going.'

Pat had given her evidence before JC gave hers, which meant that when Peter Dawson cross-examined Pat, he didn't have the benefit of first hearing what JC had to say. When he questioned Pat about the period between Christmas and New Year, he was trying to use her testimony to show that when Chris returned to the house on Boxing Day, he was a recommitted and contrite husband. Pat's evidence suggested that Chris was anything but.

'When you spoke to Lyn on the phone, was it that she gave you the impression that she was going to wait there for Chris, to see whether he came back?'

'Well, yes, that's what the impression was, she wanted to wait there in case, the words were "in case" he came back.'

'In case he came back.'

'In case.'

'And that's what she wanted?'

'That's right.'

'And you're aware that he did come back?'

'Yes, that's right.'

'And did you speak to her over the next couple of weeks?'

'I spoke to her and it was only a brief conversation . . . and that was just after New Year and I just remembered her saying about

New Year's Eve, Chris had gone out on a yacht and Lyn said to him, "We've had such a rotten Christmas, the girls and I" – no, first of all she said, could she go on the yacht with him? And he said, "No," then she said, "Oh, the girls – we've had such a rotten Christmas, could you at least drive us down and we can sit in the park in the car and watch the boats?" And he said, "No," so she stayed at home with the children and he went out . . .'

Had Peter Dawson not asked Pat that final question, we might not have found out about Lynette's miserable New Year's Eve, which revealed another instance of Chris's apparent indifference to her pain. But it also connected with something that JC said a little later. Matthew Fordham was asking JC where she and Chris would go when they went out, and she told the inquest that they would go to the Time and Tide pub in Dee Why, or to Manly Point – a secluded little park on the harbour that was a reclaimed gasworks site – where they would have sex in the car. Matthew Fordham asked JC how often they would go to Manly Point.

'Every week.'

'Over how many weeks roughly would that have taken place for?'

'Every week until we lived together or I . . . I remember him saying one New Year's Eve, it was 1981 and we were still there.'

When I first read that in the transcript, I thought JC might have got the year wrong because I had assumed, as Pat had, that Chris had gone out on a yacht on New Year's Eve, as he'd told Lynette.

I sent JC an email. 'Is it possible you were on a yacht?'

But JC was adamant that she had been staying at CC's, in Neutral Bay. Chris came over but there was no yacht. Suddenly the lightbulb went on – Chris had lied. He'd told Lynette that he was going on a yacht, meaning passengers were limited and there wasn't room for her to come along. If he'd said he was going to a party, there'd have been no reason why Lynette couldn't have gone with him. What he actually did was collect JC from Neutral Bay and drive the fifteen or twenty minutes to Manly Point, which looks south-east across the harbour and, in addition to its seclusion, is a great spot to watch the New Year's Eve fireworks. While they enjoyed the spectacle, Lynette was at home with the girls, possibly watching the same fireworks on television.

JC's detail about New Year's Eve is an important piece of evidence because it reveals that Chris was not a husband returning to his family, as Peter Dawson was suggesting. And Pat closed the circle on the lie when she was able to speak for Lynette. The evidence is clear that he had no intention of rebuilding his relationship with Lynette, and if anything, Chris's disregard towards Lynette had only intensified. The new year began with nothing changed.

Alone that night, Lynette must have known that Chris was spending New Year's Eve with JC, either on a yacht or somewhere else, and that her marriage was over. Is it possible that she was so overwhelmed with despair that she felt she couldn't face what was coming and decided to go away? As the psychologist Kirsty Levin notes, for women who leave their children, 'the decision is often reflective of an extreme form of maternal instinct – an altruistic desire to ensure their children's best interests'.[8] Perhaps Lynette's self-worth was so low that she thought that everyone, including her daughters, was better off without her. Still, if she had made the decision finally to leave Chris, it made more sense that she would take the girls and start a new life. Or, better still, would have told Chris to leave – after all, he wanted to sell the house and Lynette didn't.

CHAPTER TEN

South West Rocks

JC WAS ENJOYING SUMMER AND THE END OF SCHOOL, EVEN THOUGH her HSC results were due in a few weeks and she knew she wouldn't do well. Two of her sisters were going to stay in a caravan that Norma, her father's wife, owned at South West Rocks in northern New South Wales, and, with her father's permission, she joined them there two days after New Year's Eve. By coincidence, some of JC's schoolfriends were camping in the same spot and together they were a group of young people having a great time. JC was beginning to see the possibility of a life away from MMC, RN, school and even Chris. Perhaps anticipating this, before she left, Chris extracted a promise from JC to ring him every day, which she did, from a public phone.

Matthew Fordham asked JC about her time at South West Rocks.

'When you rang him each day, what would you talk about?'

'He'd ask me what I was doing every single second of the day. He told me he had hives and had gastric problems just like I did because he missed me so much.'

'You mentioned that before you went to South West Rocks, Chris very much wanted to continue the relationship with you. Did that point of view change during the course of those phone calls?'

'It did for me.'

'How did it change for you?'

'I was physically away from him; he couldn't get to me.'

'How did that change your opinion of whether you should continue the relationship with Chris?'

'Well, I didn't want to continue the relationship but being physically out of his reach made it easier for me to get on with it.'

'When you say "get on with it", do you mean that it was easier for you to accept a continued relationship with Chris?'

'No, it was easier for me to move away from the relationship.'

'Do you know whether Chris's intentions changed during those phone calls in relation to the continued relationship between yourself and Chris?'

'What I think happened is that he sensed that I was drifting away and, you know, I think that's why he came up [to get me].'

'You say that he sensed that he – that you believe he sensed that you were drifting away?'

'Yes.'

'You mentioned that he turned up, was it planned that he would arrive at South West Rocks?'

'He told me he was coming up.'

'When did he tell you?'

'About 10 January.'

Matthew Fordham asked about that phone call, and if Chris spoke to her about Lynette.

'Yes.'

'What did he say?'

'He said, "Lyn's gone and she's not coming back, come and help me look after the children."'

'Could it be that he said to you, "Lyn's taken a holiday" or "She's taken a break" or "She's gone away for a while" or some sort of temporary break like that? Could that be possible?'

'That's not what he said.'

'He said "Lyn's gone and she's not coming back." You sound very definite about those words?'

'Yes.'

'You have a clear recollection of those words today, is that correct?'

'Yes.'

'You obviously – it's obvious from those words that there is a permanency about Lyn's absence. Was that clear to you on the telephone that day?'

'Yes.'

'Did Chris indicate to you why Lyn was going to be permanently absent?'

'No.'

'At that time was that a matter that you discussed with Chris or did you accept what he said?'

'I accepted what he said.'

The telephone box was up on the main road, and below it sat the low-lying caravan park with scattered tents and cabins, a grey concrete shower block and, only metres away through a stand of trees, the beach.

'I can picture the telephone box,' JC told me. 'It was a red one. It was not yet dark. I remember seeing my friends walk by. It wasn't especially hot in the telephone box, so it can't have been in the middle of the day. It was definitely still light.'

If JC were to give this detailed evidence in court, anyone under the age of forty might need to be told that public telephones were once housed inside a red booth with a door, a companion piece to the red postal pillar box, and very much like Dr Who's Tardis. Coins were inserted into slots and the telephone number entered on a rotary dial. My own children can't comprehend how I managed without a mobile phone and when I tell them that I'd organise to meet friends at a certain time and place and often a week in advance, they look at me like I'm quite mad. But the other odd thing that JC remembered when we were talking about telephone calls, was that Chris had a telephone jack outside the house at Bayview. 'It was in front of the family room,' she said. 'He used to call me in secret when Lyn was still there. I don't know if it was a separate line – he used to connect a phone to it and then put it away when we finished.' It's possible that Lynette glanced outside one day and saw him, bizarrely, on the phone outside. When I next saw Damian, I told him about the phone jack outside of the house.

'Hmm,' he said. 'I didn't know that.'

The upshot of JC's phone call to Chris around 10 January – within a day or two of Lynette going missing, and less than three weeks after Chris and JC had struck out for the Queensland border – was that Chris was charging the brown Toyota Corona up the Pacific Highway again, peeling off the almost 500 kilometres to South West Rocks. I took a drive along the old highway not long ago, following its twists and turns out of steep gullies and keeping an eye out for a snake or goanna wandering across the road. The rugged terrain, in fact, reminded me of Bayview. I stopped at one of the small hamlets to buy fruit and jam. When I stepped out of the car, the dry, forbidding smell of the bush hit me, and I remembered something Carl Milovanovich told me, something that another coroner had told him: '"There'd be a body within a hundred metres of the Pacific Highway every 10 or 20 kilometres." I've never forgotten that.'

Chris arrived at South West Rocks early in the morning. JC told the inquest that he'd slept in the car the night before but was 'moved on' by police in the middle of the night.

'He had stayed the night at – in his car at the other end of . . . near Trial Bay Gaol and I don't – I suppose I must have arranged previously or I rang . . . we wouldn't have had mobile phones, I just met him on the beach with my sister, NC.' Asked how long Chris stayed before they headed back to Sydney, JC said, 'A matter of hours.'

Why all the driving? Seven hours there, seven hours back, and only a few hours of bad sleep in the car. His wife was missing, and he had two small children wanting their mother and father, but he chose to drive just under a thousand kilometres to collect JC and bring her back to Bayview. Why the urgency?

JC's sister BC gave evidence that she recalled Chris arriving at the camp site.

Matthew Fordham asked her, 'Was that the first time that you'd met Chris Dawson?'

'No, he was a teacher at my school.'

The boyfriend of one of the other girls gave this evidence about Chris coming to collect JC from the camp site:

> You know, girls talk among themselves, mate, I was the only guy there, you know, you sort of hear a bit . . . Initial impressions, sort of, yeah, pretty smooth, pretty smooth sort of fellow. I would have thought as I say, I just met him and just went, yeah, whatever, I think I just took off again, I don't know, I don't think [he was] flustered, I just thought preoccupied, I know, just, you know as I say, I didn't cotton onto him, you know, yeah.

JC's younger sister NC was also camping with the group. She told the inquest that she had travelled back to Sydney in the car with Chris and JC, but she couldn't remember any conversation in the car about Lynette.

'I don't remember, but I don't really think they talked to me about things like that anyway as a thirteen-year-old.'

NC also told the inquest that at school, students would sing a song by The Police called 'Don't Stand So Close to Me', about the sexual attraction between a young male teacher and his 'schoolgirl' student. In the video clip, Sting, the lead singer, jigs around a classroom and is wearing an academic gown and mortar board. He is young, blond and achingly handsome – much like Chris. The song came out in 1980, the same year that Chris began pursuing JC, and at Cromer High, it must have seemed like the song was written about Chris and JC.

When NC had finished giving evidence, the coroner asked, 'Just to clarify something, Mr Fordham, the reference to the song, Police, is that the name of the band, is it?'

'Yes, it is, yes, it is, yes,' he replied.

In his 1991 interview, Chris told the detectives that it took him 'almost a week' to tell JC that Lynette had left and that he wanted her to come back and help look after the children.

'I drove to South West Rocks and picked her up. Yes.'

'Do you recall what day you did that?'

'Probably a week or so after . . . I'd approximate that it was about [the] 16th or 17th, so probably a week or so after.'

JC says that she and Chris spoke on the phone about Lynette leaving, on either 9 or 10 January, and that he arrived to collect her the following morning. This timeline makes sense because Lynette's mother had taken XD and YD home with her from Northbridge Baths to stay the night, which would have left Chris free to go and collect JC. And a schoolfriend that JC flew up with gave compelling evidence about when Chris collected JC.

'Is it the case that when you were up in South West Rocks you found out your HSC results?'

'Yes.'

'And is it the case that you were able to – when the police took a statement from you that you . . . you proffered some dates as being the dates upon which you received your HSC results?'

'Mm.'

'And [did] the date upon which you received those results [assist] you in recollecting the dates upon which Chris attended South West Rocks?'

'Yes.'

'And is it the case that on the day that you received your HSC results JC and NC had already left the caravan park with Chris Dawson?'

'Yes.'

'And is it the case that 15 January is your birthday?'

'Yes.'

'And is it the case that – do you remember where you were on your birthday?'

'Yes, I was at home.'

In a statement she gave to Damian in 1998, her memories were fresher and fuller.

'It wasn't long after we arrived I remember JC saying that Chris Dawson was on his way up to pick her up and take her back to Sydney. I was quite surprised JC said this because we had only been up there about five or six days.'

JC and her friend MC arrived at South West Rocks on Saturday 2 January and this witness recalls being there 'five or six days' when Chris arrived. 'Five or six' days would mean that Chris arrived on 7 or 8 January, which can't be right because Chris arrived after Lynette went missing on 9 January. However, she also maintained that Chris arrived on a weekend, and if she's right about that, it could only have been Sunday 10 January because she clearly remembers being home for her birthday on Friday, 15 January 1982.

Like Helena at Northbridge Baths, this same girl told the inquest that when Chris arrived, he 'was very aloof and distant and quite agitated', and in her statement she repeated those observations.

'Chris appeared nervous being around us and he wasn't quite himself and he appeared agitated. He certainly wasn't his charming flirtatious self that I knew him to be . . . When I say that Chris appeared offhand and agitated, I clearly remember seeing his face and I can now visualise his face as it was so different from what I remember of him. He appeared strange and agitated.'

She also told the inquest that, 'After JC and NC left . . . I remained in the park for a couple of days. As I was waiting on my HSC results and I rang my mother from the caravan park where she told me my results. This would have been the day they were announced and I recall ringing Mum about 4 pm that day and she told me my results. I can't recall if it was either the 11th of January 1982. I can say that when I did find out my results, be it the 11th or the 14th of January 1982, JC and NC had left the caravan park. They were definitely not at South West Rocks when I got my HSC results. I also recall that as the 15th of January is my birthday I was back home in [Sydney].'

Matthew Fordham said that Chris's timeline 'conflict[s] with the solid evidence of several witnesses'. I contacted the New South Wales Education Standards Authority to see if they could give me the date that HSC results were posted in 1982. They couldn't provide an exact date but said it would have been mid-January.

On the day that Lynette disappeared, Chris had organised to meet his old schoolfriend Phil Day at Northbridge Baths as well. Phil told the inquest how he came to be there that day.

'Only a few days earlier Chris had rung me . . . to say that things weren't going so well and there'd been some problems and he'd like to talk about it . . . the purpose of Saturday, of me meeting him at the pool was to talk about it.'

They spoke for a while out of earshot of Helena, and Chris told Phil about some of the problems he and Lynette were having, but not about JC. Then Chris went to the office to take the telephone call.

'When he came back to yourself and Mrs Simms, did he talk to you about the contents of that phone call?'

'He did.'

'What did he tell you?'

'He said that Lyn had rung to say that she was keen to get away and have some time to herself and would I mind take [sic] Helena Simms and [the girls] home to the Simms residence at Clovelly.' He also told the inquest that his impression of Chris that day was that he was missing Lyn, he wished she'd return or that they'd hear from her. He didn't seem to be at peace with himself in terms of her disappearance.'

Phil lived in the eastern suburbs, so it was easy for him to drop Helena and the girls in Clovelly, or at least it was hard for him to say no.

Phil Day died not long after this second inquest. His evidence is important, and Damian has his statements and the transcript of his evidence from the first inquest.

'Chris Dawson brings him to the pool with Helena Simms so that there would be two witnesses to the phone call coming in. That's the cunningness of it,' he told me with distaste. 'I think there probably was a call set up by Chris Dawson to come in.'

If Damian is right, what he is proposing is a premeditated orchestration of events. And if it wasn't Lynette who rang Northbridge Baths that day, who was it?

JC said that Chris extracted a promise from her to ring him every day. He couldn't have taken a call from her at home that Saturday because he was working, but he could have given her the telephone number for the Baths. JC's recollection of the phone conversation in which Chris told her that Lynette had gone was that 'it wasn't especially hot in the telephone box, so it can't have been in the middle of the day. It was definitely still light,' much as it might have been when Chris said the call came from Lynette at around 3 pm. If it was JC, there would also have been STD beeps on the line.

Chris arrived at South West Rocks alone, although JC recalls the girls in the back seat at some point and thinks they may have collected them from Clovelly on the way home. After dropping NC at MMC's place, JC told the inquest, she and Chris went directly to the house in Bayview where the most notable thing was that the house was empty. Lynette wasn't there.

Matthew Fordham continued questioning JC.

'You indicated earlier, ma'am, that some weeks earlier you had to leave that particular home because of Lyn's conversation with you. It was obvious that Lyn would not have wanted you to be in the home. Is that right?'

'Yes.'

'At the time, coming back from South West Rocks, was there any conversation in relation to the potential for Lyn to see you at that home and be unhappy about it?'

'No.'

'It was never suggested, for example, that perhaps you should stay up at Paul and Marilyn's house again?'

'No.'

'Is it the case that from that moment on you began to be Chris's de facto spouse and mother to his children. Is that correct?'

'Yes.'

In his 1991 police interview, Chris agreed with the police that he had a telephone conversation with Helena Simms seven days after Lynette went missing. In that conversation, he told Helena about an implausible telephone conversation he had just had with Lynette.

'Do you recall the conversation you had with Mrs Simms when you told her that Lyn had phoned you; to be more specific, it was Friday the 15th you allegedly phoned her, so that would be the day that JC says that you drove to South West Rocks.' [In 1998 JC amended her statement to say that Chris Dawson collected her on either 10 or 11 January.] 'You phoned her and told her that you'd had a further phone call from Lyn and stating that she said that she wouldn't come home until she'd made up her mind. And part of the conversation between the two of you, you said, "How much more bloody time do you need?" And she said that she wouldn't come home at all if you spoke to, spoke to her like that. Do you recall that conversation?'

'Yes, I remember.'

'Do you also recall telling Mrs Simms . . .'

'It wasn't on the same day that I went to pick up JC, 'cause I left to pick up JC, I'm sorry. It . . .'

'Do you recall further in that conversation you said to Lyn, you asked her to come home because you needed her?'

'Yes.'

'It seems strange to me, Chris, in light of that conversation that you would also tell JC the same thing, ask her to come back to Sydney and live with you as you needed her.'

'Well . . .'

'Would you . . . well, that's just me, would you care to comment on that?'

'Yeah, I was very anxious for Lyn to come back and for us to work things out. I, at the time I thought I was being . . . in this phone call when Lyn rang me to say she needed time away, I was there looking after the two girls, I was taking time away by myself.

JC rang me and said that she was wanting to come back to Sydney, she needed to come back and . . . when I brought JC back, part of it was because I thought she was going to be returning to her family home, not my home. She ended up coming to live with me because she wasn't wanted anywhere else.'

'Mm.'

'I didn't ask JC to come and live with me.'

'So, explain to me . . . you're saying you, she has extended . . .'

'JC had . . . okay, she wasn't wanted at home because she had a dispute at home, I remember going down to [the women's refuge] with JC while they were sort of counselling her on where she could stay and go, she had the option of possibly staying there for a day or two or so, and then she had nowhere to go. And I, naively now, offered she could come and stay with me, until, you know, such time.'

'Let me get this straight, when you're referring to this time, after Lyn left or before?'

'No, no, after Lyn left.'

'All right. So you're saying that what JC says here in her statement, that you asked her to come and live with you, is not correct?'

'I didn't ask her to come and live with me, she asked if she . . . come and get her and bring her back to Sydney . . . because she was saying how she missed me and all that sort of thing, but at that stage I was still of the understanding that she was going to go back and live somewhere else in Sydney, not with me.'

Chris had been orchestrating JC's living arrangements for the last few months and knew, probably better than anyone else, that JC had nowhere to go. If Chris 'naively' allowed JC to move in, did he also naively divorce Lynette in 1983, and then marry JC in 1984?

It's also interesting that in this interview Chris gave an incomplete response, or was cut off by the detectives, when it appeared he was just about to confirm what date he had collected JC. He agreed with the detectives that he spoke to Lynette's mother on 15 January and then says that he couldn't have collected JC on 15 January, because 'it wasn't on the same day that I went to pick up JC, 'cause I left to pick up JC, I'm sorry. It . . .'

Could it have been that Chris was about to say that he had collected JC prior to 15 January?

When Peter Dawson cross-examined JC, he pressed the idea that JC had manipulated Chris by way of getting back into the house.

'What I suggest to you is in fact it was you who wished to continue the relationship and not Chris?'

'That's not correct.'

'Would it be correct to say that when Chris arrived at South West Rocks you were happy to see him?'

'I was happy to see him then.'

'Why was that?'

'Well, he told me he needed me and wanted me to come back with him.'

'So saying he needed you changed your attitude?'

'Well, it meant someone wanted me.'

'Isn't the difficulty that you at that time had nowhere to go?'

'That's true.'

'Nowhere to live?'

'As I saw it, no.'

'Where were you going to go when you came back from South West Rocks if it wasn't to live with Chris?'

'I had lots of things on my mind and I hadn't thought that through yet.'

'So you were living at your sister's place before you went to South West Rocks?'

'Yes.'

'And that wasn't an option for you?'

'It might have been. I hadn't thought – didn't think it through.'

'So, when you went to South West Rocks you had no idea where you were going to live after the holiday?'

'I didn't think about any day apart from the one that I was in.'

In the six months prior to JC moving back to Bayview, she had been moved on so many times. Her explanation for staying with Chris, that 'someone wanted me', is sad but understandable. She just wanted to be loved and needed.

Peter Dawson was trying to suggest that seventeen-year-old JC was homeless but not helpless, and that it was thirty-four-year-old Chris who was being manipulated. But it's hard to see Chris as the victim when he had made the thousand-kilometre round trip to bring JC back to the house within days of Lynette going missing. How does one reconcile Chris driving through the night to get JC when his wife was missing? Chris had told everyone, including detectives in his 1991 interview, that Lynette had said that she was only going away for a few days. If that was so, why would he have moved JC into the house, or allowed her to inveigle her way back in? Wasn't he concerned that Lynette might return and find JC taking care of her children, sleeping in her bed? How can Chris plausibly sustain the notion that he 'was very anxious for Lyn to come back and for us to work things out', when the very reason she had gone away was because of Chris's relationship with JC?

When Damian interviewed Paul Dawson, he asked him about the situation.

'We're trying to work out how . . . how it would be that JC would take up a position as virtually his wife and stepmother to his children when there was still the likelihood that Lyn would return.'

'Um . . .'

'It's a contradiction.'

'Yeah.'

'Do you understand that?'

'Well, he needed someone to look after the kids. I, I, I know what you're saying, I know.'

'I mean, even in your recollection—'

'Yeah.'

'JC was in the house in the same month, presumably living in a de facto relationship with Chris within two weeks of Lyn disappearing. How would that be if Lyn was still likely to come back?'

'I think we asked ourselves the same question at the time, by memory,' Paul said. 'I think Marilyn and I probably said the same thing, I don't know. I don't know how they were going to sort it out.'

'Because you agree that JC did return, did move in . . . at some time in January, whatever the date it was, it certainly was in January, and no matter what was said that was a fact that she moved in there—'

'Right.'

'How was he able to move [her] in with any confidence that Lyn was not coming back?' Damian asked.

'Yeah. Well, I think he, because she was the – she'd been babysitting as well, she'd be moving in, I think she, by, she used to move in from time to time anyway, I think, by memory . . .'

Marilyn's memories were clearer. She recalls how she found out that JC was living in the house again when they returned from Lake Munmorah: 'We went up to Chris's and I think JC was there and I think we just stood at the door and he's said, "Well, she's missing." My husband suggested that he [Chris] not have JC live there, that she go home and that Chris court her so that he could go through the steps of a normal courtship.'

Paul knew that Chris and JC had been in a sexual relationship for well over a year, and Marilyn had known for at least some months.

In any event, Chris didn't take the advice. Is it possible that he was unconcerned about the inevitable confrontation, when Lynette returned to find JC living in the house? Or for the children, who might be present when the grown-up hell broke loose? Is this the behaviour of a man who wanted to 'work things out'? Or perhaps he already knew that Lynette wasn't coming back.

Over dinner one night, I asked JC if she'd had any idea where she'd go when she got back to Sydney.

'Nope,' she said brusquely. 'I spent my whole childhood wanting to feel loved and needed, to be worth something, and this was the first time I felt that someone wanted me. I'd never grown up emotionally. People I trusted betrayed me. There's too much damage.'

Since leaving Chris, JC hasn't been involved with anyone else. She doesn't particularly like going out with girlfriends at night because men assume that she's looking for a partner. I wondered if men were looking at her while we had dinner.

'It's amazing how well you've done.'

She smiled at me. 'Years of therapy. *Years*,' she said. 'I had a very, very good therapist. You can talk to him if you like.'

We were slow to leave dinner and then we lingered on the footpath outside the restaurant. An icy wind had blown in from the snowfields and I had tucked my hands under my armpits to keep them warm, but JC pulled out her phone and started flipping through photos of KD's new baby boy. The next day she was going to babysit him all day.

'Look at him,' she said, proudly. 'He's magnificent!' And I had to agree that he was a terrifically handsome baby.

'I can't regret anything that happened, because if I did, I wouldn't have KD. And if I didn't have KD,' she said, tapping the little baby on the screen, 'I wouldn't have him.'

CHAPTER ELEVEN

De facto wife and stepmother

ONCE JC WAS BACK AT BAYVIEW, SHE WAS NO LONGER JUST THE babysitter – she was Lynette's replacement.

'Were you happy about that?' Matthew Fordham asked her at the inquest.

'I think I was resigned to it. I didn't believe I had any other option.'

'Were you comfortable taking on the responsibility of two young children?'

'No.'

'Did you feel as though you had enough life experience to do that job properly?'

'No, I was seventeen.'

'Is it something that you had sought to do, look after those two young children?'

'No.'

'Did you ever talk to Chris about your reluctance to take on that job?'

'I sometimes asked him, where is their mother, when is she coming back to look after them? I do remember that.'

'When you said those words, was it said in – were they said in the hope that she would come back one day?'

'Yes.'

'What would Chris's response to that be?'

'He would say "She's gone off with the religious people." Sometimes – he said different things every time about where she would be, just to shut me up really.'

'When he told you those things, did you doubt him?'

'No.'

And later: 'I didn't like being there, I didn't like looking after his children, I didn't like – I just wanted to do what people do when they're eighteen.'

JC agreed with Matthew Fordham that when Chris told her by phone at South West Rocks that 'Lynette's gone and she's not coming back', he'd indicated 'a permanency about Lyn's absence'. But that can't have been quite right, if a few weeks later she was pestering Chris, wanting to know when Lynette was coming back. Perhaps at seventeen she thought that 'she's not coming back' meant that she wasn't coming back to the house, or that Lynette would take the children and go and live somewhere else, or as others did, she assumed that it wouldn't be forever. Or perhaps the certainty with which JC accepted Chris's words increased as the months rolled by and it began to look like Lynette really wasn't going to return.

When JC met with Greg and Merilyn at Point Clare eight years later, she told them, 'I was seventeen years old and I never stopped to think how he was so sure that Lyn wasn't coming back.'

When JC arrived back at Bayview, she described the situation that confronted them all. When Lynette was still around, 'there were times when I wanted to be the only woman in his life. But I didn't want the children'. Suddenly, she had it all and more. 'When I moved in, he said, "Cook!" Well, I couldn't cook!'

Since MMC had raised her on cold cuts and bolognaise, it's not surprising that she didn't know how to make a family dinner every night. 'I remember me being in the kitchen one day and the three of them on the other side of the counter, all looking at me, waiting for me to cook. Lynette had the *Commonsense Cookery Book* and I learned how to make mashed potato. We had a lot of pre-packaged meals.'

Eventually, Chris enlisted Marilyn to come and teach her how to make a few things.

JC says she still finds cooking a perfunctory task, although she did give me the recipe for her signature chocolate caramel slice.

Back at the inquest, Matthew Fordham directed JC's attention to the pool.

'When you returned to the home after being at South West Rocks, do you remember the pool area?'

'Yes.'

'The pool was already installed – is that correct?'

'Yes.'

'Do you remember whether the paving around the pool had been completed at that time?'

'No.'

'When you say no, do you mean you don't remember or do you know that it was not?'

'Sorry. No, there was only dirt.'

'You're obviously aware now that the area around the pool had been paved after you arrived back from South West Rocks, do you know how long after you arrived back it had been paved?'

'Well, it was a process. First grass was put down, that didn't work, then paving was done as well as steps up to the house sometime later.'

'Are you able to estimate how long after you came back from South West Rocks the paving went in?'

'No.'

'It was all just dirt?'

'Yes.'

'Did you ever see Chris working around the sides of the pool where the dirt was?'

'I don't recall.'

'Were there ever times when Chris would be out working in the garden?'

'Yes.'

'Was he the sort of person who would regularly go and work in the garden or was it very much an occasional thing that he would go and work in the garden?'

'It was about weeds really, more than anything else. Just keeping the weeds away and we all participated in that.'

'Were there ever times when Chris would go and work in the garden on his own?'

'I don't recall.'

'Do you recall at any stage after you came back from South West Rocks, any changes to the dirt around the edge of the swimming pool?'

'No, I don't recall.'

'Do you recall any people working around the edges of the swimming pool, any contractors being brought in?'

'Only when the grass was being put down or the paving done. That's the only times.'

'At those times were you there when the work was done, or the paving done?'

'Given that I didn't work, I probably was.'

'Did you ever see any contractors digging in the areas around the swimming pool?'

'No.'

JC's evidence did nothing to support Matthew Fordham's theory that Lynette was buried around the pool or anywhere else on the property. It's unlikely that Chris would have got contractors to do the work if he had buried Lynette there. If he was trying to cover something up, I imagine that he would have done the work himself.

After they'd moved to Queensland, JC told the inquest, when they came back to Sydney each January, they would go back to the property at Bayview. 'Well, sometimes we both went, just on a nostalgia trip, but other times he went on his own.'

Neville and Sue Johnston, who bought the house in 1987, gave a statement to Damian in 1998. Neville recalled that in 1989,

Chris and a 'young lady with a baby' and some other small children dropped by. 'Thinking he was just an interested previous owner . . . I said, "Well, by all means have a look, if you want to go up the back, do so."

'I was certainly a little more concerned when he turned up for the second visit . . . I think it might've been close to Christmas . . . he again returned with the young lady and the same number of children and this time he did make specific comments about the landscaping and about the pool . . . he made me feel a bit uneasy [in that] during that conversation he said, "Well, of course," he said, "I've been up here before, and when I do come up I always drive by the property."'

Exactly what made Neville Johnston 'a bit uneasy' isn't clear. Perhaps he thought that Chris was 'casing' the place, planning to break in when they were out one night. 'But I didn't concern myself with it greatly, until of course your Chatswood detectives turned up,' referring to the 1990–91 investigation. 'They went over the rear of the property and they obviously contacted us at a later date for a more intensive search.'

Damian told me that the land at Bayview was rock. 'After a few centimetres you hit bedrock so any bones, if they had been buried there, they would have come up.' Nevertheless, there's one other area he'd like to test. 'It's right up the back,' he said. 'We need an excavator to dig it up. There's a large amount of soil up there because the neighbours told me when they were excavating, they asked if they could deposit it there.'

Then, a month or so after Damian told me this, I mentioned it to JC. 'They need to check the soft soil under the girls' windows,' she said. When I next had coffee with Damian, I told him what she'd said, strangely aware that I was now carrying messages between them.

'JC showed me where the dog was buried in the front yard but she's never mentioned the soft soil outside the girls' windows,' he said, with an edge of anger.

But it wasn't until sometime later that I put together that it was JC's psychic friend, who had never been to the house, who had, in JC's words, 'described very accurately' the windows and the soft soil. JC also clarified that her psychic friend hadn't mentioned the soft soil until after the dig in 2000. I let Damian know.

One evening not long after Lynette went missing, Pat was lying in the bathtub and found herself also wondering if Lynette might be buried at Bayview.

'About six weeks after Lyn had disappeared, the weather had turned cold,' Pat told me, and I had to lean in to hear what she was saying. 'I was worried about Lyn, hoping she wasn't cold. And the next thought I had was getting a helicopter and flying over the house and property to see if I could see if he had buried her.' She was whispering, I felt, because she didn't really want anyone to hear her – her suspicions a betrayal perhaps, for thinking so early on that her sister might be dead.

Years later, with this thought still weighing on her, Pat went to the Land Registry Services and purchased some aerial maps. 'One was from 1978 and the other from 1982.' She thought that by comparing them, she might be able to see if there had been any disturbance to the block. 'But to my eyes, there was so much bush and they were taken at such a height, they weren't helpful.'

When JC returned to the house, she moved into the bed that, until a few days earlier, Lynette had shared with Chris. I can picture JC wandering into rooms she hadn't been in before, opening cupboards to see what was inside. Number 2 Gilwinga Drive was more lavish than any home she'd ever lived in, and she probably enjoyed having free rein for a while. But she didn't enjoy taking care of the girls and she didn't enjoy Chris's sexual demands.

A few weeks later, JC rang her father. MMC hadn't expressed any concern when she found out that JC had moved back into the house, but JC knew that her father would disapprove, and that worried her.

'We were at Chris's sister's place when I rang. He was angry at me,' she told me. 'He was angry because he had asked me when I was still at school if I was involved with Chris and I had obviously lied to him. Dad told me that he couldn't do anything about it – he'd got some legal advice and was told that there was nothing he could do because I was over seventeen. He cut me off from that point. He told my sisters that he'd disinherited me,' she said, visibly upset. 'He did disinherit me. I was devastated.'

Like JC's father, I also found it hard to accept that nothing could be done. Surely there is a longstanding legal principle prohibiting sexual relationships between teachers and their students? I did some research, but I wasn't coming up with anything satisfactory, so I got in touch with the New South Wales Department of Education. In an email, I set out what I was after. Seven hours after I sent my inquiry, I received a reply:

> I have not been able to find the Code of Conduct that applied to teachers in the early 1980s so can only suggest you look at the

Teaching Services Act 1980, other relevant laws at the time, and anything that might be available in the history section of the Department's website.

I'd already done all that. I couldn't find any departmental policies or guidelines and although the *Teaching Services Act* did cover professional misconduct, those provisions were only introduced in 1980. Section 73 of the New South Wales *Crimes Act 1900* makes it an offence to have sexual Intercourse with someone aged sixteen to eighteen years if they are under 'special care', which includes a school teacher. But if the police didn't charge teachers with this offence, it's as if it didn't exist.

Faced with his inability to do anything, either legally or morally, XC relinquished his parenting responsibilities, most of which had lapsed years before, when he and MMC separated.

'I said to her that I couldn't tolerate it,' XC told Damian in his 1998 interview, 'and that if she didn't do something about it and stop seeing him, that I wouldn't talk to her again. And she told me point blank that she wasn't going to stop seeing him. And, well, that was it. That was it.'

Just a few pages over, he also told Damian that one of the reasons JC's marriage to Chris broke down was because of her inability to mother Lynette and Chris's girls. 'I had said to her, "Well, look, if you've taken on the responsibility of the two children, as you obviously did, you really are abdicating your responsibility by not looking after them."' I wonder if XC realised that he was telling JC to do exactly what he had not? He was chastising her about parental responsibilities, when he had as good as surrendered his own.

Could things have turned out differently for JC if he'd kept the lines of communication open? Would JC have rung him when the grind of mothering two small children quickly overwhelmed her? Could she have stayed with him? He offered to pay her rent if she moved in with one of her sisters who was living at Bankstown, but she didn't want to go so far away, not out of petulance, but because she wanted to be close to her other sisters and her friends. Could he have paid her rent closer to home? Would it have made any difference?

After a few weeks, JC decided to unpack. 'I had nowhere to put my clothes. All the drawers were completely full, it seemed like nothing [of Lynette's] was missing. I certainly packed up her clothes. He encouraged me to do it. I kept a lot of her clothes. He encouraged me to do that too. It was cheaper that way.'

JC told me this with what I can best describe as stoic shame, and I could do no more than listen quietly, as she described this disturbing incursion into Lynette's life. JC didn't say that she'd decided by then that Lynette wasn't coming back but there must have been a shift of sorts, as she moved from being a visitor in the house to putting her things in drawers and bundling Lynette's clothes into garbage bags, except for those she'd decided to keep for herself. I thought, too, about Chris dropping her back at her mother's place a few weeks earlier, when she'd arrived with her 'possessions in garbage bags'.

At the inquest, Matthew Fordham asked JC about Lynette's clothes.

'When you came back home after South West Rocks, did you go through Lyn's stuff, or had it already been gone through by Chris?'

'No, I went through it.'

'When you went through it, did you locate any pairs of glasses, or anything like that?'

'I don't recall whether I found glasses.'

'You mentioned in your statement that you placed a lot of Lyn's clothing and personal effects into some bags, is that correct?'

'Yes.'

'And how long after you returned from South West Rocks did that happen?'

'Very soon after.'

'And did the bags, did they leave the house immediately or did they stay there for a while?'

'They were put into the linen cupboard in the hallway and they were going to be taken over to Lyn's mother at Clovelly.'

'And the decision to take them over to Lyn's mother at Clovelly, how long after Lyn's disappearance was that decision made?'

'Well, it happened within, before Easter, because I didn't have the children there and after Easter I did have YD there, so I believe that it all happened quite quickly after she left.'

'That decision to take the property back to Lyn's mother's place, was that a decision made by Chris?'

'Yes.'

'At the time that the property was being prepared to take over to Lyn's mother's place, was there any discussion about the possibility, or a possibility of Lyn returning?'

'Not to me.'

Chris gave a different version in his 1991 interview. 'JC took great delight in going through the wardrobe, the reason why I packed up is because of JC's abhorrence to anything to do with Lyn in the house.'

When the bags were taken to Helena's, they sat outside the laundry on the small back verandah, which consisted of just a couple of steps that led to the backyard. Helena would have had to step around them each time she took a basket of washing to the clothesline. They stayed there for some months, reminding her each time she brushed past them that her daughter was still missing, and that all that remained of her had been bundled into garbage bags and left there like refuse.

Some months later, Greg and Merilyn visited from Muswellbrook, and Helena asked them to help her go through Lynette's things because she couldn't face doing it on her own. At the inquest, Matthew Fordham asked Greg about some of the things they found in the garbage bags.

'At page 13 you detail some of the items which had been returned in garbage bags, I think, to your parents. You describe going through the bags and that the contents of the bags included things like gardening gloves with dirt still on them?'

'That's correct. This was a while after they were delivered by Chris. I was sitting on the verandah with my father and at that stage I was – how could I explain it – I suppose, cranky. I knew JC was over in the car and I said something along the lines that "Excuse me if I don't help you" and he brought all the bags in and just dropped them and left. It was some time later, months later, that Merilyn and I were down at Mum's from Muswellbrook and we said, "We're going to leave" and Mum just asked us if we could go through Lyn's bags with her and that's when we went through them and found all these things.'

'These are the same garbage bags that you'd seen being delivered by Chris Dawson, is that right?'

'Yes, yes, yes, they were put out on the back verandah and never moved, they were in the same spot all the time.'

'Sir, the gardening gloves that you saw, was there a left and a right gardening glove?'

'Yes.'

'Do you recall, sir, whether they were a large size or a small size?'

'No, I think they could have been coloured – a colour comes up.'

'Sir, do you remember how long after Lynette disappeared that the garbage bags of her clothing were taken to the house at Clovelly?'

'I think within months. I couldn't give you an exact time.'

'Sir, you continue to describe the contents of those bags. You say that they included Lyn's nurse's badges, her contact lenses, her clothing, including a pair of pink shorts, is that correct?'

'That's correct, yes.'

'You say in your record of interview that Chris did say that when she left she had a pair of pink shorts on and that there was a pair of pink shorts in the bag. Do you remember when Chris said that she had a pair of pink shorts on when she left?'

'I think that was in the missing person's report.'

Greg and Merilyn told me they were filled with 'heart-stopping alarm' when they came across the shorts.

'We just looked at each other,' Merilyn said.

When they showed the shorts to Helena, and reminded her of the missing person report, she said, 'Lyn must have several pairs of pink shorts.'

Greg shook his head. 'Mum always had an innocent explanation for everything. She couldn't think badly of people.' But they were beginning to have private, darker thoughts about what might have happened to Lynette, thoughts that they initially pushed away, because they were too awful.

Lynette's dressing gown was there. 'It was blue velour, high at the neck and with a satin collar,' Merilyn told me, with loving detail. In the pocket of the gown, she and Greg found a sales document for the house at Bayview which had only Chris's signature on it.

Damian told the inquest, 'Evidence has been obtained that on 21 December 1981 Christopher Dawson enlisted the services of Mona Vale Real Estate, where he entered into an agency agreement between Christopher and Lynette Dawson and Mona Vale Real Estate for the property situated at 2 Gilwinga Drive, Bayview Heights, to be sold at an agreed price of $280,000. This sales agreement only indicates the signature of Christopher Dawson.'

When Pat spoke to Lynette just prior to Chris leaving on 23 December 1981, Lynette was excited because Chris had told her that he had a 'surprise'.

'She thought that perhaps he had bought tickets to White City to see the tennis,' Pat told me. 'It turned out that Chris had organised for a real estate agent to come and look at the house. Of course, Lyn didn't want to sell the house.'

Two days after Chris signed the agency agreement, he and JC left for Queensland. Was Lynette's apparent refusal to sign it the reason why Chris decided to blow it all and head to Queensland with JC? During the long drive, was Chris thinking about losing his share of the house and did that make the decision to turn around easier?

In the garbage bags, Greg and Merilyn also came across Lynette's contact lenses. Earlier, Pat told the inquest that Lynette was heavily reliant on her glasses. 'If she was passing someone, say, in the corridor where she was working she wouldn't be able to recognise them.'

'You are aware that Lyn had an appointment with the optometrist not long after she went missing, is that correct?'

'Yes, I'm aware of that, yes. In my statement, I wish to correct that part of my statement that I made because Lyn hadn't told me that she had an appointment after she went missing, but Mum had mentioned it after she went missing that she had an appointment with an ophthalmologist. Also, an optometrist, yes.'

Matthew Fordham was trying to make two points with the contact lenses. The first was that Lynette's eyesight was so poor that her ophthalmologist appointment was important, so she would have kept it or phoned to cancel. Then, given how poor her eyesight was, that if Lynette was going away, she would have taken her contact lenses with her. But Chris said at the time, and then again six weeks later when he made the missing person report, that Lynette's decision to go away was sudden and only made when she was shopping in Chatswood. She hadn't packed anything, which would explain why the contacts were in the garbage bags. When the contact lenses were found in the garbage bags, Pat must have also worried how Lynette was managing without them.

After she left, Chris said that Lynette rang him a few times in January. When people go away, intending to be lost, they don't ring home. Damian also says it's rare for a mother of young children to go missing. I couldn't find exact statistics for mothers of young children who go missing but women made up 51 per cent of the pool of missing person cases surveyed in a report by the Australian Institute of Criminology in 2000.[9] Fifty-four per cent of people who are missing were last seen in their own home, like Lynette; 20 per cent were last seen at night between 6 and 11 pm; 20 per cent were last seen on a Friday; only 9 per cent are either married or in a de facto relationship; only 8 per cent are aged between twenty-six and forty years old; and only 4 per cent of those making the missing person report were a spouse. Lynette is in a very small group.

On the day that Lynette went missing, Helena Simms had to absorb the news from Chris. First, that Lynette hadn't come to the pool as planned. Then, that she'd rung Chris to tell him that she'd decided to go away. Lynette was reliable and none of it made any sense to Helena. At times, people do things that are out of character, but my heart aches for Helena, because from that moment on, she'd lost Lynette and nothing about her much-loved daughter was ever going to make sense again.

The first of February was Helena's sixty-sixth birthday, and Lynette had organised a surprise party at Gilwinga Drive. When Pat gave evidence, Matthew Fordham asked her about the party.

'Does it strike you as strange that Lyn would organise this party and then disappear and not have any further contact in relation to the conduct of the party?'

'Yes, you can't believe it could happen but then again you couldn't believe any of that had happened. It was just – things didn't happen in our family.'

The party was cancelled.

'I came down [to Sydney] with my daughter, Pauline,' Pat told me. 'I thought Lyn might ring Mum. Chris came over with the girls. It was terrible – she was either dead, which was terrible, or she was still alive and not ringing Mum. Either way, it was just terrible. We kind of had to think these terrible things about her because otherwise she was dead.'

Some weeks after Lynette disappeared, Pat told the inquest, her mother was also pained by something Chris had told her.

Matthew Fordham asked, 'Do you know whether Lyn would have had access to any finance or any money that could assist her if she disappeared voluntarily?'

'Mum had mentioned something that Chris had said that Lyn had taken some money. My mother was so honest and to her she was absolutely devastated that Lyn may have had some money that really belonged to both of them. To Mum, this was absolutely devastating.'

The money that Pat is referring to is $500 cash, which, Chris told the police on 29 April 1982, Lynette had in her purse when she left. The $500 was also mentioned in the 1985 ombudsman's report, part of which Damian read to the inquest.

> Mr Dawson was spoken to by plain clothes constable first class Snook [?] of the Mona Vale detectives' office on 29 April but stated that he had not heard anything further since the last STD telephone call. He informed Snook that he and his wife had marriage problems for some 18 months past. They had attended a psychiatrist on the day prior to his wife leaving home to try and resolve the issue and were to attend again. He further stated that at the time of his wife leaving she had $500 in her possession.

Damian queries why it took Chris until 29 April, three months after Lynette disappeared, to mention to the police that she had $500 cash with her when she left. In 1982, $500 was such a large amount of cash that Damian would have expected Chris to mention it when he made the missing person report in mid-February. Lynette could have used the $500 to pay for hotels and food in the weeks after she went missing to avoid being traced, if that was her intention. But the cash wouldn't have lasted more than a few weeks, which would suggest that she found a job quickly, because she didn't withdraw any money from their bank account and Chris said she had only used her bank card twice. The odd thing about the bank card is that Chris said that both transactions were made at Warriewood Square Shopping Centre, 10 kilometres from Bayview. The first was at the clothing chain store Katies on 12 January, three days after Lynette had rung him at Northbridge Baths to say she was on the Central Coast, almost 100 kilometres away, and the second at another chain store, Just Jeans, on 27 January.

In his interview about that day at Northbridge Baths, he said that 'the girl who worked in the shop called me over, said there was an STD phone call for me, she'd taken the call'. Chris said that 'in the following weeks I had several phone calls from Lyn, all STD calls'. If all of Lynette's calls were long-distance, why would she go all the way back to Warriewood to shop? There would have been Katies and Just Jeans stores on the Central Coast, as well as dozens of other clothing retailers. Is it possible that she came back twice, thinking that she might go home, but changed her mind when she got there? Did she go back to the house, see that JC was living there, and leave again?

The trip would have taken her at least three hours – a train from the Central Coast, then two buses to get to Warriewood – and then another three hours in reverse. Lynette couldn't drive, so all that travelling had to be by train, bus and on foot. And what's more, Lynette lived in the area and was well connected with other mothers, with parents whose children attended the childcare centre where she worked, and with football friends of Chris and Paul's. How is it possible that no one saw her?

Barb Kilpatrick lived around the corner from JC's family in Wheeler Heights, and Barb and MMC quickly became good friends after the family moved there from the eastern suburbs. Barb had known JC since she was two, and in many ways, she'd been like a mother to her. In the 1970s, Barb set up a women's refuge in the area, and she was still running it when I started working there in 2007. Barb was willowy, with freckles and loose blonde curls. She was gentle, but her softness hid a brute determination; she'd smile and smile, but she wouldn't budge. She was a formidable advocate for women and children who are victims of domestic violence.

JC went to see Barb after she moved in with Chris, first alone, and then again with Chris. Barb told the inquest about those conversations.

'JC was very upset because she was very young and she couldn't understand how a mother would leave her little children . . . she was with this man who she thought was god and she really just wanted to be with him. She didn't want to have the responsibility of the children and she found it very difficult that if it was her and

Chris, it had to be her and Chris and the children. She was a child herself . . . she wanted their mother to come back and get them and she wanted to live happily ever after with Chris.'

'At the time that you spoke with JC in 1982 about her relationship with Chris, did you form any opinion of her willingness to please Chris?' Matthew Fordham asked.

'Yes, yes, because they came to see me together after that – we talked about lots of things and at that time I even said to Chris, "Why does JC have to be there, she should be allowed to live on her own for a little while or maybe go and live with friends." And we talked about her doing a TAFE course in childcare and I found out about it, how she could enrol, and she was quite excited about that, not moving out but going to the TAFE course. He didn't want her to move out, that was not something that was even up for discussion. So, I think she would have done whatever he wanted her to do.'

When Barb gave a statement to the police in 1998, she said that when Chris and JC came to visit her, 'I even suggested that JC should get a flat on her own,' although she made no mention of how JC might do that, and it wouldn't have been likely that an eighteen-year-old with a part-time job at Coles would be able to pay rent and support herself and go to TAFE. One of the top priorities at the refuge is to help women find a secure place to live. JC wasn't a client, but she was a family friend in need. It's hard to understand why Barb didn't offer more of this kind of help.

JC's dismal HSC results arrived in January 1982, and didn't leave her with many options. 'If you look at my grades,' she told me, 'they're a picture of my home life.' She showed me one of her school report cards with a PE grade and comment by Chris.

The childcare course that Barb had suggested was full, so she started a secretarial course at North Sydney TAFE. She only lasted three days.

'It was too difficult,' she told the inquest. 'It was too difficult from the viewpoint of dragging the children to the bus stop, it was just made very difficult. I felt as though it was made very difficult for me to do that.' Like Lynette had been, JC was now isolated and dependent on Chris and Paul to drive her places.

At Bayview, Chris, JC and the girls moved unsteadily into the new arrangements, with JC still resisting her role as mother. 'I'd put their cereal in bowls in the fridge at night because it helped with all the jobs I had to do in the morning,' she told me, seemingly surprised that she'd done this simple thing to lighten the load. 'There were times when I'd run out of the house and he'd come and find me. He'd say, "Come on. Get in the car. We need you."'

JC felt that she connected better with YD, the younger of Chris and Lynette's daughters. But even so, when XD started school a few weeks later, JC found it difficult to care for YD alone. At two years old, she was a toddler – probably the most difficult stage to be caring for a young child – so Chris paid Marilyn to look after YD until JC was able to manage.

JC could see that XD was having trouble coping at school. Most days she came home with a dirty uniform and JC resented having to clean it all the time. After a while she made XD scrub the uniform and after that it came home clean. JC knew that XD was having trouble connecting with other kids, and after school she always wandered out alone to meet her. But, in a way, that suited JC fine, as she kept to herself as well, not chatting to other mothers in the playground (although I imagine that they were chatting about her). One day, Helena turned up at the school gates unannounced. JC hurried the girls to the car and Helena was left behind, calling out to her, wanting to see her granddaughters.

Greg told the inquest that when they'd met with JC on the Central Coast, 'she apologised in relation to an episode where my mother went to give the girls a present at the school and JC pulled them away. I believe that was under – I believe she was under instructions to keep the girls away from Mum.'

Whenever JC spoke about the girls, she seemed flooded with shame and sadness. JC was only seventeen years old when she began caring for them full-time. Like XD in kindergarten, she wasn't coping. She never wanted to be their stepmother, but like a mother, she can't forgive herself for rejecting them.

CHAPTER TWELVE

The search for Lynette

WHILE JC WAS STRUGGLING WITH LIFE AT BAYVIEW, LYNETTE'S colleagues at the childcare centre at Warriewood were struggling with her disappearance. The director of the centre, Barbara Cruise, also gave evidence at the inquest.

'Ma'am, do you think that Lyn was capable of leaving her children?' Matthew Fordham asked.

'It's hard to believe, it's hard to believe of most women, there are some that – where they need to do that, but I can't imagine, knowing how much they meant to her, that she would do that.'

Barbara lives on the Central Coast, and although I told her I didn't mind driving up to see her, she said she enjoyed the train journey south and was happy to meet somewhere in the middle.

Barbara had suggested that we meet at the Hornsby RSL club. It was an unassuming blond-brick building from the outside, but inside it opened up in a kaleidoscope of flashing lights and pinging poker machines, and no hint of the sunny day outside. Her husband had come too, and I followed them as they confidently set off to the coffee shop at the back of the complex.

'I've no doubt she's dead,' Barbara said, before I'd even had the chance to open my notebook. I looked over at her husband to see if he was as surprised as I was, but he seemed unfazed. 'I came to that view only weeks or months after she disappeared,' she continued.

We discussed the childcare centre and Barbara told me that she'd originally been the acting director, but she took to the work and soon stepped into a permanent role. She enjoyed the familiarity between the staff. They were a close-knit group of women, which she said was inevitable in that environment. Her recall of staff numbers and names was impressive; and she told me that she was a practical person, which I could already see.

'I had to have a trained nurse to open the centre and that's why I employed Lyn. She started working for me in 1980. She was very popular at work.'

In the last six to twelve months before she disappeared, Barbara had noticed that Lynette had put on weight. 'Maybe 10 kilos, and in the months before she went missing, she was buying nice clothes to make herself attractive to him.' She took a quick sip of her coffee. 'I'd known of her marriage difficulties for about six months before she disappeared. One day she said, "We've moved this young girl into our place," and I said, "You're having marriage difficulties – get her out!"'

After the Christmas break, Barbara remembers that Lynette came back to work when the centre reopened on Tuesday 5 January or Wednesday 6 January. The last time she saw Lynette was Friday afternoon, when she and Chris came to collect the girls after they'd been to the marriage counselling session. On Monday 11 January, Barbara got a call from Chris.

'He rang and told me Lyn had decided to go away for a while, that she needed some space. That didn't seem unreasonable. I knew they were having difficulties. A few weeks went by and Chris rang to tell me that Lynette wouldn't be coming back to work at all.'

'The staff couldn't believe it was in her nature to leave her children and to leave us the way she did.' Beside her, Barbara's husband nodded at this. 'She came to work at the childcare centre because it fitted in with her being a mother; the girls could come too. It didn't make sense that she'd go away.'

We finished our coffees, made our way down a mirror-lined corridor and said goodbye in the foyer, with Barbara telling me about the other things they had planned before taking the train home again.

'She was a really nice person,' Barbara said, adjusting her shopping bag. 'She was very open and friendly. I can't think of anything unkind to say about her.'

I'd also arranged to meet another of Lynette's colleagues, Sue Strath. Sue worked at the childcare centre as well, and she told the inquest that Lynette's children 'were her life'. She still lives on the Northern Beaches, so a few days after my coffee with Barbara, I headed north out of Manly and up the peninsula again. I took a right turn at Long Reef Golf Club into a quiet enclave of houses locked between the golf course and the headland. A few houses back from where the street ended abruptly at a rocky inlet was Sue's white timber cottage.

She came to the door and welcomed me in.

'What a spot,' I commented, as we walked through to the kitchen.

'We're lucky,' she said, smiling at me.

We took a pot of tea to the back deck, from where I could hear the waves hitting the rocks.

'Lynette was very happy. She never grumbled. As far as she was concerned, she had everything she wanted,' Sue said, as she poured the tea. 'Our children were the same age and we'd go to the park together. Her eldest daughter was due to start school after the Christmas break and Lyn had already bought the uniforms. She was as excited as a kid.'

Sue had heard rumours that Chris was having an affair, and that Paul was 'sleeping' with schoolgirls from Forest High too.

'The insular peninsula,' she said sardonically. It was an oft-used quip about the Northern Beaches – that the locals didn't like going further south than Manly and that the rest of Sydney couldn't be bothered crossing the Spit Bridge – and consequently, everybody on the peninsula knew everybody else's business.

Then, at work one day, Sue told me that Lynette had told *her* that she'd come home from work to find Chris and JC swimming naked in the pool. 'I asked her what she thought about it, if she thought there was something going on,' Sue told me. 'And Lyn replied, "My Chris wouldn't do that." That's how she thought. She was so naive.'

A little later, Lynette told Sue that Chris was proposing that JC move in with them. 'She asked me if I thought it was a good idea. I told Lynette, "I'm not so sure I'd want an attractive young woman moving into my home!"'

When Lynette came back to work in the new year she told Sue that Chris had left her over Christmas.

Sue told the inquest, 'I remember coming back to work after Christmas and I remember her saying that Chris had left over the Christmas period and, you know, she was very upset about that, but he'd just come back again.'

Sue couldn't accept that the Lynette she knew would be capable of leaving her children. 'I used to say all the time, "Why hasn't someone come to talk to me?"' – 'someone' meaning the police. 'Within the first year of Lyn going missing I formed the strong view that he had killed her. "I bet he's bumped her off." People would laugh at me,' Sue said sternly, incredulous that anyone thought she was trying to be funny. 'I had a friend who was a detective and I kept going on at him about Lyn's disappearance.'

As I was leaving, Sue said, 'I come from a big family, five brothers and sisters, and I couldn't imagine that my family would let me be forgotten.'

I hesitated, but let the moment pass, and said goodbye. I wanted to defend Pat and Greg, Helena too. But Sue was a friend of Lynette's and she'd lived through the decades that Lynette had been missing. Who was I to tell her anything about Lynette?

I was discomfitted by Sue's parting words and pulled into the point between Freshwater and Curl Curl, not quite ready to be home. I'm in love with the ocean but on days like that, I feared it; I couldn't stop imagining what it would be like to be out beyond the break, struggling to make it ashore. Suddenly I imagined Lynette out there, swimming hard, then kicking furiously to catch a rough, frothing wave in. She'd grown up beside the beach and would have known more about the ocean than I did. Pat and Greg had told me what a great swimmer she was – better than me, and braver too, I'd bet.

I was learning that Lynette had a lot of pluck, and that she was admired and loved. There was a time when I'd imagined her as timid, and had assumed that her family were most likely the same. How else could they let twenty years pass until the first inquest was held into her disappearance? Were they estranged from Lynette, I'd wondered? Perhaps they didn't realise for some years that she was missing, rather than choosing to be out of touch? The insinuation behind each of these questions, of course, had been that they didn't care. I felt ashamed now, that I had judged them before I had gotten to know them.

What Helena was doing to find Lynette wasn't well known or widely reported at the time. Pat and Greg told me that Helena was intelligent but had had few opportunities. She'd worked in retail before she was married and then, when the children were older, as a cleaner. And then, just a month before she turned sixty-six, she found herself searching for her daughter. She didn't drive, and had only her home phone and Australia Post to assist her. Helena was doing everything she possibly could but her resources were limited.

Chris had said that when Lynette rang him in that first week after she was gone, she'd told him that she was on the Central Coast, so Helena would catch a train up there and, with no real starting point, wander around looking for Lynette. She carried leaflets with Lynette's photo on them, which she'd give to shopkeepers. With no computer or typewriter, Helena would have had to take a photo of Lynette to a printing shop, where the text would be typeset and then printed off as a flyer. Each step she took was difficult. And later, when Chris said that he hadn't heard from Lynette again,

Helena would catch the ferry to Manly with her flyers, and wander through the crowds, hoping that Lynette might have returned closer to home.

On 21 August 1982, Helena gave a statement at Mona Vale police station, where Chris had made the missing person report.

> I put an ad in the *Manly Daily* for a week, as a lady whose child she minded in the centre said she saw her standing in the Narraweena shopping centre near a car. Around about that same time or earlier another friend of Lyn and Chris's thought she saw her in a car outside a fruit stall she worked at on the way into Gosford. So I put an ad, four times in the Central Coast paper. It is her birthday on Sept 25th & I intend putting an ad in the paper then also the *SMH* [*Sydney Morning Herald*] & *Telegraph* in the hope of her seeing it.

Lynette had been missing for seven months and Helena's statement detailed her searches – the bank, Warringah Shire Council, who ran the childcare centre, the nurses registration boards in New South Wales and Queensland, previous employers, and the notices in the newspapers.

In a letter that Pat wrote to me, she detailed more of Helena's frantic search for Lynette. 'She wrote to all the major teaching hospitals, interstate also, enquiring after Lyn, in her married name, her nursing name (Sister Hewitt Simms, as there was another nurse at the Children's Hospital at Camperdown with the name "Simms" when Lyn began her training); to the police departments in each state and New Zealand. She also rang major teaching hospitals. We were always very grateful to the Salvation Army who did their utmost to help Mum.' I knew that this letter to me was one of many identical letters Pat had written over the years. Like her mother, she continued to do what she could to help find Lyn.

When Pat, Greg and Merilyn talked to me about other events – travels, news of their children, even health woes – their voices were light and cheerful, which seems to be their natural dispositions. But as soon as we returned to Lynette, the conversation felt locked-in and fraught. Guilty. They are angry that others have judged them harshly, even though my sense is that they are angry at themselves as well.

'People forget that we knew little until we heard the evidence of people who came forward and after that, we could see the bigger picture,' Pat wrote in a letter to me.

Neither Pat nor Greg lived in Sydney then, and they both had jobs and small children, so they couldn't drop everything to go and help Helena. If one of them had lived in Sydney, they might have been more concerned than Helena was by Chris's inaction in helping to find Lynette. But they'd known Chris for almost twenty years by then and had no reason to doubt him. They didn't know the truth about Lynette's marriage and they didn't know that Chris was having a relationship, although oddly, Helena did. Perhaps she was respecting Lynette's privacy, knowing that marriages can survive tough times. At a visit with the girls not long after Lynette went missing, Helena said they asked her to come for a sleepover at Bayview, as she had done in the past. Helena said that she'd like that, but there was nowhere for her to sleep, and one of the girls replied, 'You can sleep with Daddy. JC does.' Helena told Pat and Greg.

Greg was angry and confused to hear this, because he trusted Chris. Soon after, Pat had her disturbing thought about flying over the house at Bayview, looking for where Lynette might be buried.

It's hard to put these early thoughts and episodes together without wondering why the family wasn't demanding more of Chris and of the police. It doesn't make sense.

'Yes, you can't believe it could happen but then again you couldn't believe any of that had happened,' Pat said at the inquest.

She was more succinct with me. 'None of it makes any sense,' she said.

When I visited Carl Milovanovich, he told me, 'Denial is hope.' When he said that, I felt that I understood for the first time what had happened within the Simms family; I understood why Pat had whispered her early fears to me.

'Not wanting to accept the possibility that something might have happened to Lynette was denial,' Carl said. 'They just keep pushing that possibility away.'

Lynette's siblings love her dearly and they have spent over thirty years trying to find her but in those early months and years, they know they could have done more.

Chris had been asking JC to marry him in the year or so before Lynette disappeared. JC told the inquest, 'He asked me to marry him when I was sixteen and kept hassling me until I said yes. Driving in the car or maybe at school at the office, he just kept insisting that this is what he wanted.'

By mid-January 1984, Chris had divorced Lynette, and he and JC were married. The divorce and property papers were sent to Lynette's mother, and Greg and Pat remember how upset Helena was when they arrived.

'They said something like Lynette had abandoned him,' Greg told me. 'A friend of Chris's, Jeff Linden, did the work for him.' He was also a friend of the Simms family, which made it more painful for them.

I tracked Jeff down to Lismore, where he was a magistrate, and sent him an email. I expected him to say that he wouldn't speak to me, but like Carl, he replied straightaway. 'Give me a ring. The best time is just before I go into court around 9 am.'

Jeff told me that he'd grown up in the eastern suburbs of Sydney and knew Chris through rugby. 'He was a better rugby player than me.' Damian had said the same thing the very first time I met him.

'I knew Lyn really well,' he said softly. 'When they married, in the early days, we socialised a bit, my then-wife and Chris and Lyn. I'd been to Lyn's house – they had a pool.' A pool meant something in the 1970s. They weren't common, and having one was a status symbol. Jeff noticed. And everyone who visited the house noticed that – from the pool to the light fittings – every detail was hand-picked by Lynette.

Jeff continued. 'When Chris came to see me, he wanted to dissolve the marriage and also the property.'

When the documents were served to Lynette's mother, she rang Jeff. 'She was distraught. I said I was just doing my job, but Helena never accepted that Lyn had just walked out and that he was doing this so soon.'

Jeff asked Helena to forward an enclosed envelope to Lynette, if she knew of her whereabouts. In a reply letter, Helena wrote:

> It would be my dearest wish to be able to comply with your other request but I last saw my daughter on Jan 3, 1982 and last spoke

to her over the phone on Jan 8, 1982, and up to this very minute neither her parents, brothers and sister or friends have had any contact from her.

Yours in despair,

Helena Simms

Jeff said he couldn't remember exactly when Chris came to him. I told him that Chris and JC were married on 15 January 1984 and that Greg thought the divorce papers were sent to Helena around April 1983, fourteen months after Lynette had gone missing.

'I'm surprised to hear that,' he said, and was silent for a moment. 'To be brutally honest, I really liked Lyn.'

Another pause opened up between us and into that circumspect quietness, I think he was signalling a deep distress over Lynette's disappearance.

'At the time, I had no idea what was to follow. Far more information has come out now. It wasn't my job to question what I was being told. Now, it's beyond my comprehension that she would have just walked out. With the benefit of hindsight, I find it difficult to believe.'

In court, Matthew Fordham asked JC about their marriage plans and about the wedding and engagement rings.

'When I was going through Lyn's things in 1982, I found two rings which Chris told me were her engagement ring and an eternity ring and we had those rings made up into one ring, for me.'

'And that was to be your wedding ring, is that correct?'

'That was to be my engagement ring.'

'Do you still have that ring?'

'Yes.'

'Do you have it here today?'

'Yes.'

'The ring that was given to you as an engagement ring, has it changed in appearance since it was worn by Lyn?'

'Yes.'

'How has it changed?'

'Well, it was two rings and now there's just one.'

'You're indicating there a fairly substantial ring with I think three rows of diamonds is that correct?'

'There's twelve diamonds.'

JC had told Greg and Merilyn about the rings when they'd met at Point Clare and it was one of the things they'd decided to not tell Helena.

Pat told me, 'After Lyn had gone [Mum] asked Chris, "Does my Lyn have her rings?" Chris said yes. Mum thought Lyn could sell them if she needed money.' Of course, Helena did eventually find out about the rings. And although the Simms already knew, JC recalled the family gasping when she was giving evidence and then as they passed the ring box between them. I asked JC why Chris didn't buy her a new ring. 'He would have thought, "Why get new ones when I have perfectly good ones right here."'

I wonder if YD and XD had also gasped when they found out. They would have read in the paper, if they didn't already know, that Chris had refashioned their mother's rings for JC, rather than give them to the girls when they were older. Perhaps Chris assumed that they'd never know because, as JC said, 'Chris tried to *make* me the children's mother.' He might have thought that JC would pass the ring to the girls one day and if they wanted, they could divide Lynette's diamonds into two rings again. JC thinks he was just too stingy to buy another one and wasn't thinking about the meaning of the rings at all. At the time, JC didn't think about their significance either. Did Chris ever wonder what he would say about them to Lynette if she did come back?

'I guess he'd just say the rings were lost,' JC told me. The rings also made me wonder if the decision to have Peter Dawson represent Chris and Paul at the inquest was because it was cheaper. Later, JC told me that she had passed the ring on to KD, and KD had it reworked to commemorate the birth of her son. She divided the diamonds and, with white gold, had them made into two rings, which JC approved of because they were no longer a reminder of Lynette.

'Was there any conversation in relation to – that Chris had with you about the use of that ring for your engagement ring?' Matthew Fordham asked.

'No, we were just . . . he was just going to use it, he didn't have to buy me another one because there were diamonds there to be used.'

'You obviously knew that this was Lyn's engagement ring, is that correct?'

'Yes.'

'Did Chris talk to you about the possibility of Lyn coming back and claiming this property?'

'No.'

'Does it strike you as strange that Lyn would leave items such as her engagement ring behind?'

'Well, I didn't think about it at the time, but obviously now it does.'

Chris and JC married on 15 January 1984, two years and six days after Lynette went missing. The wedding was at the house at

Bayview, by then a sorry shell of the home that Lynette had lovingly created. JC was nineteen and Chris was thirty-six.

'At our wedding, he wanted me to have the same dress as Marilyn's. He wanted me to cut my hair short like Marilyn's too. He wanted me to look older than I did.' JC rolled her eyes, probably at the irony of it, I thought. 'It rained.'

'He said that his family would accept me, just as they had accepted that Lynette was gone. We both wrote letters to our fathers because they were both angry with us. My father didn't respond.'

Despite Chris's anxiety that JC appear older, there was no disguising that she was a teenage bride. JC showed me photos of the wedding. There was no professional photographer, so they were just like the holiday happy snaps she'd shown me that time in her flat. In them, she has a childlike look of uncertainty, as if she hasn't taken full possession of proceedings. Her hair is pulled back into a ponytail and she is wearing no makeup.

JC and Marilyn are in identical dresses that look homemade – JC's pale pink, Marilyn's pale blue. The Dawson twins are wearing white pants and matching short-sleeved shirts – Chris's is pale pink, Paul's pale blue, to match their wives. Everyone is twinned.

In one of the photos, five little girls stand tallest to shortest in front of the wedding party – XD and YD with Paul and Marilyn's three. Paul and Marilyn's oldest daughter isn't much shorter than JC and she doesn't look that much younger, either. A grey-haired woman in a high-necked blue frock and sensible shoes is the celebrant, and not twinned or matched, she looks the only adult in the party. Behind the bridal party, bamboo blinds are wonkily pulled up over sliding glass doors.

One of the photos is of JC with her three sisters and MMC. They are a handsome group but there is no sign of giddy happiness. They stand side by side, rather than close together, and their lips are parted to suggest a smile rather than actually smiling. Chris's parents were there too, but JC doesn't have a photo of them.

'My gran came. MMC bought the wedding cake,' JC told me. The wedding cake was chocolate but it's nowhere to be seen in the photos. There is no sign of festivity at all: the room is conspicuously bare, as if a rugby player woke up on the morning of his wedding, looked around and thought, 'We'll get married over there.' And JC didn't know how to brighten the room either, although she surprised me one day by describing in detail how Lynette had furnished the house.

'You can't imagine how beautiful it was. It was a magnificently appointed and furnished place. Everything in that house was hand-picked – the curtains and window coverings, every cushion and feature. Just incredible. From the entrance with the latch-door handle, to the skylights and vaulted ceilings, the sunken lounge, the colour of every wall and tapestry, brass fittings in the bathroom, even the towels in each bathroom – all perfect!' She was laughing warmly as she told me this, still astounded and amazed by the detail. 'And the girls' rooms were just beautiful. You could see the love.'

Was it what she would have chosen?

'I see that there was a lot of planning that went into the home so that it would be exactly how she wanted it to be. I don't really think it was to my taste, but I liked it. I didn't change anything.' Then she laughed raucously. 'Chris Dawson would have had nothing to do with it – he was colour-blind! Paul was too. Both brown-green colour-blind!'

JC may not have changed anything, but she couldn't keep the house exactly as Lynette had. She didn't know how to. You could see that from the wedding photos. JC only married once, and I felt sad that she'd missed out on the dress and the love and the whole palaver. After they were married, Chris told the girls to call JC 'Mum', and within six months she was pregnant.

In the first twelve or eighteen months after Lynette disappeared, Sue Strath continued to express her alarm about Lynette.

'I tried to soothe Sue's outrage,' Barbara Cruise had told me. '"[Lyn's] brother's a policeman. I'm sure he's doing everything."' But Sue wasn't comforted, and Barbara was keen to catch up with Lynette when she came back, even if she never returned to work at the childcare centre. 'I phoned Chris more than he phoned us. No one else had heard from Lyn and there he is with the girlfriend, the house, the money.' But after a while, Barbara stopped ringing.

Sue was also pestering her friend Paul Hulme, the police officer who many years later became the commander at Dee Why and brought Damian Loone onto the case. Paul told her that there was nothing he could do. A few years went by and Sue didn't let up, so in 1985 Paul suggested that she make a complaint to the ombudsman about the lack of a police investigation into Lynette's disappearance. But Sue thought they should speak with Lynette's family first. So she approached Barbara, who was able to look up Lynette's maiden name on the copies of her diplomas, which she had on file.

'I rang every Simms in the phonebook until I found her mother,' Barbara told me. 'I rang her, and I said, "We don't believe that Lynette's disappeared of her own free will."'

At first, Helena told Barbara that she didn't believe Chris had anything to do with Lynette's disappearance.

'As the conversation wore on,' Barbara told me, 'Helena said, "Now I do."' So, with Helena's permission, Sue complained to the ombudsman.

When I told Greg about the conversation Barbara Cruise had with his mother, he tilted his head and leaned gently towards me.

'I never knew that,' he said, quietly, then he sat back and smiled, not at me, but in a private way. It was satisfying to pass this news along to Greg, but I also felt sad that a small act meant so much. If Greg and Pat hadn't known about the conversation Helena had with Barbara three years after Lynette disappeared, perhaps they also didn't know that Helena was having doubts about Chris in those early years. Like Lynette, it seemed that Helena was only comfortable admitting her worst fears to an outsider. And I understand that inhibition. In families, some things are obvious and don't need to be said, and sometimes things are said that can't be put away. If Helena admitted her worst fears to the family, I think she would have felt that she was betraying Lynette and that she was giving up hope. But I came to admire Helena's refusal to define Lynette's disappearance. She was the emotional centre of the family and if she said that Lynette was dead, it gave the rest of the family permission to say it too. Perhaps Helena didn't want Lynette's fate to become part of the family lore, because lore is a story that has lost its urgency.

Sue's handwritten letter to the New South Wales Ombudsman's Office is undated, but is stamped as received on 5 February 1985.

Dear Sir,
It is 3 years since my friend Lyn Dawson of Bayview Heights was reported as a missing person by her husband, Chris Dawson.

Lyn was a devoted mother of 2 small children. I worked with her at Warriewood Children's Centre. It was known by all her workmates that she was having marital problems, we had all heard about Chris' relationship with a (then) 16 year old student of his, who was staying at the time with the Dawson family. Lyn – although she probably suspected – didn't want to believe this of her husband – whom she idolised.

She accepted her marriage was 'shaky' and on the Friday before she was last seen, she and her husband went to see a marriage psychologist. She and Chris came back to work excited about 'better understanding' and 'working out problems' together.

The next day what happened????

Chris told work friends she packed a few things while he was out and just left without goodbyes to anyone. She lives on an acre isolated block at Bayview Heights which has no public transport, so she would have to leave the house by cab as Lyn was not active enough to walk and she cannot drive a car.

Chris has told another friend of mine that Lyn found he and his girlfriend in bed and just 'freaked' – so I can understand that – but I don't believe she could walk out on her 2 girls and leave them for another woman to raise.

She loved her home and was a very materialist [sic] person. Why would she walk out on a home worth over ¼ million dollars?

Chris reported she left to join a religious group and is believed to be living on the North Coast. As far as I know, she had no religious beliefs at all and didn't attend church. A person cannot become religious overnight and most religious groups are very family oriented so a woman with children would be acceptable rather than a woman without. Her husband was so sure she would not return, his girlfriend was moved in the following week. He has now married his schoolgirl lover, has a beautiful house and established family. Everything seems too easy. He got exactly what he wanted and his wife, who wasn't up to standard, has vanished from the face of the earth, having no further contact with any family or friends. Chris has said he received a phone call but I put that down to the extended story.

It doesn't seem possible that a person can be swept under the rug and forgotten. I would like to know what the police have done in this matter? Why weren't her workmates interviewed as to her last 24 hours? Why were her husband's words used as sole evidence as to her whereabouts?

It appears to me the police have taken the view that Lyn left her husband, family and work friends of her own free will – I wonder if this is true?

I'm concerned as I was one of the last to see her on the Friday but was never questioned by the police. Can a person just disappear and [have it accepted that] because she is over 16 years, she did so willingly, when we only have her husband's word that this is what happened?

Could you please throw a little bit of light on this mystery? I've seen her 'Missing Person' poster and just cannot accept the explanation or reason of whereabouts.

Yours faithfully,
Susan Browett [now Sue Strath]

Sue Strath's letter to the ombudsman is crafted with clarity and with tenderness for her friend Lyn. But her tone is also deferential, as she astutely sidesteps accusations, and instead submits troubling and unanswered questions. As required by law, the ombudsman referred Sue's complaint to the commissioner of police, who in turn tasked an Inspector Shattles to conduct a review of how the police handled Lynette's missing person file. Inspector Shattle's 1985 report contained uncorroborated statements by Chris that appear to have been accepted as fact. Those statements included that on the Saturday morning that Lynette went missing, Chris dropped Lynette off at Mona Vale at 7 am to catch a bus to Chatswood; that Lynette rang Chris at Northbridge Baths that afternoon, 'by an STD call stating that she was on the Central Coast'; that Lynette rang Chris again the next day; that Lynette rang him again on 15 January; and, that Lynette's bank card was used twice after she disappeared.

Damian had told me that police relied on families a lot more in missing person matters then, so I wavered on whether or not it was reasonable that the police had accepted what Chris told them. Should they have checked telephone records, and spoken with staff at Northbridge Baths to confirm that an STD call came in for Chris? Should they have pulled Chris's home telephone records to verify that an STD call came in from Lynette the following day? Even if Lynette was only treated as a missing person, it's hard to accept that the police didn't speak to the last people to see her, to see if they had any insight into her state of mind, or to ask them if she'd given any indication that she was going away. It's difficult to second-guess the police response, although checking just one of those details might have made a difference. It's harder to accept that Lynette was still treated as a missing person when her file was reviewed three years later.

The alleged use of Lynette's bank card continued to be a significant issue. Barbara told me that Lynette had her bank card statements sent to work and that after she went missing, 'I do remember the bank card statements continued to come.' She gave evidence at the inquest about the bank card statements as well.

Matthew Fordham asked, 'Ma'am are you aware that Lyn had her bank card account forwarded to her at the childcare centre?'

'Yes, because she asked was that okay and I said, "Yes, no problem."'

'Do you know why she had it forwarded to there and not at home?'

'As I say, I don't know whether there were financial difficulties, or just exactly what the problem was at home, but she didn't want Chris to know what she was spending, and basically that was why she did it.'

Barbara said that she contacted Chris to come and collect Lynette's bank card statements, but he never did. How did Chris know that Lynette's bank card was used after her disappearance if the statements continued arriving at the childcare centre? If Lynette's bank card was an ancillary card on Chris's account, there would have been no point having her statements sent to work because Chris would also be receiving the statements at home. If the police had interviewed Lynette's work colleagues at the time that she went missing, Barbara would have told them about the bank card statements coming to work. She also would have told them about JC.

Damian read Inspector Shattles' 1985 report into court. The report detailed the inquiries that were made by the police:

'the Registrar General's Department, transport records, electoral offices and fingerprints section . . . with the Nurses Registration Board in all States . . .' Having made these inquiries, it's hard to understand why staff at Lynette's workplace weren't spoken to.

Damian continued to read from the inspector's 1985 report.

> On 14 August, 1982, [an officer] of Mona Vale Police Station contacted both Mr Dawson and Mrs Simms and requested them to prepare a full profile of the missing person and include all sources of information, friends, associates and relatives etc for information of the Missing Person Unit. These profiles were received (copy attached) and forwarded to the Missing Person Unit, nothing appearing in them to lead to any suspicion of foul play.

Chris Dawson and Helena Simms were asked by police to provide a follow-up profile to add to Lynette's missing person's file. Although Inspector Shattles said that Chris Dawson's and Helena Simms's follow-up profiles were attached to his report, only Helena's handwritten profile dated 21 August 1982 was in the missing person file that Damian was given. Damian included Helena's handwritten profile in the first brief of evidence for the coroner in 2001. It read:

> As requested I am forwarding a statement about the disappearance of my daughter Lynette Joy Dawson. My daughter had been uptight and very tense over the latter months of last year, she and her husband had struck a bumpy patch in their marriage and partnership of 17 years. Complicated by the taking in of a teenage student seeking help. She had babysat for them, my daughter had

> offered her hospitality in good faith, which she later regretted when she caused her so much anguish.

And her closing comments:

> Until recently I have held my son-in-law in high esteem and got along well with him but my faith has been shaken when for all his talk of wanting only to look after his two little girls, Lyn 'goes' + he has introduced the teenager back into the house as early as Feb 6th that I heard of it, so if Lyn has been in the vicinity and seen them so often together she has cut herself off from us all totally and completely. I'm sure she can't be thinking straight.

Helena might not have explicitly expressed her worst fears, but her meaning was clear. It is so difficult to reconcile Inspector Shattles' conclusion that a man moving another woman into his house within weeks of his wife disappearing is not suspicious behaviour.

His report concluded:

> It might be noted that at no time has Mrs Simms ever hinted that there were ever any suspicious circumstances regarding the disappearance of her daughter. Further to this, the brother of the missing person is a senior constable in the New South Wales Police Force and he at no time contacted police at this station in regard to any suspicions he had regarding the disappearance of his sister.

The inspector's report to the ombudsman's office points to Helena and Greg for any inadequacies in the police investigation. Specifically, the report noted that the police didn't talk to Sue Strath in 1982 because she hadn't been mentioned by Greg or Helena. How could Helena and Greg know the names of Lynette's work colleagues?

Greg wrote me an explosive email about the inspector's conclusions.

> I did on a number of occasions contact them and asked what the position was. I was put in my place saying I was not the next of kin and I couldn't be told anything. (Even after telling them I was a cop.) Dawson was the contact. It was only when he divorced Lyn in her absence and married JC. Sometime after that I made a call to M.P. section. They still had Dawson as the next of kin. I told them that he had relinquished that position when he divorced my sister. My parents were now the next of kin and all M.P. inquiries should be directed to me. It would have been common sense for the police to check with her work colleagues. I feel Mum would have mentioned Lyn's workplace friends to the police. She was desperate to find her daughter. Not much was done in the early years as Dawson was still the next of kin and Missing Persons went through him. *He had control!*

The last time Lynette was seen by anyone other than Chris was Friday afternoon at work. Had police contacted the childcare centre, Barbara Cruise, Sue Strath and Anna Grantham would have told them that Lynette would not have left her daughters, and they would also have told the police about Chris's relationship with a schoolgirl. The police might then have interviewed JC, who could have told them how she came to be living in Lynette's house.

In 1985, when Lynette's missing person file and the police's handling of the case were reviewed, it was three years since she'd disappeared. The longer she was not heard from, the more certain the police seemed to be that she was a missing person.

JC told the inquest more about moving back into the house at Bayview. 'He had access to me twenty-four hours a day. I tried to get away several times but again had no options. I didn't speak to anyone about it, except for Barbara Kilpatrick at the refuge.'

'When you tried to get away several times, what happened then?' Matthew Fordham asked JC.

'He was violent.'

'And how was he violent towards you?'

'There were some times where I locked myself in one of the rooms, one of the bedrooms, and he would try to break the door down to get to me.'

When JC became pregnant in mid-1984, Chris's behaviour became more controlling and aggressive. Then, in late December, they moved to Queensland along with Paul and Marilyn and their children. In a replay of the set-up at Bayview, the twins bought land at Yawalpah, in the hinterland behind the Gold Coast, and built two houses 500 metres apart. In January 1985, KD was born, one month premature. Then, in late 1985, Chris and Paul's parents followed them north.

After KD was born, JC suggests Chris's behaviour towards her escalated sharply.

'Were there ever times when Chris would restrict, for example, the clothing you wore or anything like that?'

'He chose what I wore.'

'And did he choose what you wore every day?'

'If I was going somewhere he had to approve it.'

'And were there times when you believed you wanted to wear something and he would disagree with that?'

'Well, I didn't – if he was becoming aggressive I just did what he wanted because of the consequences.'

By the time she was twenty, JC was at home with two small children and a newborn. The move to Queensland took her away from her sisters and friends and left her with no one for company, or to ask for help, except for Paul's wife, Marilyn, who was sixteen or seventeen years older. She was isolated, and she became depressed.

'It was a nightmare,' she told me over lunch one day, her eyes full of tears. 'Often I only ate Coco Pops at the beginning of the day and then I'd eat nothing else.'

JC told the inquest that KD's arrival made her relationship with Chris 'quite different'.

'He was very possessive, even more possessive of me, and sort of rejected KD because he wanted me to himself.'

'When you say that he was wanting you for himself, what sort of behaviour would cause you to say that?'

'He wanted the girls to look after KD while we spent time together. He, yeah, just wanted her out of the way lots of the time.'

'When you were living up in Queensland with Chris, were there ever times when you would talk about what happened to Lyn?'

'No.'

'Were there ever times when you would come into conflict with Chris?'

'Yes.'

'Can you tell us about those times?'

'There were times when he was violent because, I don't like violence, so I just did as I was told. But there was conflict around my ability to look after his two daughters.'

'What was Chris's point of view about your ability to look after YD and XD?'

'He wanted me to be their mother, treat them like a mother does.'

'And what was your opinion of that?'

'Well, it was very confusing for me, because I didn't feel like their mother. I felt like a mother to my own child but also his view of how I should treat them was quite different to a mothering thing. It was just impossible to do what he wanted.'

'Were you able to discipline XD and YD in the same way that you could discipline KD?'

'No.'

'How was it different?'

'He would stand over me, in front of them and, you know, if I didn't treat them as little princesses, which they were, but they weren't always like that, and if I treated them, if I disciplined them in any way he would yell.'

Reading about this conflict, I remembered Pat telling me, 'To my mind they had a perfect mum. How could he just replace her?' JC agreed. She told me that Chris had tried to make her the girls' mother and he wanted her to mother them the same way that Lynette had. He kept no photos of Lynette, and JC felt that Lyn had been wiped from their lives. The girls not only had to make do with JC for a mum but after Lynette disappeared, they also lost Lynette's family – their grandmother and grandfather, aunts and uncles and cousins – because Chris cut them off.

She told the inquest more about this period in her life.

'I didn't leave what we called "the compound". It was surrounded by 6-foot-high fencing and I only saw Marilyn for most of the time, for the first couple of years I think, and the only time I went out was with him or up to their house. He wasn't very sociable. When KD got old enough to go to playgroup, then I took her down to the local playgroup.'

'And what was his reaction to KD going to playgroup?'

'Well, his reaction to me going to playgroup was severe because I came back and said, oh, you know, they get to do X, Y and Z in their marriage and she can do this, and you know, they do separate things. Why don't we do that? Because I didn't know any better.'

'And how did Chris behave towards you when you talked about those things?'

'He was aggressive.'

Nonetheless, JC was emboldened by the mothers she met at playgroup, and through one of them, she joined an indoor cricket team. JC is naturally athletic and was good at cricket. She made friends and her confidence grew. Still, this small liberty didn't come freely. She had to trade sexual favours to be allowed out, or to buy shoes for indoor cricket.

From the beginning, when JC was sixteen, she was ill-equipped to deal with Chris's demands. It appears that the conduct persisted from when she moved back in after Lynette was gone until the end of her marriage. JC told the inquest about a fight they had in the car, with KD in a baby capsule in the back.

'We were driving into the driveway of the house that was yet to be completed and he was again complaining about, why can't you be a mother to my children, why don't you do this, that and the other, and I was just at a loss for words and he became so irate that he punched the windscreen and [it] shattered and it was a laminated windscreen which is not so easy to do.'

Evidence of Chris's violence was patchy. When Peter Dawson cross-examined JC, she acknowledged that when she had lived with Lynette and Chris, 'I didn't see any violence.' Nor had Pat, Greg, Merilyn or Helena.

When Peter Dawson cross-examined Pat, he pressed her on the issue. 'Did Lyn bruise easily?'

'I can remember – I don't know. I can remember my mother commenting on bruises on Lyn which is a further part in my memories here and my mother put it down to "Oh, she must have had something wrong with her blood."'

'But certainly Lyn never made any complaint to you or, as far as you're aware, to your mother, that Chris had assaulted her?'

'No, she didn't, but Lyn and Chris as a couple were always held up as – they always dressed well, they looked good, they had a beautiful home. I wonder if Lyn would have said anything to us because the image, the image that everyone had, "Oh Lyn and Chris, everything's okay" and "beautiful couple", perhaps she'd wanted to try and handle [it] herself and thought that it wasn't as bad as it was, the whole situation, and didn't want to mention it to us because of that reason, that she wanted to have this image of them still being the perfect couple.'

'But certainly she never mentioned it to you or her mother?'

'No, only his anger, she mentioned his anger in those phone conversations.'

Pat had told me, again in hushed tones, that she was sure there was violence and that Lynette didn't say anything because 'she didn't want the dream shattered'. And Greg had said, with a drawn look of incredulity, 'Lyn would say she'd bumped into this or that. It never occurred to us that he was hitting her.'

I thought back to Pat's story, that not long after Lynette and Chris started dating, Lynette had asked Pat what she thought about Chris. 'I don't know why she cared what I thought,' Pat said. And yet Lynette did care what others thought.

At the inquest, there were only two witnesses who had direct evidence of Chris's violence: JC and a woman named Julie Andrew. Julie was a neighbour and good friend of Lynette's and although she didn't give evidence at the inquest, Damian had taken a statement from her.

He told the inquest: 'Evidence is also available [from] a neighbour, Mrs Julie Andrew, who saw and heard Christopher and Lynette Dawson arguing in the back corner of the Dawson residence. At the time, Lynette Dawson was crying. This witness observed Christopher Dawson shaking Lynette Dawson by the shoulders.'

In her statement to Damian, Julie gave distressing details about what she had seen:

> One day I was outside when I heard Lyn crying. I looked up towards Lyn's place and I saw Lyn leaning with her back against the trampoline. I saw Chris standing very close to her and they appeared to be arguing. I heard Lyn cry very loudly and I noticed that Lyn was very upset. I heard Lyn say something like, 'Chris, how could you do it to us?' I saw Chris shaking Lyn by the shoulders. I saw one of Lyn's children come out to where they were standing and Lyn picked the child up and hugged her to her chest. Lyn was holding the baby and saying something like, 'What's Daddy doing

to us?' Lyn was very upset and then walked back inside the house sobbing.

Later that afternoon I went over to Lyn's house to see if she was alright. We spoke and Lyn told me that there were problems because of JC moving in. I advised Lyn to get rid of JC because I knew that Chris and JC were having a sexual relationship. Lyn didn't seem to want to accept what was happening, but Lyn did say that Chris told her that everything was going to be OK . . .

From her house, Julie said that she could see Lynette's swimming pool. 'JC would sometimes be only wearing a G-string and would be topless around the pool . . .'

JC gave the same evidence.

Matthew Fordham asked her, 'One of the neighbours made some observations in relation to one time when you were swimming with Chris, did the two of you remain fully clothed during those times?'

JC replied, 'Lyn even accepted that I went topless. That was just the way I was.'

Julie recalled another conversation she'd had with Lynette. 'Lyn told me that she walked up the driveway to the house and then into her bedroom where she caught Chris and JC in a compromising position. Somehow Lyn told me that Chris had talked his way out of what was happening. This would have only been a couple of weeks prior to Lyn disappearing.'

The scene that Julie painted of Lynette in the backyard was disturbing and completely at odds with the splendid home at the front. But as the Australian social scientist Lyn Richards has observed, 'Suburbia has two faces, the dream achieved and the nightmare of dreary living, deprivation and isolation.'[10]

For two years before Lynette disappeared, Roslyn McLoughlin played weekly tennis with a group of women that included Lynette. In the months before Lynette disappeared, Roslyn told the inquest, she 'appeared to be under a lot of stress and not just presenting how she would' and she took 'less care of herself'. The last time she saw Lynette was just before Christmas, and she told the inquest that she 'had a very large bruise on her upper thigh' and 'upper arm marks – I can't remember whether they were on both or one arm'. Paul's wife, Marilyn, was also part of the tennis group. When Damian interviewed her in 1999 she didn't mention seeing any bruises on Lynette at tennis, and she declined to give evidence at the inquest.

A year or so before Lynette disappeared, Anna Grantham told the inquest, she and Lynette held a 'boot sale' together at her place. When Chris came to collect Lynette, 'he had wanted to go straight away, and she wanted to wait a bit longer or something. And I saw he was very, very cranky and also aggressive, and she looked very frightened.' When they spoke about it later at work, Lynette confided an even more disturbing incident, which Anna also gave evidence about.

'And I said to her the first time that I saw Chris to be aggressive towards her, being nasty towards her, she said that he could be quite aggressive at times. And then she told me of the time when he actually . . . they were building a swimming pool apparently and they had an argument where they were just around the pool, and I don't know what the argument was about, but he actually picked her up by the back of the hair and held her into the mud. And I remember that time saying to her, "My god, he could have – he could have killed you, that sounds terrible." I was horrified. She said, "He could very well have done that, I could hardly breathe, and I was gasping for breath."'

'When Lyn was telling you about this incident around the swimming pool, did she describe . . . you mentioned that Chris allegedly grabbed hold of her hair and held her down into the mud – do you know which part of her came in contact with the mud?'

'Her face.'

'And did Lyn describe how long she was being held in the mud for?'

'No, but he held her there with her face into the mud, and she was gasping for breath, and she couldn't breathe.'

Greg told the inquest that he hadn't seen or suspected that Chris was being violent towards Lynette. But Greg did also say, 'When something hadn't gone the way he wanted it he gave that real dark death stare. I call it "a death stare" because, you know you've done something that he didn't really like.'

When Matthew Fordham had finished questioning Greg, Peter Dawson promptly rose to cross-examine him.

'Mr Simms, you're not suggesting that Chris Dawson stared your sister to death?'

'Well, I've heard of rats dying of shock from a rat trap going off behind them, so it's quite possible, isn't it?'

It was an ugly exchange. It was clear that even before Greg was rattled by Peter Dawson, he was struggling to give evidence. When Matthew Fordham had asked him what he thought had happened to Lynette, Greg's words had tumbled out.

'Well, like most of the family, I believed that Chris wasn't capable of anything. As we got into a length of time with all the information all one side from Chris, my father initially said that "the bastard's done her in", they were his exact words, after Lyn disappeared, and my mother also was very soft-natured and she couldn't see evil of anybody and on a number of occasions I had said to her, "Mum, under any circumstances, anyone is capable of anything" and at a time after that she just sort of . . . I think she just relinquished the thought she'd never see her daughter again. My idea, as I said to Damian Loone, all the information has always been one-sided, and I feel in my own heart and my gut feeling that he has murdered her.'

Peter Dawson continued with his questioning. 'You see, Mr Simms, up until the conversation with JC the family was angry with Chris Dawson, weren't they?'

'Yes, well, everything coming from Chris – everything was coming from Chris. You had a sister who loved her family, who organised everything, would always ring everybody for a different occasion, no contact, cut off from that date and all the information coming from your brother.'

'Yes, but you were angry with Chris because he had taken up with JC weren't you?'

'Well, wouldn't you be, sir, if you had a sister and someone had taken up with a young lady?'

'You were pretty disappointed in Chris because he'd done that?'

'Extremely disappointed,' Greg said.

'And that's why you didn't help him with the bags of Lyn's belongings?'

'It could have been one of the reasons, yes.'

'Well, at that stage that was the only reason, wasn't it?' Peter asked.

'Well, you look at the way my mother was being treated. I didn't like the way her grandchildren had been cut off from her, especially in the date in question at the pool at Northbridge, the . . . I believe that Mum took the girls home that night with Phil Day and then your parents came over the next day and took them to their place. So I don't know what your brother was doing.'

'Did you ask him?'

'No, because I wasn't aware of the situation then.'

Later, Peter asked Greg about JC's hit-man evidence. 'And that was one of the things that turned you into shock that day?'

'I think anyone in their right mind, if they were in hope of seeing their sister alive and hearing this sort of thing, you would be in some form of shock. Why wouldn't you be?'

I can sense Greg's rage. Rage that he has to answer to Chris's brother, rage that Chris doesn't have to answer to anyone. Rage that Helena, his mother, died without knowing what happened to her daughter.

Perhaps Lynette felt the same kind of rage. Or despair. When Roslyn McLoughlin gave evidence, she said that the last time that she'd seen Lynette was at the tennis get-together before Christmas, when she'd noticed the bruises and Lynette had asked her to come home with her.

'I declined to go back because it was Christmas week, or around that time, and we were all really, really busy . . . but she actually begged me to go back with her to have a cup of coffee, and – which I felt even on that day was very unusual, because not knowing her that well . . . it was quite out of context, it was unusual, and she seemed quite distressed when she asked me.'

Roslyn said that she wasn't the only one Lynette asked. 'That day no one went back with her, but she basically did not want to return by herself.'

Was Lynette scared? Desperate? Was she asking for help? Unable to fully confide in those closest to her, was she reaching out, if not to a stranger, to someone she didn't know well? When no one came, did she give up?

In Queensland, things were getting worse for JC. 'I took KD with me everywhere I went,' JC told me. 'She came when I played or trained. She sat and waited for me. She was incredible.'

Paul and Marilyn took sides with Chris, naturally enough, and JC felt that they blamed her for all the problems in her and Chris's relationship. 'I deliberately kept KD separate from his girls. I don't know why I did that. I was nothing for so long. I didn't think. I didn't act. The only thing I was was a devoted mother.'

JC had slowly been reassessing everything that had happened. A few years on, she was now a young woman and a mother, and her perspective had changed. She could see Chris's behaviour, both towards her and Lynette, with different eyes. From the time KD was born, she realised that the way she felt about her was very different to how she felt about Chris and Lynette's girls.

'Would you agree that your behaviour towards Chris's daughters changed after KD was born?' Peter Dawson asked.

'Yes.'

'Would you agree that you felt less able to act as a mother towards them?'

'I didn't feel that I was a mother to them.'

'But up until that time you acted as a mother towards them for a number of years?'

'Well, I don't think I'd acted as a mother because I don't believe I knew how to act as a mother.'

'Didn't they call you "Mum"?'

'They did, but that doesn't mean I'm their mother.'

'Well, don't you think they regarded you as a mother?'

'I can't vouch for what they regarded me as.'

Most significantly, through her experience of motherhood, JC came to understand Lynette's love for XD and YD. 'She molly-coddled the girls. All that makes it more unbelievable that she would leave them.'

More and more, JC was thinking about leaving the marriage. In June 1989, her grandmother gave her money to fly to Sydney with KD for her sister NC's twenty-first birthday party. She caught up with girlfriends from school and when she told them about life in 'the compound' they encouraged her to leave. When she flew back to Queensland, Chris met her at the airport wearing lycra shorts with no underwear. He told JC that he thought she'd like it but when she told me about this, she squirmed uncomfortably. They saw a marriage counsellor, and she hung on for a bit longer. And then she and Chris had a fight. Mathew Fordham asked JC about the fight.

'I'd been to a lingerie party with a friend of mine who I played cricket with and when I got home – I bought a G-string, you know, as you do, and I put it on and he said, oh, you know, you're only going to wear that for me aren't you, and I said, "No, I'm just going to wear it if the need arises" and he became very angry and grabbed me around the neck and subsequently tore it off me.'

'When Chris grabbed you around the neck, how did he grab you around the neck?'

'Like strangling.'

'Did he use one hand or two?'

'Two.'

'And how did you feel when your neck was being grabbed?'

'Frightened.'

'Could you breathe properly?'

'He let go before I passed out, obviously.'

JC told me about this incident a few times and each time, she included a detail that wasn't in her testimony. She told me that after Chris let go of her, she'd said, 'Why don't you get rid of me like your last wife.'

'And he said, "Don't say that." And I could just see that it was true. And my reaction was like, "My god. Maybe this is what really happened."'

It troubled me that this exchange wasn't in the transcript, so I asked Damian about it. 'It doesn't matter,' he said, 'it's in her statement.' For some reason, Matthew Fordham didn't prompt her about it, but Damian was clear that if JC were to give evidence in another court, the prosecutor would be able to question her about it because it was there in the statement she made to him.

Annette Leary, who also worked with Lynette at the childcare centre, gave chillingly similar testimony. She told the inquest about her interaction with Lynette on the Friday afternoon before she disappeared.

'Lyn was coming out of a change room and I noticed a bruise on her neck and I said to her, "Gosh, what happened to your neck?" and she said, "Oh, when we went to the marriage counsellor, we got in the lift and Chris said . . .", [apparently] he gripped her just by the throat and he shook her a bit and he said, "Look, if this doesn't work, I'm only doing this once. If it doesn't work, I'm getting rid of you."'

Matthew Fordham was questioning Annette Leary at the time. 'Ma'am, you made a motion in the witness box there with your own hand outstretched towards the front of you with your fingers away from your thumb. Is that correct?'

'Yes, it's only because there was a large mark on one side of her throat and, you know, that was what I presumed he just held her by the throat, which is what she said.'

'Did she indicate to you any conversation from Chris at the time that this was happening?'

'Only what she said that he said to her: "I'm only doing this once. If it doesn't work, I'm getting rid of you."'

'Did it appear to you that Lyn was concerned about what had happened at the marriage counsellor?'

'I think she was a bit stunned about that but she did say she hoped it'd work out – the counsellor.'

This is a particularly affecting detail, given that her other colleagues said that when she returned from the counselling session, she was happy and optimistic. For the last year or so, Lynette was in denial, refusing to accept that Chris and JC were in a sexual relationship, even though it was happening under her nose. This episode suggests that she may have been in a dissociative state that day, telling her colleagues that her marriage was on the mend despite the fact that Chris had choked her in the lift a few hours earlier. There is a sad disconnection between reality and the image she has of herself as a happy wife and mother.

Not long after Lynette had disappeared, Annette also told the inquest that she and Anna Grantham ran into Chris at Warriewood shopping centre, next to the childcare centre. Chris was with JC, YD and XD.

'I'd never met JC before, so I didn't know her, but the two little girls were there as well and we said to Chris, "Have you heard from Lyn?" and he said, "Yes, I've had a letter from her, she's in Queensland and I don't know when she's coming back."'

'Do you remember the T-shirt that was being worn by Chris at the time?'

'Yes. When they walked away from Anna and I, we watched them go and Anna gripped my arm and she said, "Good Lord, look at his T-shirt." I said, "Why, what's wrong with it?" and then she pointed out the emblem, which was an advertisement for a rubbish removal company and it had a motto on it: "We get rid of anything."'

In the 1991 interview, the detectives asked Chris if he'd run into Annette and Anna, and also about the letter.

'I do recall now . . . but I wouldn't have said that I received a letter, I would have said I'd received a phone call, but I wouldn't have stated I received a letter from her because I wouldn't have – I didn't receive a letter from her.'

The T-shirt was alarming but realistically of no probative value, but the letter was interesting because Annette and Anna recalled that Chris did mention a letter. If there was a letter, it's possible that JC had seen it, or had heard Chris tell Lynette's family or Paul about it. But JC never mentioned a letter to me and Matthew Fordham didn't ask her about it either.

Despite everything that Lynette had confided to Annette, and despite what Annette had seen, Matthew Fordham asked her if Lynette had 'faith in her marriage being repaired'.

'She was always hopeful.'

After the choking incident, JC resolved to leave. KD was five, XD and YD were twelve and ten, and JC and Chris had just passed their sixth wedding anniversary. JC had a credit card attached to Chris's account, which JC said he cut up when he could see that she was thinking of leaving. So over the next few months, she began squirrelling money away in her handbag from the small cash allowance that he gave her. One day she caught him riffling through it – JC thought to see how much money she had. From then on, she slept with her handbag under the bed. She got some advice from a solicitor who told her that, compared to what Chris gave her, she would be financially better off with single parent benefits and child support. Nonetheless, she was scared. She was twenty-five and about to be a single mother. Again, she had nowhere to live. She had no money, no bank account or credit card in her own name, no job, and her only work experience was her part-time job at Coles during school.

'Eventually, Chris said, "Don't prolong this. If you're going, just go,"' JC told me. 'KD helped me pack the car. Chris's daughters were there, and the oldest one said, "I don't want you to leave," which I took to mean something practical like, "Who will make us dinner?" I drove away anyway. I didn't think about them once KD and I were gone.'

That may have been true at the time but in the years after she left, she thought about the girls a lot. From the time JC was installed as their stepmother, she was tough on them. Chris could see it and they argued about it. In the beginning, JC expected Lynette to come back, so she did the bare minimum for the girls, but as time passed, she grew to resent them. JC is heavily burdened by the effect she must have had on the girls, both when she was their stepmother and then after she left, and they were abandoned for the second time.

'I try not to think about them because I feel such guilt,' she told me.

JC had rung Barb Kilpatrick before she and KD left Queensland to ask for help finding a place to live. RN had died in 1982, so Barb arranged for JC and KD to live with MMC until JC sorted something else out. So, in late January 1990, they moved in with MMC.

'MMC wanted to appear to Barb to care about me,' was JC's assessment of the situation, which was perhaps unfair, because MMC may have genuinely wanted to make amends. JC also suspected that Barb felt guilty and wished that she'd done more, both when JC was younger and MMC was such a mess, and then later, when JC had had to leave home because of RN.

I'd worked with Barb, and I wondered if JC had misread something, because the Barb I knew would walk over hot coals to help a woman or a child in distress. Barb had retired by the time JC was telling me all this, so I gave her a buzz and she warmly invited me over.

In her townhouse, Barb and I sat in the sun by the windows that looked onto a small courtyard. I'd told Barb that I was writing a book about JC and Lynette, and without so much as an offer of a glass of water, she began to talk.

The husband of a good friend of Barb was a teacher at Cromer High during JC's final year of school, and he had told Barb that he was worried by what he saw going on at school between Chris and JC.

'I talked to MMC about it and she was beside herself. So upset,' Barb said. 'MMC said she had begun to wonder about their relationship. RN was there when I spoke to MMC and he said, "Of course JC's having an affair with him."'

JC's sister BC gave a statement to Damian in 1998 about what MMC knew. 'I recall being with my mother . . . at our unit in Dee Why. This was before Lyn went missing as I saw Lyn in the car, I'm not sure if she was seated in the driver's seat. My mother went and spoke with Lyn and I could hear Lyn saying words to the effect that she was worried about Chris being unfaithful and concerned about JC's apparent relationship with Chris. I remember Mum saying to Lyn that it couldn't be possible for JC to be having an affair with Chris because JC wasn't brought up like that, or words similar, meaning that JC wouldn't be having an affair with a married man at her age, which was sixteen.'

At the inquest, BC repeated this story to the court. 'I deduced that it was about Lyn expressing some worries about Chris and JC and I believe I heard Mum say something like "Oh – JC wouldn't do something like that."' BC doesn't put a date on the visit from Lyn but in the questions leading up to it, she says she is referring to events in 1981 and 1982.

But in the statement that MMC gave to Damian in 1998, her recollection of Lyn's visit didn't square with what BC had overheard, or what Barb had told her about JC and Chris.

> In early 1979 I met Lyn Dawson. She had driven over to my unit at Dee Why and I can remember her sitting in the passenger seat of a car. I assumed that Lyn wanted to meet JC's mother. I can't recall the exact conversation however I do recall that Lyn had just had her hair done and it appeared as if she wanted someone else's approval to see if she looked nice for her husband. It seemed she wanted a compliment for the way her hair looked.

It's hard to view MMC's statement as anything other than self-serving, wanting to appear to be a good mother. The purpose of visits like this are usually to scare off a competitor or, in this case, to ask MMC to get her daughter to stand down. How else could an unexpected visit from Lynette seeking a compliment about her hair be interpreted? Chris had only arrived at Cromer High in 1979 and it wasn't until 1980 that JC began babysitting for Lynette and Chris. MMC did get something right: Lynette would have been in the passenger's seat. But, then, who was the driver? And if BC is right, instead of confiding in someone close to her, Lynette told a stranger that she was 'worried about Chris being unfaithful'. Having overheard Lynette's concerns and knowing that Lynette was fighting to save her marriage, I wonder if, later, BC ever raised the possibility with JC that Lynette's disappearance was suspicious – if not right away, then perhaps when JC married Chris, or in the years that followed. Did she tell JC that Lynette had confronted MMC?

At Cromer High, JC and Chris were called into the principal's office and told that they'd been seen together out of school. The principal asked them if they were involved, which of course they both denied. The principal also spoke to MMC but nothing happened.

'Everyone knew they were in a relationship,' Barb told me. '*Everyone*.'

From the way she stressed 'everyone' I knew she meant MMC. I wondered if it was unreasonable of me to think Barb should have gone to see the principal. Barb sat back quietly, and I wondered if she was asking herself the same question.

In time, she leaned towards me again. 'The violence between RN and MMC was horrendous. They were both drinking and one of the girls came to me crying, on more than one occasion. There were terrible incidents. I spoke to MMC about it and said, "If one of the girls comes to my house one more time I'm calling the police."'

But Barb never called the police and the girls were left to fend for themselves.

'MMC at that time was pathetic,' Barb said. 'JC left the apartment because RN hit her. He did. MMC told me that RN hit her. It was just terrible. MMC was devastated when JC went to live with Chris and Lynette. She was probably embarrassed and ashamed.'

MMC could have gone back to the principal and said, 'JC is about to move in with Chris Dawson. Now do something.' She could have gone to the Department of Education or the police. She could have gone to see Chris Dawson. Or Lynette. There were actions she could have taken, but they all would have required MMC to explain why JC couldn't stay at home with her – MMC, her mother.

Years later, when JC left Chris, it's unsurprising that she didn't want to go back to stay with MMC, but she didn't have a choice. JC didn't know where her father was living but she wanted to be near her sisters and her friends in Sydney. MMC had moved out of the apartment and into a small house at Wheeler Heights, and although RN had died by then, JC felt the memory of him, of the drinking, the abuse and her mother's choice to let RN stay instead of her. There were other memories too, tied up in MMC's strictness with her granddaughter. KD wasn't allowed to play in the house, and her dolls and toys had to be kept in the bedroom – the same rules that MMC had imposed on JC and her sisters, as if MMC wanted to eliminate any sign of the children from the house. It had left JC feeling unwanted.

Within a couple of days, JC felt she couldn't cope. 'On the phone, I was telling Chris I was coming back. I wrote a letter to my [cricket] batting partner and told her I was coming back because the love I got from him was better than no love at all.'

But she didn't go back.

'I knew it was over,' JC told me emphatically.

She and KD ended up staying with MMC for two years.

A few weeks after arriving back in Sydney, KD started kindergarten. 'She cried for the first eight weeks,' JC said. 'So I got involved as a class parent, did canteen.'

JC sent KD to her old primary school, which surprised me, but I was genuinely shocked to discover that KD then went to Cromer High. When we'd gone to the open night, JC had pointed out a photo on the wall of the 2002 prefects, with KD sitting at the end.

'She wanted to go,' JC told me with a shrug. 'All her friends were going.'

I wondered if KD would send her son there.

'I'd be horrified,' JC said. 'He is so sensitive. He'd get eaten up.'

CHAPTER THIRTEEN

JC goes to the police

IN MAY 1990, JC TOOK HERSELF TO CHATSWOOD POLICE STATION and gave her first statement to detectives about Lynette's disappearance. I'd seen a copy, which was held together by a rusted paperclip that had bled its shape into the top left-hand corner. She hadn't read it for some years, because she gave Damian another statement when he took over Lynette's case. When I told her it was dated 17 May 1990, she quipped, 'I didn't waste any time, did I.'

When I first saw the date, it didn't strike me as rash, but later when I was putting all the pieces together, I wondered. JC and KD had only arrived back in Sydney on 30 January 1990. At twenty-six, JC's life was enormously stressful. She had no money and was working her way into life as a single parent. KD was having trouble settling in at kindergarten and soon, JC and Chris were arguing about custody.

Several times, I tried to tease out of her what led her to Chatswood police station less than four months after coming back to Sydney but she wouldn't explain it, not to me anyway.

JC's police statement did kick off an investigation into Lynette's disappearance. When I'd met with Sue Strath, she'd told me, 'I spoke to a detective from Chatswood after my complaint to the ombudsman,' which I took to mean around the time of her complaint in 1985, which resulted in the police review and report on Lynette's missing person file. But after reading JC's 1990 statement, which was also made to a detective in Chatswood, I emailed Sue to check the date.

'It was 1990,' she replied.

I emailed her straight back, because it didn't make sense that no one had spoken to her as part of the 1985 review. She was the person whose complaint had instigated it, after all.

'I have a file about Lyn,' Sue replied, 'and I just checked it and found a business card from [one of the detectives] from the homicide squad in Chatswood.'

Barbara Cruise told me the same thing – that the first time she spoke to the police was when she was working at Gosford Council in 1990. 'Two policemen from Chatswood came to see me.' But the ombudsman's file says that on 23 March 1985, a detective 'interviewed Mrs Browett at her home in Collaroy' and 'Mrs Barbara Cruise of the Warriewood Children's Centre . . . was spoken to on the 25 March 1985.' It's curious why Sue and Barbara were adamant that they didn't speak to the police until 1990, when the ombudsman's file says otherwise.

In 1990, in addition to speaking to Sue Strath and Barbara Cruise, the detectives also spoke to Anna Grantham and Annette

Leary, but none of those interviews were in the file that Damian inherited eight years later. Damian also didn't know that they had conducted a ground-penetrating radar search at the house in 1990 until he spoke to the owners. There were no records of that either.

On 15 January 1991, homicide detectives went to Queensland and interviewed Chris Dawson. In the interview with Chris, the detectives asked him about events surrounding Lynette's disappearance and challenged him when he gave an inconsistent answer. They then asked him directly if he had murdered Lynette, which he emphatically denied. But having been asked the question, Chris was put on notice.

'It ensured he would never give another interview to the police,' Damian told me.

The police investigation was substantial – after all, they were considering a possible homicide. Their investigation began nearly nine years after Lynette had disappeared and, although unlikely, it's possible that telephone records or bank statements from 1982 might still have existed. Along with the statements from JC and Lynette's work colleagues, the detectives might have been able to locate someone who was working at Northbridge Baths on 9 January 1982. Could that person have verified the telephone call that Chris said came in from Lynette? Could that person have also verified that three beeps sounded when the phone was answered, denoting that the call was STD? Most regrettably, it was the only opportunity to question Chris Dawson. There may have been other interviews and material that were lost before Damian was given the file eight years later. Where had it all gone? And why was the case dropped?

When Damian took over Lynette's file, he tried to contact the Chatswood detectives 'without success', he said. I asked him what he thought had happened to the investigation.

'Glover was running around the North Shore then, so any other work was put aside.'

Sue Strath told me the same thing. 'When I made mention to a detective about them not following up, it was said that the Mosman Granny Killer was taking up their time during that period.'

John Wayne Glover, the so-called Granny Killer, was a middle-aged man who killed six elderly women on the North Shore of Sydney, from 1989 to 1990. He was arrested on 19 March 1990, ten months before Chris Dawson was interviewed in January 1991.

The Chatswood detectives' investigation was significant enough for them to ask Chris directly in that interview if he had killed Lynette, which he denied.

I wanted to know more about the investigation because they'd done a lot of work, good work. I tracked down one of the detectives to where he was now based at Tweed Heads and sent him an email. In it, I told him that I'd spoken to Damian Loone several times and that I'd like to speak to him about the investigation. But he never replied. I couldn't find the other detective, so I rang the New South Wales Police Media Unit. A friendly officer asked me to put my request in writing. Two weeks later, I got a reply:

> As discussed last week, the officer in charge on this matter [. . .] is no longer working for NSW Police. I'm afraid we won't be able to arrange an interview for you on this one.

What about records and files? And why can't the other detective talk about the investigation? He still works for New South Wales police. Police are regularly asked about historical investigations and I couldn't understand why someone wouldn't talk to me about this one. I went back to the media officer and told him that.

He replied with more of the same:

> As I said in my previous email [. . .], the officer in charge of the original investigation no longer works for NSW Police. As a result, I'm not in a position to arrange an interview for you with him.

I wrote back again. 'It would be helpful to understand the decision not to pursue the investigation and/or to understand how and why the matter was concluded.'

I never heard back.

It's perplexing why the investigation stopped when the summary the detectives gave Chris Dawson at the end of the interview was that Lynette was dead and that they regarded her death as suspicious.

> [W]e've already done a lot of work on it, and Lyn just doesn't show up anywhere. She doesn't show up on taxation records, she doesn't show up on Social Security records, she doesn't show up on Medicare, her nurse's registration . . . It's rather strange that she's disappeared out of sight like that. And when people disappear out of sight like that we can only hazard a guess as to what has happened, what's happened to them and usually you can be sure that they're deceased. In which case we're going to have to put this to the coroner.

But they never did. That was left to Damian after he inherited the file in 1998.

After the last witness was called at the 2003 inquest, and before Matthew Fordham and Peter Dawson made their final submissions, the coroner laid out the task before him.

'I think the position would be that we start back from square one, notwithstanding that the former Senior Deputy State Coroner made a finding in relation to the fact that she was satisfied that Lynette Joy Dawson was deceased. Having had a fresh inquest I think that that is a further finding that I need to revisit so that will also encompass my findings as well as any other submissions that I will need to deliberate on.'

In other words, he wouldn't be relying on the first inquest's findings – not even that Lynette was deceased.

Matthew Fordham summarised the lengthy chain of circumstantial evidence that he and Damian had followed. Lynette was a devoted mother, daughter and friend, he told the inquest, and she was also a wife who was fighting to save her marriage. JC had spent more time than anyone else inside the Dawson home in the two years before Lynette went missing, including living there in Lynette's final months, and Matthew Fordham quoted her when she described Lynette as 'a devoted wife and mother deeply involved in the care and attention of her children and husband'.

By contrast, he described Chris as a promiscuously unfaithful husband who developed an infatuation with JC, his student, who he groomed for sex while he was still her teacher and 'exercised a position of trust and power'.

He noted that Chris proposed to JC while she was still at school and he was still married to Lynette. When JC moved into the Dawson home, she gave evidence, she had witnessed Chris taunting Lynette and other witnesses gave indirect evidence of Chris being violent towards her. Later, JC detailed her own experiences of his 'domineering and aggressive' behaviour, as well as physical abuse. Matthew Fordham reminded the coroner of JC's testimony that towards the end of 1981, about three months before Lynette went missing, she was with Chris when he went to get a hit man to kill Lynette, but at the last minute changed his mind.

In January 1982, in the week or so before Lynette went missing, Matthew Fordham told the inquest, JC was camping at South West Rocks, celebrating the end of school with friends and that during that period, Chris knew that he was 'losing' her.

'It is my submission that that alarm of the prospect of losing JC overwhelmed Chris Dawson and he began to plan the murder of Lynette to allow the relationship with JC to proceed.'

Matthew Fordham then focused on two critical time periods. The first was the sixteen hours after Lynette spoke to her mother on the phone around 9 pm on Friday 8 January 1982, through to 3 pm the following day, when Chris said that Lynette rang him at Northbridge Baths. The second period concerned Chris collecting JC from South West Rocks and bringing her back to the house in Bayview.

JC testified that when she was babysitting and later, when she was living in the house, if Chris wanted to be alone with JC so they could have sex, he would make Lynette a drink and she would go to sleep. The evidence in Helena's statement was that Lynette sounded groggy when they spoke on the Friday night because, as Lynette told her, 'My husband has made me a lovely drink.' This should be read, Matthew Fordham said, as suspicious. 'Why would Chris be making Lyn a drink on 8 January when JC was not living at the home at that time?'

Fordham asked Carl Milovanovich 'to reject the version proffered by Chris Dawson', that he dropped Lynette at Mona Vale to catch a bus to Chatswood on the morning that she went missing. Rather, he invited the coroner to consider why Chris appeared agitated to Lynette's mother, Helena, when she arrived at Northbridge Baths that afternoon. 'Not only did Helena think that Chris was agitated but he also asked her "if she had heard from Lynette", and, sir, this begs the question that if Lynette was expected to be out shopping, why would he ask her this?'

Matthew Fordham then turned to the telephone call at the Baths.

'According to Chris himself, the call was supposedly from Lynette at which time she informs him for the very first time of her intention to "have a break".

'In my submission, the phone call received was in fact not from Lynette Dawson but rather from another person. It is my submission that Chris Dawson has invented his version – that Lynette had called him – in order to disguise her murder. Had what Chris told Lynette's mother and Phillip Day been true, that Lyn was having a break, then it begs the question as to why Chris would tell other people different stories about what had happened to Lynette.'

Matthew Fordham then moved on to the second critical period. JC's testimony was that Chris told her by telephone, on either

9 or 10 January, that 'Lyn's gone. She's not coming back' – words, he said, that JC recalled 'with certainty'. Following that conversation, 'Chris Dawson drove to South West Rocks the next day and collected JC. They returned to Sydney where she immediately took up the role of de facto wife and mother to two young girls.'

Fordham continued. 'If we accept the version of events given by Chris to investigating police it took almost a week for Chris to inform JC of Lynette's disappearance. This is borne out by the evidence contained in . . . affidavits. I think in those affidavits he describes that it was 15 January that he actually went to South West Rocks to collect her. Sir, this is in conflict with the solid evidence of several witnesses who were able to pinpoint the date when Chris arrived at South West Rocks to collect JC . . . Chris Dawson's affidavit states that he arrived at South West Rocks on 15 January 1982. Sir, this cannot be true given the unchallenged evidence of [the witness] who told us that Chris had taken JC and NC back to Sydney before she returned to Sydney in time for her birthday on 15 January.'

Of this evidence, Matthew Fordham said, 'Chris was clearly embarrassed about the speed with which he took himself up to South West Rocks to retrieve JC.' That lie, Fordham continued, was to cover up for the unpalatable haste with which he collected JC and installed her at Bayview. If Chris had collected JC on 15 January, it was still only six days since Lynette had said she was going away for a few days. Most husbands would be worried and making all efforts to find their missing wife. Instead, Chris was driving nearly 500 kilometres to get JC. Having done that, he made no active effort to find Lynette and seemed unconcerned that she would come back to find JC in the house.

Matthew Fordham recapped other events which, he said, when taken together, give weight to the circumstantial case. He reminded the coroner that Chris gave JC an engagement ring using diamonds from Lynette's rings within a year of her going missing; that Chris had divorced Lynette in June 1983 and then married JC on 15 January 1984; that when Chris returned from Queensland for visits, he would jog past the house in Gilwinga Drive, where the new owners said they saw him 'looking around the pool area'; that records to substantiate the fact that Lynette used her bank card in the days following her disappearance have never been produced by Chris; that Chris asked JC to pack Lynette's clothes into garbage bags within months of her going missing; that Chris was violent and had choked JC, and that one of Lynette's colleagues said Lynette told them that Chris had choked her in the elevator on their way to see the marriage counsellor the day before she disappeared; and that many witnesses had said that Lynette was not capable of leaving her children. Of all this evidence, Fordham said that Peter Dawson 'only challenged the allegations about hiring a hit man and Chris's later assaults upon JC'.

He also noted JC's credibility as a witness.

'JC has absolutely nothing to gain from assisting the police investigating Lyn's disappearance and nothing to gain from coming to court both in February 2001 [the first inquest] as well as this week, and when you take into account the fact that on both occasions she has had to endure a bright public spotlight of the media as we focused upon the most intimate and personal aspects of her formative years. She was subjected, sir, to a vigorous cross-examination by my friend. Her evidence was tested and it is my submission that JC [h]as not budged an inch.'

Of the evidence given by those closest to Lynette, Fordham said, 'in relation to the unanimous evidence of those witnesses who were close to Lyn I ask this court to find that Lyn was not capable of simply walking away from all her friends, her workmates, neighbours, members of her family and, most significantly, her children. If that is accepted, then the only available rational hypothesis is that Lyn Dawson was murdered.'

And finally, Matthew Fordham addressed the attacks that Peter Dawson had made about Damian's investigation, including an allegation of bias.

'At the first inquest my friend took issue with the quality of the investigation by the police and, sir, during this inquest has made some fairly serious allegations of bias against the officer in charge. Your Worship, if my friend is genuine in those complaints I can only encourage him to take them to the appropriate authority.'

Peter Dawson did not make a complaint about Damian.

Ironically, Peter Dawson mentioned to the inquest that at one point he had lost his practising certificate. JC gave evidence that she was in the same room as Chris when he had rung Peter, wanting to know what his legal position would be if he left the matrimonial home. Peter asked Damian if he was aware that he wasn't practising as a solicitor at the time of that call and Damian said, 'Yes, I am aware of that, sir.'

Matthew Fordham continued his closing statement, noting that the DPP had declined to lay charges after the first inquest, but said that this second inquest presented a stronger case.

'I am mindful of the director's initial reluctance to proceed with charges due to the fact that evidence of the witnesses had not been tested. I submit that the evidence of witnesses who would be relied upon by the prosecution has not changed, and in particular JC was rock solid. A properly instructed jury would have an abundance of evidence available to it to allow it to conclude beyond any reasonable doubt that Lynette Joy Dawson was murdered on the evening of Friday, 8 January 1982 or in the early hours of Saturday, 9 January 1982.'

He returned to the drink that Chris gave Lynette on the Friday night.

'Sir, why would Chris be making Lyn a drink on 8 January when JC had been up at South West Rocks since 2 January and was not living at the home at that time? I submit that a jury will have absolutely no doubt about why Chris was giving Lyn a drink that night.

'Finally, sir, I would like to record my sincere condolences to the family of Lynette.'

Without a break, Peter Dawson got to his feet.

'Your Worship, Detective Loone's alleged that Christopher Michael Dawson, with counselling and assistance from others unknown, murdered Lynette Joy Dawson between the hours of 9 pm Friday, 8 January 1982 and 8 am on Saturday, [9] January 1982. My friend has conceded in his address to you that the evidence in support of that allegation is entirely circumstantial. The brief of evidence that has been submitted to you, sir, contains statements from and interviews with about thirty persons. Unfortunately, Your Worship, I'd submit that those statements include matters which are irrelevant, comment in the guise of evidence, inexpert opinions, prejudicial hearsay and statements, the prejudicial effect of which outweighs their probative value.

'I submit, sir, the brief contains a morass of material which would be totally inadmissible at a trial.'

All of that is true. Pat, for example, would not be permitted to read her notes to the court, and material about the Dawson sexual liaisons with students wouldn't be allowed because it has no relevance to Lynette's disappearance. The standard of proof in a criminal court is stricter than in civil proceedings. In a criminal court, the charges need to be proved 'beyond a reasonable doubt', whereas in civil courts the issues being contested need to be proved on the 'balance of probabilities'.

Peter addressed the lack of physical evidence.

'A great deal of time and expense has been expended on such matters as ground-penetrating radar, police rescue squad, cadaver dogs, site excavations, telephone taps, but no physical evidence whatsoever of injury or harm to Lynette Joy Dawson by any person has been located [. . .]

'My friend's suggested that I should produce the bank card statement. There's no evidence, Your Worship, as to what happened to that bank card statement but there's clear evidence that it existed. It's referred to by Chris Dawson. It's referred to by JC. It's referred to by Helena Simms. Heaven knows what happened to it, Your Worship. I don't think any of us have any evidence of that but it's obviously more likely, Your Worship, that it was included in the matters that were forwarded to the Simms family and retained by Chris Dawson for nineteen years. I would be much more suspicious if he was able to produce it.'

Chris had raised the bank card use and, with or without the statement, it's problematic. If Chris had kept only that one statement for nineteen years, there could be an inference that he'd done that to prove that Lynette was alive after 9 January 1982. But the real problem is that Chris said Lynette had rung him twice from the Central Coast in the week after she disappeared and it's hard to accept that she would have travelled back to the Northern Beaches twice to buy something, and then go away again.

Peter Dawson then tried to characterise Lynette's disappearance as an unfortunate but everyday event.

'It's natural that when a woman such as Lynette Joy Dawson leaves home, fails to contact her family and friends, fails to have any contact with anybody else, obviously suspicion will fall upon her husband and it's also natural for that suspicion to increase when shortly after her departure Mr Dawson establishes a de facto relationship with his teenage lover and in due course marries her.'

Damian had told me that he sees couples fight all the time. 'One goes away for a while but they always come back.' For Lynette to leave in the circumstances outlined by Peter Dawson is as troubling as it is rare. Could the unified force of this string of rare circumstances give rise to what Matthew Fordham described as 'an abundance of evidence' that might enable a jury to convict?

Circumstantial matters aren't unusual, but they are more difficult without a body. There have been two recent murder convictions in New South Wales without a body. In December 2010, Keli Lane was found guilty of murdering her two-day-old daughter Tegan. Two days after Tegan was born in September 1996, Keli discharged herself and Tegan from hospital and arrived alone at her parents' home in Manly a few hours later. That afternoon she attended a wedding. Lane gave several versions of what happened to Tegan, including that she gave her to her biological father, and then to a couple from Perth, but none of these people could be located. The defence argued that Lane could not be found guilty of murder, because without a body there was no evidence as to how Tegan died, but the jury found her guilty. When Lane appealed her conviction, the court said that while her many lies about Tegan's whereabouts didn't establish murder, when put together they formed 'one powerful item of evidence in a circumstantial case'. In 2006, Bruce Burrell was found guilty of murdering Kerry Whelan in 1997, though her body has never been found. Much of the circumstantial evidence was excluded, the public later found out, and it took one hung jury and a second trial for Burrell to be found guilty, making it a very expensive verdict. He appealed, but his conviction was upheld.

Budgets are tight and the DPP is reluctant to prosecute matters unless there is a good chance of success. But you can never predict the behaviour of a jury. They thought they had a strong case with Robert Xie, who stood trial in 2015, charged with the murders of five of his wife Kathy's relatives. The five victims were bludgeoned to death in their leafy, suburban home. The crime scene was so gruesome that the police gathering forensic evidence were photographed looking distressed on the grass verge outside the house. With so much evidence, many expected the trial to be a formality but at three separate trials the jury was unable to reach a verdict. It took a fourth trial for Xie to be found guilty. Perhaps the forensic evidence was so overwhelming that the jury couldn't process it. Perhaps there is an optimal amount of forensic evidence, combined with a strong narrative, for a prosecution to succeed.

'So much of the evidence in Lynette's case is hearsay,' Coroner Carl Milovanovich told me later, and with a few exceptions, hearsay evidence is excluded. 'Even the direct evidence that JC was throttled by Chris isn't direct evidence of Lynette suffering violence.' Even so, the coroner, Damian Loone and Matthew Fordham were confident they had enough to proceed.

———

When I read Milovanovich's findings, I was struck by his obvious concern for those who had grieved for Lynette for twenty years. Carl had told me that he would regularly 'unashamedly shed a tear in the courtroom', especially when young children were involved, but I still expected a drier account in his written findings. Legal process and language tend to dehumanise events, but he put Lynette at the centre.

His first duty was to determine if Lynette was, in fact, deceased. He read his findings in court.

'The fact that there has been no contact from Lyn Dawson and if one adds the further factor that there has been considerable media interest . . . if Lyn Joy Dawson was in fact alive, one would have thought that she would have contacted somebody.

'Her children turned eighteen years of age. They turned twenty-one years of age. Her mother passed away. She did not attend the funeral . . . Checks with all agencies can find no trace of her and, in this day and age, unless one lives in a cave and lives off the land, you cannot be undetectable having regard to the perhaps necessary intrusions that exist in our lives such as Medicare cards, access to bank accounts, doctors, social service agencies, et cetera . . . Even if we accept that there were some unconfirmed sightings of Lyn Dawson shortly after her death and some alleged contact between her and Chris Dawson . . . there is no suggestion that she had any contact with anybody since.

'Accordingly, I make formal findings that I am satisfied that Lyn Joy Dawson is in fact deceased.'

Damian was surprised that Peter Dawson accepted the coroner's finding that Lynette was dead. 'We expected an argument but never received one,' he told me. Had she left voluntarily and then died, or her remains been discovered, her death would have been noted, an inquest held, family contacted.

Next, the coroner noted that at the first inquest in 2001, Coroner Jan Stevenson read the brief and, without calling any witnesses, terminated the inquest and referred Lynette's file to the DPP with a recommendation that charges be laid. Of that referral, he said: 'The Director of Public Prosecutions elected not to file a bill on that recommended indictment. One of the reasons, amongst others being given, was that the evidence had not been tested. I am of the view that the evidence has now been tested.'

He continued: 'I feel compelled also to make comments on the failure of Christopher Dawson, Paul Dawson and Marilyn Dawson in not attending this inquest. It is true that they, as was the case at the last inquest, were legally represented and it was indicated, as in this case, that they would not give evidence. There is a distinction, however, between coming to court, getting into the witness box and exercising one's right not to answer questions that may incriminate oneself, and not attending at all.'

I really admired the way that the coroner acknowledged the humanity in his court, as well as the facts. Their absence suggested they had no interest in learning more about the circumstances of

Lynette's disappearance; and their love and respect for Lynette, who had once been wife, sister-in-law and a good friend to them all, was also insufficient to get them there. After Lynette disappeared, Chris had said that he wanted her to come home; twenty years later, no one expected that she would come back, but if events had been as he said they were, he surely must have still wanted to know what became of his childhood sweetheart, wife, and the mother of two of his children.

When I met Carl Milovanovich at his home, I asked him about Chris's and Paul's refusals to give evidence. 'I was hoping that the Dawsons would give evidence,' he said, 'but I would have to have given them a warning and a certificate of immunity, so there's no point then giving evidence.'

Section 61 of the *Coroners Act 2009* deals with privilege and self-incrimination. If the coroner believes that a witness might incriminate themselves by giving evidence, then the coroner must caution the witness against self-incrimination, meaning they cannot be compelled to give that evidence. The coroner can, however, offer the witness a certificate of immunity, which guarantees that any evidence the witness gives cannot be used against them. In other words, a witness could confess to a crime but would be protected from prosecution.

I thought about the certificate of immunity as I drove home from my meeting with Carl. When I got in, I sent him an email, asking if a coroner could grant Chris, Paul, Marilyn, or anybody else, a certificate of immunity now, to give Lynette's family a chance to hear from them, even if it meant they would be protected from prosecution. He replied:

> Even if Chris Dawson was prepared to give evidence (most unlikely) as to what he knows about her disappearance, no Coroner would grant him a Certificate of Immunity in regard to an indictable offence. Hypothetically, if [dealing with] a co-accused, e.g., a person who may be guilty of being an accessory after the fact to murder, or being a person who has committed an offence, such as assisting in the disposal of a body, the Coroner may be prepared to give that person a certificate of immunity on the basis that that person would provide evidence that may lead to the arrest and conviction of the principal perpetrator.

When I started writing about JC and Lynette, ten years had passed since the inquest and it had been over thirty years since Lynette disappeared. I wondered if Chris might have something to say now. I didn't know how to contact Chris, so I sent Peter Dawson an email on 20 May 2014:

> Dear Mr Dawson,
> I am writing a book about Lynette Dawson's disappearance. I would like to interview your brother Chris Dawson and I note that you represented him, and Paul and Marilyn Dawson at the coronial inquest in 2003. I am therefore asking through you if Chris Dawson would speak with me. I would also be interested in speaking with you about anything that has transpired since then.

Three days later, I received his reply. He wrote that it was Lynette's decision to leave her husband and children and said that the Dawson family had no intention of assisting to perpetuate the myth that there was any more to the story.

At the end of the coroner's findings, he gave a short catalogue of the inadequacies of the historical police investigations, both missing persons and homicide. That sad list, he said, included: 'losing documented material, some of which has been referred to in these proceedings, some of which we are told is no longer in existence . . . the passage of time, the fact that such records like bank card transactions, insurance policies are destroyed after a given period of time . . . The real impetus in relation to this investigation did not start until possibly ten years after Lyn's disappearance and then a more comprehensive [. . .] investigation did not really start until approximately 1998. I have little doubt that had this missing person report been prioritised differently at the time and some preliminary inquiries made in relation to the various persons that were involved and associated with Lyn Dawson at the time, the investigation might have taken a different course.'

He repeated his criticism of the witnesses who chose not to appear.

'Those witnesses have chosen not to come before this inquest, and they have chosen not to get in the witness box and seek the immunity of section 33, and they therefore leave themselves open for criticism, and they are factors that weigh heavily on my mind in relation to the irresistible inference that must be drawn that they are in possession of information, material, perhaps even documentation which they are refusing to provide to investigators or to the coroner. This is the sort of matter, in my view, where I can be satisfied that on the tested evidence that has been presented before this inquest, that it is evidence which is capable of satisfying a jury that a known person has committed an indictable offence . . . [and] that a jury is capable of convicting on that evidence . . . I feel that for the family and for the community, this is a matter where the appropriate course is that a jury should decide whether there is an indictable offence committed by any known person rather than an administrative decision being made by the Director of Public Prosecutions.

'I accordingly terminate the inquest and I will be recommending to the Director of Public Prosecutions that a known person be charged with the charge of murder.'

The inquest concluded on Friday, 28 February 2003.

PART THREE

CHAPTER FOURTEEN

Still looking for Lynette

IN AUGUST 2003, SIX MONTHS AFTER THE INQUEST HAD FINISHED, THE ABC's *Australian Story* aired an episode called 'Looking for Lyn'. The next morning, Damian received a call from Lorraine Watson, a retired seamstress who'd had *Australian Story* on in the background as she pottered in the kitchen.

'You should go and talk to her,' he told me.

I had trouble getting a hold of Lorraine by phone, so I wrote her a letter. When she rang me sometime later, she said she'd gone to Melbourne for a funeral and had come down with a flu that was so bad she'd had to put off flying back. She sounded frail but when I visited her in her swanky apartment by the beach, she was anything but.

'Damian was talking about Lynette Dawson's mother, Helena, looking for Lynette, how she would just go out and wander around leaving flyers everywhere,' Lorraine said, before we'd even sat down at her kitchen table, which was covered in white and cream fabric and pins. 'I do wedding dresses and christening robes now,' she said, leaning on the table as she lowered herself into the chair. 'On the television, they showed a picture of Lynette, the picture of her on her wedding day. I was shocked,' she said, gazing at me with eyes enlarged by a pair of thick glasses. Two days later, she went to Dee Why police station and told Damian what had happened in her dress shop in the Strand Arcade in Sydney in late 1981.

'I've got to tell you something,' she said, then reached across the table and raised one of her red-painted nails close to my face. 'I've got an incredibly good memory. You can imagine in my business you meet thousands of girls, but I never forget a face.

'One day, Lynette had come into the shop. She'd seen a bridal dress in the window. She told Dee, my salesgirl, that she had a beautiful black skirt at home and she wanted to get the lace top in the window made in black. She said she had a formal function to go to, and the top and skirt would be perfect.'

Lorraine had a busy high-end business and didn't like doing small work. 'I thought to myself, my god, I don't want to do it. I couldn't be bothered,' so she told Lynette it would cost $1000, hoping the price would scare her away. 'She must have had some money because she didn't quibble with that at all. I was surprised because she was wearing sensible shoes and I wondered if she was a nurse.'

I sat up a little straighter in my chair, noting her seamstress's eye for detail.

'I got her to take off her top to take her measurements, and she had purple finger marks on her arm. They were vicious marks. Really vicious.' Across from me, Lorraine winced. 'You could see the fingers in purple clearly. But I didn't say anything to her then because I didn't know her at all.'

Roslyn McLoughlin said that Lynette had 'finger marks on her arm' and 'a very large bruise on her upper thigh' when she'd seen her at the last tennis get-together before Christmas. I wondered if the function Lynette was having the top made for was her mother's surprise sixty-sixth birthday party. She was planning it for the beginning of February 1982, which turned out to be only a few weeks after she went missing. The timing would make sense and no one else had mentioned any other occasion that was coming up.

A week later, Lynette went back for a fitting and when she got undressed, Lorraine saw a massive bruise on her buttocks.

'I said, "Christ! What have you done to yourself?" I'm no shrinking violet! She looked sad and she said, "It's a long story."

'We had a couple of lounges in the shop and in the afternoon one of us would go and get coffees. So, on this day, one of the girls went down and got one for Lynette as well and we all sat down and started talking. She told me, "I'm in a very violent marriage." She said that when she first got married things were great. She said he was a footballer and he was extremely good-looking and that women really liked him. She said that he had lots of affairs and that he would "smack her across the mouth" if she asked about them or said anything about them.

'Then she told me that her husband was having an affair with a young girl. She said that she'd asked him about the young girl once, when they were in the kitchen and she was cooking and that he'd "backhanded" her and hot water went everywhere. She said, "He loves young women. My time with him has run out."'

I remembered JC saying that Chris wanted her to look girlish. 'If he noticed any minuscule fluctuation in my weight he put me to work, made me go for a long run. He wanted me to be gorgeous forever,' she'd told me, rolling her eyes.

'I knew that Lynette lived on the Northern Beaches,' Lorraine continued, 'because she'd left her address and phone number, so I offered her a lift home. My husband Ron would pick me up. We dropped Dee [one of her employees] at her place in Fairlight and we dropped Lynette home. I remember the house was out of the way. I thought it was the back of Mona Vale. We got to her house and it was a big new house and I said to her, "Why don't you piss him off?" and she said, "I can't. I've got two girls and the house." So, she took the top, gave me a kiss and said goodbye. I wished her luck.'

Lorraine picked up an ivory christening robe and flattened it out with her big hands. 'I know a woman who went to Cromer High. She was in the same year as JC. She said everyone could see that Chris and JC were involved. If that happened now, they'd lock the bastard up.'

I could see that Lorraine wanted to get on with her work on the little robe, so I packed up my things and thanked her. At the front door, she said, 'I liked this girl. I never normally got involved with clients. I was there to make money. But with her, I couldn't help it.'

On my way home from Lorraine's, I was agitated. Roslyn McLoughlin's evidence about Lynette's bruises – the finger marks and the bruise on her thigh – was an exact match with the bruises Lorraine had seen in her dress shop that day and, as far as I was aware, those two pieces of evidence had not been put together. It was significant. And, like Lorraine, I wondered how many other witnesses there might be who hadn't come forward yet. Carl had told me that press coverage of an inquest often brought out new information and it seemed unfair that *Australian Story* hadn't gone to air before the second inquest so that Lorraine could have been called as a witness. Would her testimony have made a difference to the DPP's decision?

I rang Damian to tell him that I'd met Lorraine. 'She's fantastic, isn't she?' he asked.

It must have been disappointing, I said, to not have had her evidence at the inquest, but he didn't seem bothered by that. He'd taken her statement and he could use it if he managed to get the matter to trial. 'We keep in touch every now and again. Fantastic witness.'

In late 2003 a psychic named Debbie Malone came forward claiming to have 'made contact' with Lynette. Damian checked with Pat and Greg, and they decided to give her services a go. At Pat's place, Debbie was given some of Lynette's belongings – a ring, a bangle, some photos. There's an article in the *Manly Daily* called '"Body in Bush" Tip: Body in Bush, Says Medium',[11] with a photo of everyone gathered around Pat's kitchen table. After holding Lynette's personal items, Debbie said that Lynette was 'lying on her back with a plastic bag over her head, buried under tightly packed earth, somewhere near her former Bayview house'. I asked Damian if he believed in Debbie Malone's abilities and he was non-committal, but he had told me once that every time Lynette's disappearance is in the paper, or her face is on the television, there's a chance that someone might come forward with more information. Perhaps that was his aim. Interestingly, I came across a 2009 article in the *Daily Telegraph*, 'Dead Men Do Tell Tales After All, Says Clairvoyant Debbie Malone'.[12] Debbie had written a book about the surprising number of police cases she has been involved in, including Lynette's.

In April 2013, the *Daily Telegraph* ran another article: 'Lynette Dawson – Painting a Picture of a Woman Murdered'.[13] Just before Christmas 1981, Lynette had commissioned an artist to make charcoal drawings of the girls.

'[The artist] told me that in January 1982, she went to the house to see Lynette to give her the sketches,' Damian told me. 'Chris came to the door, she asked for Lynette and Chris told her she wasn't there. She explains to him that's she's got the drawings to give to her and he tells her, "Lynette's not here. We don't need them anymore." Unbelievable, isn't it?' Damian was clearly delighted with this piece of evidence.

Included with the article are copies of the sketches, which show two happy little girls.

'This was a wonderful mother who commissioned these drawings, got the girls to pose for photographs for the artist and then is supposed to have vanished before seeing them?' Greg is quoted as saying. 'She would never have left her children and this is something solid from around that time that shows she had no plans to leave them.'

CHAPTER FIFTEEN

What remains

BY THE END OF THE INQUEST, DAMIAN LOONE, MATTHEW FORDHAM and Carl Milovanovich all believed that the DPP would act. And Pat, Greg and Merilyn were quietly confident that charges would follow too. This time, they thought, the DPP would have to proceed because the second inquest had come to the same conclusion as the first. JC had also assumed that the second inquest was 'the beginning of the end'.

Giving evidence was stressful but also easy, she told me, because she knew all the answers. What wasn't easy was the attention from the photographers, who chased her around that week. In the foyer afterwards, Pat and Greg embraced her. 'She was a victim too,' Greg said.

But the DPP didn't like the case.

'The DPP knocked it back again,' Damian told me, without rancour. 'No reasons given. They just don't think there's enough there to get a conviction.'

But Carl thought there was enough there. 'I think it should have gone before a jury,' he told me. 'I think, "What a shame the evidence was never tested."'

When Carl referred Lynette's file to the DPP for the second time, it 'offered the family momentary closure', he said. But when the DPP declined to lay charges, it was almost too much for Pat, Greg and Merilyn, and their grief rolled on. They were angry that the system had let them down again.

'We were absolutely devastated,' Pat told me, her voice drained and slow. 'They said that JC was an unreliable witness.' She and Greg were especially perplexed by this assessment, seeing as so much of what happened, and what JC gave evidence about, was indisputable. And JC was just disappointed.

Carl agreed that JC was a credible witness and he too was surprised at the DPP's decision. 'We examined her evidence under oath. I think I was impressed,' he told me.

'Everything has fallen the wrong way,' Greg said. 'The inquests, the DPP. We think we're getting somewhere and then we take three steps back, then one forward, and another three back.'

Pat feels that Chris and Paul have been treated like a 'protected species', while the Simms family has been judged at every step, as if it's somehow their fault that Lynette hasn't been found.

When the police reviewed Lynette's missing person file in 1985, the report detailed the checks that the police made and I go back and forth on this, trying to understand if it's only with hindsight that Lynette's disappearance seems all wrong. Was it reasonable for the police to rely on Helena to raise the possibility of foul play? Should the police have been suspicious? Should they have considered other possibilities – for example, that after Lynette left Bayview, she might have met with foul play somewhere else?

When Trudie Adams went missing in 1978 after a night out at Newport Surf Club, which is just around the corner from where Lynette lived, the police maintained a highly visible media profile from early on. She was never portrayed as a missing person. The circumstances were more worrying, perhaps, but Lynette's profile, as a mother of two small children who hadn't been heard from in six weeks, would also have been a rare and worrying occurrence. Was it reasonable that the police saw nothing unsettling when they made the following entry in Lynette's missing person file?

> On 10 November 1983 Mrs Simms was again contacted as to any further sightings and stated that she had nothing further other than that Mr Dawson had obtained a divorce from her daughter, she believed in July, and was about to marry JC, who had been the babysitter at the home.

Why was JC characterised as the 'babysitter at the home'? Did the police mean that JC had been the babysitter since moving in a few days after Lynette went missing? Or did they mean that JC had been the babysitter, as well as Chris's 'lover', for up to eighteen months before Lynette disappeared? By the time that note was made in November 1983, the police must have known that the relationship began when JC was Chris's student at Cromer High. Should their relationship have concerned them? Was there a period when a new relationship might raise a red flag? Did Chris's divorce from Lynette, initiated fourteen months after she went missing, appear hasty? Sue Strath was telling her friend, policeman Paul Hulme, about her suspicions. He most likely mentioned it to his colleagues. There might be answers to these questions, but there's no record of them.

Greg and Pat are also bewildered that nothing came of the allegations that Chris was sexually involved with students. Damian said that he didn't press those issues at the time because he wanted to focus on the bigger investigation.

'I didn't want this to become all about the sex. I knew that's all the media would talk about. They would have forgotten about Lyn.' Many of the women were also mothers by then and they didn't want to give evidence; they didn't want their children learning about those events, and possibly their husbands too.

After the inquest, JC contacted the Department of Education and Training and made a Freedom of Information request for anything they might have on file about her, or about what had gone on at Cromer High. They told her that they had nothing. She also explored the possibility of suing the department, but in the end, that came to nothing as well.

When the inquest was over, the Queensland Crown Solicitor considered Chris Dawson's and Paul Dawson's registrations as teachers, and contacted JC to give evidence. Later, she received a letter from the Crown Solicitor's Office advising her that Chris and Paul had requested that their names be removed from the Teachers Registration Board.

In a long, handwritten letter that I have carefully placed into my file about Lynette, Pat expressed her enduring heartache and anger at the DPP's decision not to proceed.

> My cousin Wendy rang the Office of the Department of Public Prosecutions to seek information on the decision. She spoke to a representative . . . and my cousin was totally shocked to be told that the 'most telling factor' in the decision was the fact that my Mum

> had seen Lyn after she went missing! My cousin went into meltdown on hearing such nonsense. I spoke to Ms [. . .] the following day . . . she again repeated what she had said the previous day, using the words 'telling factor in the decision not to go to prosecution' and 'the fact that Mum saw Lyn after she went missing' . . . Thinking that the DPP's decision was primarily based on the untruth of Mum seeing Lyn, as was told us, caused us much upset over the years. It was just so wrong, and so unjust, and that was the sort of thing we were battling.

Pat and Greg were worn down. At times, they were angry and would have liked to reverse the burden and have the DPP explain to them what could have happened to Lynette. What their best explanation of Lynette's disappearance would have been? But it wasn't about what the DPP did or didn't believe, it was about the quality of the evidence. Was the evidence strong enough to get a conviction?

Pat's letter spelled out for me again the detail of what had happened, where she felt the family had been let down, where she felt she'd let Lynette down, revisiting it all. And one day when I was with Greg and Merilyn, they asked me what I thought about the relevance of the pink cardigan. I was weighing it up aloud and was just about to say something about the violence of being stabbed, when I looked up and stopped speaking.

'It's okay. It's okay,' they said, encouraging me to continue. 'We want to hear.'

Lynette's parents both died in 2001. Len died first and then Helena, a few months later. Len's funeral was held at the naval base chapel at South Head, where the mouth of Sydney Harbour opens into the Tasman Sea. The naval base is at the top of towering sandstone cliffs, watching over the ocean that rolls off to the east. During the service, Helena kept looking down the aisle to see if Lynette might come, because she was certain that if she were still alive, she would come to her father's funeral. When she didn't show up, Pat and Greg said that Helena was forced to accept that Lynette was dead. She didn't last long without Len. Perhaps she couldn't face her grief without him, or more likely, she'd lost the final thread of hope that her daughter was alive.

Over the years, at family get-togethers – birthdays or a new baby coming along – Pat says that she always thinks, 'Lyn should be in all of these places.' The family's grief was unresolved for many years, but in a letter, Pat told me that its nature has changed more recently.

> Whenever I heard of a body being found in a National Park or along the Pacific Highway the first thought was with trepidation that it might be Lyn – then relief to find that it wasn't. I know Greg had the same reaction when an unidentified body was discovered. Now what we most desperately want is to find her body and 'put her to rest'.

Lynette is trapped at thirty-three. Sometimes I imagine that she might yet come back and look at her siblings and wonder, 'How have they got so old?'

One day I came across an article about the Family and Friends of Missing Persons Unit (FFMPU), a part of the New South Wales Attorney-General's Department, whose role is to help the families of people who are missing long-term. I got in touch with the unit's coordinator, Liz Davies, who invited me to come in for a chat.

There was a thick fog the morning I set out for Parramatta.

The FFMPU website defines a missing person as 'anyone who is reported missing to police, whose whereabouts are unknown, and there are fears for the safety or concern for the welfare of that person'.[14] For the 30 kilometres from Manly to Parramatta, the six lanes of traffic were jammed, and as I looked over the sea of congestion, it didn't seem that there was anywhere in this city to get lost.

I was late and apologetic, but Liz Davies was unconcerned. 'Rebecca, hi, hi, come in,' she said, keen to get going. We talked a little about Lynette and what I was doing, and although I looked for signs that she might know Pat and Greg, she gave nothing away. She was energetic and passionate about her work, and I liked her very much.

'Each week, 160 people go missing in New South Wales alone. Sixty-five per cent of them are under eighteen,' Liz said, which I quickly calculated to be about 104. There'd been a piece in the morning's paper about two teenage girls who had disappeared. Liz took me through the stats. In New South Wales, 87 per cent of missing people return within forty-eight hours, and within a month 98 per cent are located. 'The remaining one to two per cent are the long-term missing,' she said. Of that small group, I remembered Carl Milovanovich telling Peter Dawson, 'most are subject to homicide'.

'There are lots of families who have someone go missing for a short time. They can be lost or disoriented, as many older people are, they can choose to leave and want to be left alone, some suicide and some meet with misadventure. Those people are found,' Liz said. 'But for those families that just don't know what happened, we have 650 missing persons to date. I don't presume to know what the families are going through,' she continued, looking at me steadily. 'Missing is a trauma like no other. We aim to help families be as comfortable as they can be without knowing what has happened. They call it an "ambiguous loss", meaning that a person can be physically present but psychologically lost, like dementia. Or, the person can be psychologically present, but physically missing, like Lynette. It's a hard place to be.'

Liz told me that more than 50 per cent of people who go missing have a mental health issue, and I thought back to the man making the missing person report at the police station at The Rocks when I first went to meet Damian. 'But people with a mental health disease can also meet with foul play or misadventure,' she went on, waiting while I wrote it all down. 'The families whose loved one is missing and has a mental health issue are fearful of disclosing that for fear that the police will think that they've run off to kill themselves, that they won't look for them. They're protective of their loved one's reputation.'

In one of Pat's letters to me, she expressed that exact sentiment. 'People had attempted to assassinate the character of Lyn, with Lyn having no right of reply to any slurs or false allegations.'

The police also kept telling the family, 'It's not a crime to go missing,' like they were urging the family to accept that Lynette had simply decided to leave. Pat said she got sick of hearing it. She felt that the police were pushing back, as if they knew Lynette better, and she got angry that the police didn't want to hear about the Lyn they knew so well, who would never have left her children.

I'd tried to imagine what it must have been like for XD and YD too, how they might have fared over the years. I asked Liz for her opinion.

'It's not recognised how much children suffer too,' she said. 'A mother is a person who is there for you. If your mother goes missing, there's anger and loss and children ask, "Why didn't she choose to stay with me?" It's like a suicide. The self-blame for the child is profound. They can't make sense of what's happened.'

We talked about Judith Bartlett, a New South Wales woman who had been missing since 1964. Human bones were discovered in 2009 near where she disappeared but it took another four years for them to be identified as hers, sparking a homicide investigation. Judith's daughter, Frances, was ten years old when she was told that her mother had left and fifty-nine when her bones were identified. In 2013, an article appeared in the *Australian* about the case:[15]

> 'Our mother didn't leave us,' her eldest child Frances Ryan said in Sydney today.
>
> 'She didn't stop loving us. She was taken by a thief in the night. I had a mother that I thought loved me. I had a mother that was my friend. I was told she had gone away. I thought she had left me.'
>
> 'I spent 49 years looking for a face in the crowd,' she said.
>
> She also said that her brother Darrell spent 49 years 'almost hating' his mother for walking out on him.

A few years ago, JC told me that Lynette's older daughter, XD, rang her to say that she forgives her. 'I took that to mean that she forgives me for leaving them,' JC said. It's hard to imagine what losing their mother, and then JC, had done to XD and YD.

After a lot of thought, I sent XD an email via Greg, who is still occasionally in touch with her. I asked her if she would speak to me, not about what she thought had happened to her mother, but what it had been like growing up without her and not knowing what had happened.

She politely replied, 'Thank you for the invitation to contribute to your book. However, after careful consideration I've decided it's not the best thing for me at this time.'

When I visited Carl, he pulled out a folder of newspaper clippings about inquests he'd presided over. We set it down on the coffee table and he told me a little about each one. I was surprised by how many I remembered. For some of the families, there was no resolution because, like Lynette, there was no body. For others, the cause of death might be clear but the circumstances surrounding the death remained unknown. I'd spent a lot of time thinking about death, and I asked Carl if he thinks we've got worse at confronting it. Past generations had death all around them – accidents on the farm, in childbirth, disease – people died at home and were laid out in the front room. Modern Western culture rejects death, and possibly to our detriment. 'Have we overvalued life?' I asked Carl.

'I don't think we value life enough,' he said. 'People need to know about the death of a loved one because it helps us understand their life; it helps us understand our life better. With Lynette, the family will never know. What else could have happened to her?' He shrugged. 'She wasn't out at night, at a nightclub or something. Even if she went away she would have had to stay somewhere and there's no evidence she ever accessed any money. She doesn't contact her mother, her daughters. Is she dead or alive? The answer is dead.

Then, was it random, did she have enemies? Unlikely any of those. Who had reason to kill her?'

In the months after Lynette went missing, Chris would still occasionally take the girls to Clovelly to visit their grandparents. Helena would bring the albums out and show them photos of their mum.

'She wanted to keep their mother alive for them,' Greg told me. Then she might take them to the beach to look for shells and to have a swim.

On the day we visited Clovelly, Greg pointed to where a telephone box had once stood in the tiny park in front of the house. Chris would ring from there and Helena would come out and get the girls.

'Did anyone confront him about this odd behaviour?' I said, wondering if the girls were afraid because their father was unwilling to go inside.

'No. I don't like confrontation,' Greg said. 'Also, Mum wanted to keep the girls in her life.'

For a while after Lynette's disappearance, Helena continued to go to Chris's football matches, which she'd always attended with Lynette and the girls, but in time she felt that the Dawsons 'closed ranks' and so she stayed away. Soon, Chris stopped bringing the girls over to visit, and then not quite three years after Lynette went missing, Chris and JC moved to Queensland.

Pat, Greg and Merilyn still miss the girls and regret that their own children weren't able to grow up alongside them. They always made a point of telling their children about their aunt Lynette, and their cousins XD and YD.

'We've never tried to hide anything,' Merilyn said. 'We always try and keep her memory alive.'

But it was Helena who suffered the most. 'Mum not only lost Lyn but she also lost Lyn's girls too,' Pat told me, bitterly. 'I can never forgive him for what he did to Mum.'

Helena kept small diaries her whole life and Pat wrote to tell me about them.

> Mum had always kept diaries. Just those little pocket-sized books with brief notes on who had rung, letters replied to etc but the entries after Lyn's disappearance were heart-wrenching . . . Mum unable to sleep, nightmares, depressed . . . She showed me a black plastic bag one day and said it contained her diaries. She asked me to destroy them, 'undisturbed' when she passed away. It went against all my principles and it was with great guilt to not do as she had requested but maybe she will forgive me. I still feel sad that I didn't follow her wishes. I've not looked at the other diaries, just the relevant one and I felt her words at the time were too important to destroy.

Helena could have thrown them away while she was alive, but she had recorded so many things in them about Lynette from before and after she went missing that I wondered if she'd hung on to them as contemporaneous notes about who said what and when, in case someone was charged with Lynette's murder one day. But if Helena died before someone was charged, perhaps she didn't see the point of keeping them.

Over the course of our acquaintance, we spoke about many things, but Pat and Greg had said little about their father, Len, and their oldest brother, Philip. Philip had given Damian a statement for the first inquest's brief of evidence, but he wasn't called as a witness at the second inquest, probably because his statement didn't really add anything of evidential value. But in a family that had already lost one of four children, his absence seemed more significant. In one of our email exchanges, I asked Pat about Philip.

> Phil and his wife came to the two coronial inquiries, and Phil to one of the first television interviews, *A Current Affair*, which didn't go ahead as they were afraid of legal implications then. I think *Australian Story* broke that barrier. At the time of Lyn's disappearance, he was living in Singleton, so far away from Sydney as we all were, with no mobile phones, no computers in those days . . . He was busy with work and his immediate family, and maybe he wasn't really in touch with what was going on before and after Lyn's disappearance. He seems to keep his 'head in the sand' about Lyn I think, and maybe it is self-preservation not to go over those times. Maybe it is partially Greg and my fault too as Damian or the media would contact either of us, and Phil, who wasn't as involved, slipped under the radar. I guess I should have invited his participation more.

I never got far trying to understand their father, Len, either. Things were said – that he was 'old-fashioned', a loner, who wasn't to be interrupted when he was reading the newspaper or playing cribbage on the front porch. Greg said that he went to work and 'everything else was left to Mum', including searching for their missing daughter. Greg also told me that he was an angry man who Helena was always trying to placate, and who the kids knew to leave alone. But Pat remembers good times too – that he had nicknames for all the kids, that he could be kind and he helped her with her maths. He died nineteen years after Lynette went missing but Pat and Greg never mentioned a single thing he did to help Helena in her desperate search for Lynette. Perhaps he really meant it when he said, 'The bastard's done her in.'

One day, I stopped in on Lynette's childhood friend Tricia Hartley. Tricia lives in Maroubra now but she grew up in Clovelly, on the other side of the beach to the Simms family, and she and Lynette spent all their spare time together as kids.

'We had so much fun,' she told me. 'The beach was our life.' She talked about Len too. 'Her dad was very dominating. He was just scary. He was nice to me, but he wasn't nice to Lyn. I don't know why he wasn't nice to Lyn.'

Tricia's mother, Clare, was also good friends with Helena, and Tricia said that he wasn't nice to Helena either. 'She'd come to our place just to get out of the house. They'd go shopping at Bondi Junction a lot too, to get away from Lyn's dad.'

I wondered if the pall of Lynette's father was that he was more than angry. Pat and Greg's automatic response whenever he was mentioned was that he was very sick with diabetes towards the end of his life, but it was such a reflex that it seemed like a shield against his full character, that perhaps there were times when he was domineering.

Nonetheless, Greg maintained that Lynette would stand up to their father, and Tricia said she found it hard to imagine that Chris would dominate Lyn.

'I can't see that,' she told me emphatically.

But Lorraine Watson's evidence is that 'he "backhanded" her' and that Lynette had told her that she was in a 'very violent marriage'. If Chris was violent, I wondered if Lynette accepted it, in part, because there was discord in her childhood home, and possibly more so for her because she did stand up to her father. Women, and men, who come from a violent home often accept that it is normal. That was certainly the story of many of the women who came through the refuge. But this was no more than my own speculation.

After JC left Chris, she drove KD to Queensland every school holiday to spend time with her father and half-sisters, and when KD was old enough, she would fly up alone. KD was seven when Chris married for the third time, and she flew to Fiji for the ceremony. Even so, JC feels guilty that she didn't do more to facilitate KD's relationship with the girls.

Now, KD only sees XD and YD occasionally at Dawson family functions and she sometimes gets angry if JC asks about them.

'KD feels in the middle of it and she says, "It's got nothing to do with me," which is and isn't true. She sometimes says, "Why me?"' JC told me.

KD knows that JC doesn't want to see Chris, so if he's visiting, she'll tell JC not to come around or to stay home between such and such time.

One day when JC and I were having lunch, JC accidentally left her phone on silent and when she did check it, found seven missed calls from KD.

'If KD can't get in contact with me she panics,' JC explained, as she held the phone to her ear, waiting for her to pick up. 'I'm with Rebecca,' she said. 'I'm fine. I'm not murdered.'

After she moved back to Sydney, JC enrolled at North Sydney TAFE to do the Tertiary Preparation Certificate – the mature-age equivalent of the HSC. She wanted to do a subject that was only offered at the Randwick campus, so once a week she'd trudge to the other side of town, leaving KD with her great-grandmother, XC's mother, who lived in Coogee. When the class was over, she'd collect KD and schlep all the way back to MMC's in Wheeler Heights.

'It was worth it. I topped the subject,' JC told me proudly. 'And in biology I came fifth in the state. In my HSC,' she tells me for comparison, 'I got 33 per cent.'

Once JC was finished with TAFE she enrolled at Macquarie University and after she finished her psychology degree she started working at the refuge, where she stayed for many years. Apart from her part-time job at Coles during high school, it was the only job she'd had and leaving wasn't easy, but it was also a part of everything she'd been through and it was time to move on. Now she's in a workplace that is free of anything to do with MMC or Chris or domestic violence.

'I work hard. They treat me well. I go home happy,' she told me chirpily. She's doing other things that she missed out on, especially travelling. Every couple of years she goes overseas –where as she told me in one of our first chats over coffee, no one knows her.

JC and I most often met at the beach. One day, as I approached the café, I could see her waiting on the corner outside. It was easy to spot her loose blonde hair, and when she caught sight of me, she broke into a joyful smile and gave me a hug.

On the southern side of the beach, a stand of Norfolk pines marks the spot where Chris had parked his car over thirty years ago and confessed his feelings to sixteen-year-old JC. MMC lives nearby, and although JC doesn't visit her, she sees her occasionally at family functions. Also close by is the apartment where RN assaulted her. And not far away is the beautiful home where Lynette devoted herself to her daughters and to her husband. All reminders. It was a stomping ground that contained so much pain and I wondered why JC stayed.

'It's safe,' she explained. I was surprised by that, because so many bad things in her life had happened there in a pretty tight radius. I'd also been surprised when she told me that she and Chris had turned back at the Queensland border because she wanted to go home, even though she had no home to go to. I remember her telling me when we had our first conversation about Lynette that, 'whenever something like *this* comes up, they always drag me out,' and I imagine that if she were living in a state other than New South Wales, she wouldn't feel this so keenly. Still, being in Queensland with Chris was one of the worst periods in her life, and I could understand that by comparison, it was safe here. Now, KD and her husband and their two children live nearby, and JC is a doting and very involved grandmother.

In 2011, Damian submitted another brief to the DPP and for the third time they declined to prosecute the case. Damian was moved from The Rocks to central command, near Chinatown. I met him for coffee a couple of times after he'd moved but I didn't like the heavy traffic and construction noise at that end of town. Neither did he.

'I've worked on this matter since 1998,' he told me in late 2012. 'I was lying in bed the other night thinking of the jury coming out. I was trying to think how I'd feel if it was guilty. I think I'd break down. I'm tired.' Like Greg, I could hear his weary hope for a resolution.

The following week I was heading out early for a swim when a friend rang. It was about Barb Kilpatrick, who had started the refuge.

'Barb's been found dead,' she said, sounding distressed. 'It's just awful. I'm not sure if JC would know. Do you think you could call her?'

JC hadn't been in touch with Barb for a few years. Still, Barb had been a mother figure to JC for most of her life, and I was afraid she'd take the news badly. I rang her straightaway and as always, she was stronger than I gave her credit for.

Barb's funeral was held at St Kieran's, a hexagonal 1970s blond-brick church in Manly Vale. It was a beautiful autumn day. The crowd spilled across the church's driveway and pressed up against the black hearse in the forecourt. JC was there with KD, who had a pram, and I could see her chatting to one of Barb's children. People from our time at the refuge were there, which must have brought back a lot of memories, and I admired JC again for doing what was right, instead of what was easy.

Inside, I sat next to the friend who'd rung me with the news of Barb's death. Along the walls, people stood two-deep, and others blocked the doorways, trying to get inside. Barb had been a towering figure in a mostly clandestine world. She worked in the intimate space of women, children and family, but she was well known in so many communities. Her funeral was attended by people from the refuge movement, police and politicians, as well as her five children, grandchildren, and many, many friends, including MMC. For every woman that Barb had helped, others in the community benefited, especially children. She devoted over half of her life to helping women in need but I still found it strange that she couldn't help JC more when she needed it most. I could see JC on the other side of the church and I wondered if things would have turned out differently if Barb had helped her more. I wished too that Lynette could have somehow found her way to Barb.

One day, after getting our takeaways from JC's favourite café, she and I walked north through the park that leads onto Dee Why Lagoon, a wetlands and wildlife refuge. We sat on a weather-beaten wooden bench and laughed as we took stock of our ballooning middle-aged ailments. JC is such easy company – funny, warm and interested in other people and ideas. Despite everything she's been through, she has determinedly, and remarkably, made a better life for herself and KD, and now for her grandchildren. She thinks that she wouldn't have left Chris if she hadn't had KD, because she would never have known how much she could love her own child. Since KD was born, everything has been about being the best mother she could be.

'I tell KD every day that I love her,' she said to me.

PART
FOUR

CHAPTER SIXTEEN

A podcast takes form

IN SEPTEMBER 2017, I THOUGHT I HAD FINISHED WRITING THIS BOOK. I was going to Melbourne, to see Shakespeare's Pop-up Globe. As I was about to scan my boarding pass, my mobile phone rang. 'Hi, Rebecca. It's Hedley Thomas. I'm not sure if you remember me?'

I'd only spoken to Hedley once before but he called me that day with a bold plan: he was going to make a podcast about Lynette Dawson and was hoping that I would help.

I had accumulated a folder of articles about Lynette Dawson's disappearance in the course of researching this book. In 2001 Hedley Thomas had written a lengthy article in the *Courier-Mail* about the inquest into Lynette's disappearance. His article stood out from the others. It was the human loss at the centre of this story that he got right, so I contacted him as part of my book research. He didn't have any further leads about Lynette's disappearance but he told me, 'It will be a great book.' He must have meant that because a few years later, in 2017, when Hedley was working for the *Australian*, he decided to take a right-hand turn away from print journalism and make a podcast about Lynette's disappearance. He told me that I was the first person he rang.

When I got back from Melbourne, Hedley suggested we meet for lunch at Icebergs restaurant overlooking Bondi Beach. Business lunches at Icebergs can be a power move, so I was wary, but over lunch we got on well and I decided to take a risk with a guy I knew little about, and who had never made a podcast.

I was in.

Not much had happened on Lynette's matter in the previous few years. In December 2014 Damian sent me an email in which he told me he was working on another brief to go to the DPP. 'This is my last go. I would like to think I've given it my best.' He hoped that Lynette's family understood that 'if the DPP elects not to proceed then I've done as much as I possibly could'. But in 2015, before Damian finalised the brief, Lynette's file was transferred to NSW Police Force Unsolved Homicide Unit and a reinvestigation began. Still, by mid-2016, Greg told me by email, 'Nothing happening on the Lyn front.'

In September 2017, just after Hedley and I spoke, Hedley rang Greg and pitched his idea of making a podcast about Lynette's disappearance. Greg was keen to give it a go, in the hope that a podcast might bring renewed interest in Lynette's disappearance and a breakthrough in the case.

A week or two after our lunch, I picked Hedley up from Newcastle Airport and drove to Greg and Merilyn Simms's place. Greg and Merilyn repeated the stories they had told me. Greg was the keeper of all that had happened since Lynette disappeared, and as we sat in their cosy lounge room, I wondered how many times he had repeated these stories in the thirty-six years since Lynette disappeared.

That summer of 2017–18 was one of the hottest on record. Hedley and I spent long and exhausting days in my car. We interviewed members of Lynette's family and her work colleagues, the retired deputy principal from Cromer High School, two past New South Wales coroners, a retired policeman and many, many others. Behind the scenes, Hedley worked the voodoo that journalists do, to locate people and to convince them to speak to him for inclusion in the podcast. With each interview, we magnified each piece of evidence, and later, we spent hours on the phone dissecting it further. It often felt like we were the only native speakers of a language that no one else understood. We mapped dates and places, and we knew the details of so many people connected to Lynette's disappearance and how they fitted into the big picture.

I was only a casual podcast listener, but I could tell that something special was coming together. When I told Hedley that I thought it was going to be the most successful podcast in Australian podcasting history, it made him visibly anxious. Hedley thrives on the pressure of filing a news story every day and it unnerved him that he had been working on the podcast for six months and no episodes had been released. In early May 2018, he rang to say that he was going to release the first episode of *The Teacher's Pet*, even though only three were finished. I asked him if he was nuts.

On the day that the first episode was released, Hedley and I were fretful. Early on, the analytics recorded three downloads, and two of them were mine. But soon the downloads were off the chart. As each episode aired, Hedley invited anyone with information about Lynette's disappearance to contact him. A tsunami arrived and kept on coming. It seemed like truth serum had been released into Sydney's drinking water. 'If I was writing this in the newspaper,' Hedley told me, 'people wouldn't be contacting me. It's the medium; they can hear me.'

The Teacher's Pet quickly became something that had never been seen in Australia. Hedley recruited other journalists to fact-check information, to follow up leads and to write follow-up pieces for the *Australian* newspaper. Producing a weekly episode was a seventeen-hour-a-day, seven-day-a-week undertaking. Everything else in Hedley's life was put on hold.

The Teacher's Pet became part of news cycles and conversations. Lynette's family and friends, who had fought for so long to keep Lynette's disappearance in the news in the hope that a new lead would emerge, were suddenly overwhelmed by the avalanche of information and by media requests for interviews. The phenomenon knocked on to the police, who were under pressure to answer questions about their investigations into Lynette's disappearance. Hedley was shining a light on Lynette's disappearance, but as the podcast progressed, the scope widened to include the culture of teachers across the Northern Beaches who preyed on their students. Now in their fifties, those students wanted to tell their stories. To many, Hedley's warm voice felt like they were already in a conversation with him.

Of all the interviews, it was the one Hedley and I did with Lynette's older brother Philip that has stayed with me. We interviewed Philip on our first day, just after we'd seen Greg and Merilyn. Philip lived with his wife, Linda, only a 20-minute drive from Greg and Merilyn, but they were uncertain about when they'd last seen him, although they knew that his health was not good. I knew that there was an undercurrent of disconnection. Over the years, in indirect ways, I'd asked Greg and Pat about Philip. In an email, Pat had told me she blamed herself for Philip not being 'included' in the decades-long publicity campaign to keep Lynette's disappearance alive.

Philip Simms was a retired engineer: self-contained and softly spoken. Philip's wife, Linda, was more outgoing, and she watched over Philip throughout the interview, as if there was something fragile about him that needed protecting. Like everyone who knew Lynette, Philip said that she would never have left her children. 'She just wouldn't. She adored them.'

Philip was measured and gentle but there was also a hint of control. As the interview progressed, it was clear that he was struggling to manage his distress. Linda was nearby but Philip sat alone on the sofa and determinedly gave a full account to all of our questions.

'I believe she's on the block,' he told us, even though we hadn't asked and would never have asked that question.

'I believe she was initially buried where the soil had been excavated for the swimming pool. It was the easiest place because that area was excavated already. Then some time in the next few days, they moved her again. That's what I've always thought. I'll take it to my grave.

'If this bloke put rock over the top of her, they'll never find her. If we won Lotto, Greg and I said we'd buy the house at Bayview and demolish it. I'd get permission from the Parks and Wildlife people and bring a digger through the back of the block. I'd pull all of the material back down to neutral surface. Ground-penetrating radar would then find her.'

Philip's lips quivered as he described his reasoned and brutal plan. There wasn't much that I didn't know or hadn't read about Lynette's disappearance – digs, sniffer dogs, doomed hope that she might return – but still I found what Philip told us confronting. Specific and unsparing, these were the thoughts that he had lived with.

Before we left, I walked around the lounge room looking at Philip and Linda's extraordinary art collection. The reasons for his estrangement from Pat and Greg remained elusive but it was clear that he had struggled with a deep grief over Lynette's disappearance without his siblings.

When the last episode of *The Teacher's Pet* was released in August 2018, it had more than 18.6 million downloads. Other podcasts had achieved success but *The Teacher's Pet* became a cultural touchstone.

But it wasn't quite finished.

On 12 September 2018, jackhammers and concrete-cutters descended on Gilwinga Drive and disturbed the peace that had returned to the residents after the podcast finished. The previous digs were conducted discreetly, but following the podcast, a discomfitting public excitement took hold around the site. Sightseer cars and television broadcast vans blocked the street, on the evening news journalists reported from the bottom of the steep driveway, helicopters flew overhead. Greg, Merilyn, Pat and Phil endured another brutal dig to look for Lynette, as well as invasive and often inappropriate public interest.

But after five days of digging and sifting, nothing was found. The diggers and police in dark blue field uniforms packed up, and the journalists and media vans pulled out of Gilwinga Drive. Lynette's family were again left with nothing. When I spoke to Greg and

Merilyn a few days later, they said that they were trying to remain hopeful, but I could hear that hope was some way off yet.

Hedley and I spoke less often but the intensity of what we'd been through stayed with us. There was a winding down, as if we needed to wean ourselves off each other.

My book – covering the decades following Lynette's disappearance and before the podcast had picked up the story – was due to be printed and in bookshops in time for Christmas. I was excited and full of anticipation about its release.

CHAPTER SEVENTEEN

Charged with murder

ON WEDNESDAY 5 DECEMBER 2018, I WAS HEADING HOME FROM AN early morning walk. As I passed South Steyne Surf Club, a flurry of text message pings interrupted the podcast I was listening to. *Ping, ping, ping, ping.*

After *The Teacher's Pet* had finished, and following the dig in September, there was anticipation that charges would follow. It was a rare day that anyone would ring or text me so early, so when my phone lit up that morning, I guessed immediately what had happened.

By the time I got home, the news that Chris Dawson had been arrested had rocketed around Australia. Every radio news bulletin led with the story and every television breakfast show aired footage of the moment he was arrested in Queensland. Wearing shorts and thongs, Chris Dawson was shepherded through the carport of a modest weatherboard house with detectives behind him and one on either side. At the open door of an unmarked police car, he bent forward with a hand on each thigh, seemingly overcome. After thirty-six years, he might reasonably have thought this moment would never come.

Detective Senior Constable Daniel Poole had rung Greg and Merilyn Simms just after the arrest to tell them the news. I hadn't heard of Daniel Poole before but I was keen to understand his work and the evidence that had led to Chris Dawson's arrest. A few hours later, Greg and Merilyn rang me. They were aware that the murder charges might affect the publication of my book. I was amazed and possibly a bit embarrassed that in the midst of this momentous event they had thought of me.

Then New South Wales Police Commissioner Mick Fuller held a press conference. The police had been criticised for not doing enough; now, he was going to make sure they took the credit. He wore his full police uniform and two plain-clothes detectives stood behind him.

'Can I thank the public and the media for the partnership in solving this matter. While New South Wales police since 2015 has worked tirelessly, I recognise that it is an important and ongoing relationship not just for solving this crime but many, many other crimes,' he said.

By thanking the media in 'partnership' with the police, the New South Wales police commissioner had elevated podcasting from entertainment to investigative journalism. But it was not clear what the 'tireless' work was. When the September dig at Bayview failed to turn up anything, it seemed that without physical evidence, charges would never be made. It appeared that the police investigation into Lynette's disappearance had reached the end of the road. What had happened in the four weeks between the end of the dig and charges being laid? What new evidence had come to light? Were the charges no more than a public relations exercise?

Chris Dawson was brought before a Queensland magistrate that day, as required by law. A sketch in the *Australian*[16] depicted him in court with his elbows on his knees and his hands over his ears, while the murder charge was read out to the court. Police applied to extradite him from Queensland to New South Wales. After a night in the Southport watchhouse, he was extradited to Sydney by plane, still wearing the same shorts and thongs. Photos emerged of him looking disconsolately out the window, with Detective Senior Constable Daniel Poole beside him. Anyone with a mobile phone was a press photographer now.

In Sydney, he was driven to Surry Hills Police Centre and charged with murder. Later that day, the criminal lawyer Greg Walsh spoke to the media from the forecourt of Sydney Central Local Court, with its grand sandstone balustrade behind him. Wearing a well-cut suit and glasses with transparent frames, he made his first, and somewhat softly spoken, defence of his client. 'His brother came and saw me, who is a solicitor, and I was given a huge amount of material, so I worked most of the night and today to try and read as much as I can, but it's a very important application for bail and it's an important charge against him, and it has to be prepared properly. There's no point in rushing cases like this.'[17]

Bail was slow coming. In New South Wales, bail conditions include where the accused will live, how often they are required to report to police, and a security is often required, particularly for serious offences. There had been rumours while the podcast aired that Chris Dawson had separated from his third wife. Now there was speculation that she was unwilling to have their house used as security. On 24 December, nearly three weeks after he was arrested, a $1.5 million security was obtained and Chris Dawson was released on bail and made it home in time for Christmas.

Hedley Thomas had gone overseas with his family for a holiday. In Berlin one night, he snuck into the hallway to phone me so that he wouldn't wake his family. Years before, I had come across a document that may have had a bearing on the case and we decided that I should let the police know about it. The next day, I rang Detective Senior Constable Daniel Poole.

'Hi Daniel. It's Rebecca Hazel. I'm not sure if you know me?'

It was a complex investigation, and Daniel Poole didn't so much as pause when I told him my name. 'I know who you are,' he said.

I told him about the document in my possession. 'I'm aware of it,' he said. I felt that it was my civic duty to let him know about the document and I felt relieved to have done my part. I thought that would be the extent of my involvement. But the next day while I was shopping in Coles, my husband rang to say that two detectives had just been to the house. A few hours later they came back, and I sat with them at my kitchen table.

The detectives asked me if I was prepared to make a statement, which of course I was. Was I also willing to produce the material I had accumulated while writing this book – interview notes, newspaper clippings, emails, text messages, every draft and the final manuscript, as it then was – as well as anything relating to *The Teacher's Pet*? Before I could say yes, they said that it could all be subpoenaed. They might have thought I would object, but I didn't regard myself as a journalist.

Hedley was asked to do the same, as well as all of the audio for *The Teacher's Pet* – not just each episode but all the unedited interviews, including the recordings of Hedley and me as we tooled around together in the early months, when we didn't really know what we were doing and we mostly forgot the audio guy sitting silently in the back seat of my car, recording everything we said. Chris Dawson's solicitor, Greg Walsh, also subpoenaed material from each of us.

PART FIVE

CHAPTER EIGHTEEN

The slow wheels of justice

IN NEW SOUTH WALES, MURDER TRIALS BEGIN IN THE LOCAL COURT. The Downing Centre Local Court in Sydney is housed in the original 1909 building of what had once been the Mark Foy's department store. The building ostentatiously takes up a large city block, and from its marble entrance, Chris Dawson's solicitor, Greg Walsh, gave fired-up, post-court media stops for his client. At each appearance, his tone of indignation on behalf of his client escalated, perhaps evocative of the saying that a confident person has 'more front than Mark Foy's'. Also there were Chris Dawson with his brother Peter, loitering 3 metres behind Greg Walsh and wearing dark sunglasses.

At a first court mention (when a case is first brought up in a court of law) in a criminal matter, the accused attends court, usually with their lawyer, and enters a plea of guilty or not guilty; or the prosecution lays out the precise charges. Court processes are complicated and legal language can be impenetrable. Often the first mention is also the first time an accused person has been inside a court room – they are uncertain, overwhelmed. At Chris Dawson's first mention in February 2019, he wore his sunglasses inside the court room and his brother Peter was again by his side. Tall, tanned and upright, Chris Dawson moved like a man used to being observed. He stood with his brother against the back wall, not seated near his solicitor as other clients generally were, which gave an impression of arrogance. The Dawson brothers weren't deferential to anyone, including the law. Greg Walsh, meanwhile, had joined the line of solicitors shuffling forward to mention his client's matter and get directions from the magistrate. He chatted happily to colleagues.

Crown Prosecutor Craig Everson told Magistrate Megan Greenwood that the DPP was 'struggling' to gather and organise the brief of evidence – the evidence the Crown would rely on to prove the charge of murder, which already included 4500 pages and 100GB of audio. The word 'unprecedented' was heard at every stage of the proceedings. Magistrate Greenwood extended the deadline for the brief of evidence to be served on Chris Dawson to 9 May 2019. When the mention was over, journalists and photographers gathered on the steps of the courthouse. Greg Walsh emerged and addressed the media. Chris and Peter Dawson fell back a discreet 3 metres behind him. Notably absent was Chris Dawson's wife.

Greg Walsh eloquently laid out Chris Dawson's defence to the media: that memories of events that occurred thirty-six years ago are unreliable, and *The Teacher's Pet* had contaminated memories even further and also prejudiced potential jurors. He said, 'Human memory is a reconstructive process – so what a person learns from others, what they read, what they discuss, can all become encoded in their memory. I think it's a matter of common sense that the risk of contamination is a very real one in the context of modern communications as well.'[18]

In a move he may later have regretted, Greg Walsh mentioned the diaries of Lynette's mother, Helena Simms. 'We have now been provided with the actual hand-written copies of the diary and they are very significant. That type of evidence is critical in a case like this, it helps my client significantly.'[19]

The next stage was the committal hearing. A committal hearing determines if the evidence to be relied on by the prosecution is sufficient for the matter to proceed to the next stage.

The witnesses who gave evidence at Chris Dawson's committal hearing were an incongruous bunch. The court heard from Debbie Malone, the psychic who had contacted Damian Loone in 2003. Ms Malone told the court that through clairvoyance, Lynette Dawson had told her that she was dead and also where she was buried.

The final three witnesses gave conventional evidence of seeing Lynette after she had disappeared on 9 January 1982. Chris Dawson's brother-in-law, Ross Hutcheon, said that three to six months after Lynette disappeared, he saw her standing on the side of the road. Jill and Peter Breese were former neighbours of Lynette and Chris Dawson and they told the court that they saw Lynette working as a nurse at Rockcastle Hospital six to eighteen months after Lynette disappeared. Neither Ross Hutcheon nor the Breeses spoke to Lynette.

Crown Prosecutor Craig Everson asked the magistrate to commit Chris Dawson to trial. Chris Dawson was seated in the front row of the public gallery. The magistrate asked him to stand and formally ordered him to stand trial for the murder of Lynette Dawson in the New South Wales Supreme Court.

A few hours after Chris Dawson was committed to stand trial for murder, he was charged with the historical sex offence of carnal knowledge by a teacher of a student between the ages of ten and seventeen years. In 2019 sexual offences no longer used this language. But Chris Dawson was charged with the offence as it existed in 1980, at the time when he was alleged to have committed it. It is a serious crime, punishable by up to fourteen years in jail.

Chris Dawson's first appearance in the New South Wales Supreme Court was like every appearance he made in the magistrate's court – that is, it was unprecedented. On 11 March 2020 the World Health Organization declared COVID-19 a pandemic. On 30 March 2020 New South Wales residents were ordered into lockdown and for a while, the court system shut down. Chris Dawson was at home in Queensland, where there were relatively few restrictions. Lynette's progress was slowed down again.

Chris Dawson made his first appearance in the New South Wales Supreme Court on 3 April 2020 from Queensland via videolink – a practice that was introduced to accommodate the pandemic – and he formally entered a plea of not guilty to the charge of murder. He applied to the Supreme Court to make an order to stay, or stop, proceedings because the prosecution was 'irredeemably unfair'.

He cited three reasons: an incompetent police investigation, the thirty-six-year delay in prosecuting the case and the 'contamination and collusion of evidence'.

In July 2020, the stay application was heard in the Supreme Court. Phillip Boulten SC was the barrister representing Chris Dawson. Five witnesses whom Phillip Boulten had removed from the witness list at the committal hearing would be called to give evidence. By agreement with the prosecution, the defence called me as a witness.

A severe weather system drenched Sydney on the day that I gave evidence. By the time I got to the Supreme Court building on Phillip Street, near St James railway station in the Sydney CBD, I was wet, but in the way of courts I had time to dry out while I waited to be called to give evidence. COVID-19 restrictions had emptied the usually busy pale-wood-panelled corridors and the closed courtroom doors seemed to have hermetically silenced the proceedings inside.

Detective Senior Constable Daniel Poole came to say hello. We had spoken on the phone several times by then, but this was the first time we'd met, although I knew what he looked like from the footage of Chris Dawson's arrest.

The courtroom door opened and then quickly shut but I immediately recognised Damian Loone's voice. I had not considered that he would give evidence, but it was lovely that I would get to say hi as he left and I came into the courtroom. I recalled our conversation about the possibility of Chris Dawson ever facing a trial. Damian hadn't committed either way, but nor had he been prepared to say 'never'.

A court attendant opened the door and bowed to the judge and came over to me. 'Would you like an affirmation or an oath?' A few minutes later, when I was called in, I realised that Damian had given evidence remotely.

The judge had left the bench for a few minutes. I sat down and looked around the room. Everyone except me and the lawyers wore a blue COVID-19 mask. I was seated only 10 metres or so from Greg Walsh, and Chris and Peter Dawson.

Chris Dawson knew I had been writing a book and by now I presumed he would have read my manuscript, which his defence team had subpoenaed. My eyes settled on him and for a few seconds he held my gaze, and what I saw looking back at me was red-faced hatred. I was unperturbed and in that fleeting eye contact I thought, 'You are here because you have some questions to answer.' He thought he was here because of Hedley and me.

Phillip Boulten SC has a formidable reputation as a barrister so I was curious to see him in action. He began with simple questions. How did I meet JC? What were the financial arrangements I had with her? I agreed with the question he put to me that, on balance, I thought that Chris Dawson had murdered his wife Lynette when I set out to write my book. Then he moved on to the real reason he'd called me as a witness: to show that Hedley Thomas, through *The Teacher's Pet*, had depicted Chris Dawson as a murderer. Who had I introduced Hedley to? Was I present when Hedley conducted interviews?

The defence had called Hedley and me as witnesses to support Chris Dawson's argument that he could not get a fair trial and the court, therefore, should allow the stay application and stop the trial. Courts are loath to grant stay applications because only a full trial can weigh all of the evidence. The judge presiding over the stay application hearing, Justice Fullerton, allowed it in part by ordering that the trial should not commence before June 2021, to give time for any prejudice created in the minds of potential jurors by *The Teacher's Pet* to fade. Justice Fullerton also made a non-publication order which prohibited the media from reporting on the stay application decision.

The non-publication order meant that my evidence was essentially given in a vacuum. I was unperturbed when I was giving evidence, but later that day and in the days that followed, I became distressed. I knew that the police, the prosecutors and the defence team had all read my notes and emails and had also listened to *The Teacher's Pet*, including all of the audio of Hedley and me discussing things in the early days. In court, Phillip Boulten SC had projected a couple of my emails and pages of my notes onto a large screen, and when I went over my evidence in the hours and days that followed, the invasive reality that so many people had scrawled through my documents filled me with shame. I also felt that I had disappointed everyone. Our legal system is adversarial – that is, a contest between two sides, to reveal the truth to a judge or to a jury. Witnesses are in the middle of the contest, and it can be a brutal experience.

Hedley Thomas and I are very different people but I still thought that he was the only person who would understand my upset after I had given evidence. When we spoke a day or so later, Hedley reported feeling more anxious before he gave evidence. In the stand, Phillip Boulten turned up the heat on Hedley, who was well prepared and bellicose in reply.

Had Chris Dawson been charged while the podcast was being aired, Justice Fullerton said, 'a number of individuals and publishers would inevitably have been found liable and likely convicted of a criminal contempt'.[20] And although Chris Dawson had not been charged with murder while the podcast aired, she said that it was a fact 'that all media interests were well aware that question was under active consideration by the [Office of the] DPP'.[21] To some extent, it felt like a circular argument. The DPP had declined to prosecute Chris Dawson before – twice after the coronial inquests in 2001 and 2003, and in 2011 after Damian had submitted another brief – so the most likely outcome was that they would decline again. When the DPP made the decision to prosecute Chris Dawson in late 2018, it appeared that it was the podcast that had forced their hand. On the other hand, Daniel Poole is an exceptional detective, and his brief had gone to the DPP in April 2018, a month before the first episode of *The Teacher's Pet* was released.

Justice Fullerton allowed Chris Dawson's stay application in part by ordering the trial to be delayed but Chris Dawson wanted her to permanently stay, that is to stop, the proceedings. Dawson appealed the decision to the New South Wales Court of Criminal Appeal. On 11 June 2021, the Court of Criminal Appeal refused the appeal. He appealed the Court of Criminal Appeal decision to the High Court of Australia. On 8 April 2022 the High Court refused to hear the appeal of the Court of Criminal Appeal decision. With all of his options exhausted, Chris Dawson was now facing a murder trial, due to begin on 9 May 2022.

CHAPTER NINETEEN

The murder trial

MURDER AND OTHER SERIOUS INDICTABLE OFFENCES ARE HEARD BY a jury. But a week before Dawson's trial got underway on 9 May 2022, he asked the Supreme Court to make an order that his trial be heard by a judge alone. He argued that *The Teacher's Pet* was so prejudicial that he could not receive a fair trial with a jury.

Supreme Court Chief Justice Beech-Jones, who presided over the application, agreed. He said, 'The nature of the podcast and its extremely wide distribution raises real concerns about the fairness of a trial before a jury that might include persons who had heard, or at least heard of, the podcast or the associated publicity.'[22] He made an order for Chris Dawson to have a 'trial by judge' alone.

In doing so, Chief Justice Beech-Jones singled out the 'extraordinary feature' of three senior public officials voicing their opinions of 'the accused's guilt' in *The Teacher's Pet* podcast[23] – namely, then

New South Wales Commissioner of Police Mick Fuller; former Deputy State Coroner Carl Milovanovich; and retired magistrate Jeff Linden, who was formerly a solicitor and had acted for Chris Dawson in 1983, when Dawson divorced Lynette so that he could marry JC.

I had been surprised when Carl Milovanovich and Jeff Linden readily and openly spoke to me for the research for this book, but I was even more surprised that they spoke to Hedley Thomas a few years later, knowing that parts of their recorded interview would be included in *The Teacher's Pet*. Why the then New South Wales Commissioner of Police, Mick Fuller, spoke to Hedley is unclear.

Monday, 9 May 2022. Three and a half years after Chris Dawson was charged with murder, the trial began. After forty years, Lynette was finally having her day in court.

I arrived early and took the lift to level 9. I expected a crush of spectators, but the corridors were empty. A few unhurried court attendants settled papers and checked the audiovisual link.

Craig Everson SC and the prosecution team arrived first. I'd met Craig in 2020 when I was called as a witness in the stay application hearing. He'd invited me to the DPP to discuss the stay application procedure and his colleague Emma Blizzard had joined us. Emma said nothing throughout the meeting. She leaned towards me with her forearms on the table and looked at me with what felt like a penetrating and sceptical eye, as if to test me as a witness under pressure.

Several floors below, Chris and Peter Dawson made their way through the crush of media up the stairs and into the Supreme Court building.

'Are you pleased to be getting underway?' a journalist asked.

'Very pleased,' Chris Dawson replied with unconvincing bravado. When he entered the courtroom a few minutes later, I felt I saw dread behind his blue COVID mask.

At 9.30 am Justice Ian Harrison, the judge who would hear the case, appeared. Everyone stood and bowed, and like a swimmer diving off their block, he launched into the trial.

The prosecution and the defence made a joint application for a suppression order over the entire trial. A suppression order prohibits the publication or dissemination of information in any way, which in Chris Dawson's murder trial would mean the media would be unable to report on the trial or even report that the trial was underway. The issue was that in June 2019 Chris Dawson had been charged with the historical offence of carnal knowledge of a seventeen-year-old student when he was her teacher, and that trial was due to start in the District Court in a few months' time. The Crown and the defence argued that a suppression order over the entire murder trial was needed to ensure that witnesses in the carnal knowledge trial would not be influenced by evidence in the murder trial. Both sides wanted the suppression order to include the audiovisual coverage of the trial because some witnesses might watch the trial remotely.

'Who are these witnesses?' Justice Harrison asked tersely. I was surprised to hear Craig Everson mention my name. As far I knew, I was not going to be called as a witness.

Dauid Sibtain SC argued against a suppression order. I'd seen Mr Sibtain act for the *Australian* before. On this occasion he was representing several media intervenors – that is, clients who were not party to the proceedings but who wanted to be heard. Justice Harrison summarised Mr Sibtain's argument that Chris Dawson had already lost his right to a fair trial in the District Court 'by reason of the extensive, uncensored and egregious publicity'.[24] It was a bold argument from Mr Sibtain because the 'egregious publicity' was the podcast *The Teacher's Pet*, produced and published by the *Australian*, who he was representing in court. To underscore the size of the horse that had already bolted, Mr Sibtain submitted an affidavit that noted that an internet search for 'Chris Dawson murder' produced several million results. Justice Harrison refused to grant a suppression order noting that it would 'simply make no difference'.[25]

Justice Harrison's decision had an interesting domino effect. It meant that the suppression order over Justice Fullerton's 2020 decision to temporarily stay the murder trial until after June 2021 could now also be lifted.

Arguing the defence's case for a suppression order was Pauline David, who had replaced Phillip Boulten SC as Chris Dawson's barrister. No sooner had Justice Harrison denied the application for the suppression order, Pauline David was on her feet again, asking for more time to prepare the defence case, including conferring with Chris Dawson, who, she told the court, was now in Sydney until the trial was over. Justice Harrison was visibly annoyed by the request. It had been four years since the defendant was charged, he curtly reminded the court, and the issues before the court should not be delayed any longer. Justice Harrison ordered the Crown to make their opening statement.

Craig Everson told the court the story began when Lynette and Chris Dawson met as teenagers, fell in love and later married.

Two children followed. It was an everyday story until 1980, when Chris Dawson groomed and lured a schoolgirl into a sexual relationship. By January 1982, Chris Dawson's infatuation with the schoolgirl had become an obsession, and he murdered his wife Lynette so that he could have what Craig Everson called an, 'unfettered relationship' with the schoolgirl. 'The Crown alleges that on or about the 8th of January 1982 the accused alone or with the involvement of another person murdered Lynette Dawson.'

A day or so later, I was in court with two friends from Melbourne. One was a judge, the other a barrister who is now a judge too. Craig Everson came over. 'I don't want to embarrass you, Rebecca, but there will be argument about the defence wanting to cross-examine you. You will be asked to leave.'

When proceedings got underway, discussion about witnesses, including me, went back and forth between the Crown, the defence and Justice Harrison, just as Craig Everson had said. It was pointless waiting for them to tell me to leave. I put my notebook away, put on my rain jacket because Sydney was beset by another deluge, and left the courtroom.

Hedley Thomas and I had dismissed the idea that we would be called as witnesses in the murder trial. At the stay application in 2020, the defence hoped that my evidence would help prove three things: that I had included JC's supposed lies in the book I'd written, to help sell more copies; that my notes of interviews with Damian Loone were evidence of a biased police investigation; and that Hedley and I had cooked up a fantastic story for *The Teacher's Pet* to ensure that the podcast was a success. But the murder trial was about what happened to Lynette in 1982. Hedley learned of Lynette's disappearance and suspected murder twenty years after she disappeared. I first heard about Lynette from JC, twenty-five years after she disappeared. Perhaps witnesses we interviewed had given different accounts over the years, but if that was the case, the best person to ask about that was the witness. We were annoyed that we were locked out of the courtroom, and we doubted that either of us would in fact be called to give evidence.

As potential witnesses, we tried to avoid media coverage of the trial, but it wasn't easy. Print, radio, television and social media were saturated with news of the trial.

Then, seven weeks into the trial, Hedley and I were called as witnesses. I spent the weekend fretting, fearing a repeat of how I'd felt after the stay application, or even worse. Reporting on the stay application had been suppressed, but this time it was likely that my evidence would be reported in the media.

Upstairs in the Supreme Court building, I waited alone outside the courtroom until I was called to give evidence.

The courtroom was quiet – not even a ruffle of paper from the volumes of documents on the bar tables and the bench. Everyone was wearing a mask except the lawyers, the judge and me. I felt very little when I looked at the judge while I gave my affirmation.

Pauline David suggested to me that JC had cooperated with me because I had offered to give her some money from the sales of my book. I told her that we never discussed money until I'd just finished writing the final draft of the manuscript. When questioned by Pauline David, I agreed that my book might sell more copies because of my involvement in *The Teacher's Pet*. I agreed that JC had used the term 'sex slave' and that she also told me that Chris Dawson chose clothes for her to wear.

Craig Everson SC objected several times to the relevance of the questions.

Two days later I was sworn in again and the questions and their relevance continued. The journalist David Murray was in court, and he described my head bouncing between the bar table and the bench as if I was watching a tennis match. In the end, it seemed to me that Pauline David gave up questioning me rather than finished.

Pauline David's main attack on Hedley Thomas was that he had recklessly interfered with witness evidence. Hedley was in the witness stand for two days. It was almost irrelevant what Justice Harrison thought of him and the allegations put to him. The real test was how Justice Harrison assessed the evidence of the witnesses who the defence claimed were unreliable because of Hedley.

A few days after Hedley gave evidence, my son and I took a road trip to western New South Wales. I drove across flat wheat plains and my son brought up playlists of his favourite music. We didn't listen to the radio, watch the news, or read a newspaper. We bushwalked and at night looked at stars, but it was the slow red, pink, then grey sunsets that we liked best. By the time we got back to Sydney, the trial was nearly finished.

I went to court to hear final submissions. Craig Everson SC delivered the Crown's closing submissions with the same metronomic clarity he had sustained throughout the trial. Pauline David struggled with closing submissions for the defence – Justice Harrison commented that her submissions 'had become like a pinball' and were 'all over the shop'.[26]

She told the court that Chris Dawson could have loved Lynette and JC at the same time. On the other hand, she urged Justice Harrison to reject JC's evidence that Chris Dawson had groomed her. Justice Harrison immediately asked if Chris Dawson had utilised his position to take advantage of a person who he did care about. Justice Harrison wanted to know when Chris Dawson and JC resumed a sexual relationship after Lynette disappeared. Pauline David said it wasn't clear but they were not in a committed relationship for some time. Unsatisfied with this response, Justice Harrison replied, 'Anyway, I've asked the question.'[27]

It was an important question. The Crown's case was that Chris Dawson murdered Lynette to have an unfettered sexual relationship with JC, which he achieved within a few days of Lynette's disappearance. Justice Harrison asked Pauline David to tell him what was wrong with the Crown's case. 'I want you to help me, that's basically what I'm saying.'[28] The court's role is to find the truth through contesting arguments. The Crown had presented one argument and Justice Harrison wanted Pauline David to present an opposing one. It was Friday afternoon and he told her to take the weekend to prepare that.

When court resumed on Monday, Justice Harrison suggested to Pauline David that it was a good opportunity, in fact it was the last opportunity, for the defence to present a reasonable hypothesis about what might have happened to Lynette Dawson. In a circumstantial case, the Crown has to prove beyond reasonable doubt that Chris Dawson murdered Lynette and that it is the only inference that can be drawn from the evidence. If the defence could present a rational alternative hypothesis of what could have happened to Lynette, then Chris Dawson would be acquitted.

Pauline David told the court that one alternative hypothesis could be that Lynette killed herself. Justice Harrison gave the same response that Carl Milovanovich, as the coroner at the 2003 inquest, had given to the idea many years before: that it would have been difficult for Lynette to kill herself and then dispose of her own body. In lieu of that, the defence submission was that they simply did not know what had happened to Lynette Dawson.

Just after midday on Monday, 11 July 2022, Justice Harrison said to the few of us still in the courtroom that he wouldn't take long before he would deliver his judgment. 'Not by tomorrow, I can assure you, but relatively quickly.'[29]

In court, there was collective exhaustion. Craig Everson looked tired but happy.

Greg Walsh packed his books and files in his roller bag and was keen to leave. Rumours had swirled throughout the trial about the lack of harmony within Chris Dawson's defence team. As the trial wore on, it was clear that there was discord. One day, not long before the trial finished, I was standing with Greg and Merilyn just outside the courtroom. Chris, his brother Peter, Pauline David and Greg Walsh were in one of the glass-fronted conference rooms in the corridor. Suddenly, Greg Walsh burst out of the room and, as he slammed the door behind him, let out a loud expletive.

At last, the *R v Dawson* decision was listed for 30 August 2022. By then, I had come to the conclusion that Chris Dawson was going to be found guilty. I scribbled down lists of witnesses and crossed off their names as I discounted their evidence. Each time I kept coming up with the same result. Guilty. I spoke to Hedley Thomas in the days before the verdict and he thought it was going to be a guilty verdict, too. Damian Loone and I exchanged text messages and he said that he wasn't confident. Regardless of the verdict, I encouraged him to be proud of what he had done because without his work in the early years, there wouldn't have been a trial.

After seven weeks of deliberations, we were about to learn if Chris Dawson would be found guilty of murdering Lynette.

CHAPTER TWENTY

Justice Harrison's long decision

AT 10 AM ON TUESDAY, 30 AUGUST 2022, JUSTICE IAN HARRISON entered the court through the small door behind the bench wearing the arcane red and white judicial robes and wig. He took his seat in the middle of the long honey-wood bench, where he had sat alone throughout the trial, ready to read his judgment. The decision was to be broadcast live to anyone who wanted to tune in, including on a wall-mounted monitor in the courtroom and in an overflow courtroom, to accommodate the large public contingent expected to exercise their right to observe court proceedings.

A tight lens of scrutiny was on Justice Harrison. As a judge sitting alone, he'd told the court at the outset that he would admit all evidence and assess its admissibility when he wrote his judgment. Most of the evidence to be assessed in his judgment was witness evidence. Who impressed him? Who didn't?

He began with the offence.

> Christopher Michael Dawson is charged that on or about 8 January 1982 at Bayview or elsewhere in the State of New South Wales he did murder Lynette Joy Dawson. Mr Dawson has pleaded not guilty to that charge. His trial before me, sitting as a judge alone, commenced on 9 May 2022.[30]

Justice Harrison outlined the background and stated: 'The Crown case is that Lynette Dawson was dead by no later than sometime on the morning of 9 January 1982.'[31]

He went on to explain:

> The Crown must prove [this] beyond reasonable doubt . . . If there exists a reasonable possibility that Lynette Dawson was alive after 8 January 1982, Mr Dawson is entitled to be acquitted of the charge of murder.[32]

The Crown's first witness

The first prosecution witness was Julie Andrew. Listeners of *The Teacher's Pet* were familiar with Julie Andrew's faltering voice pleading for justice for her friend Lynette, which was spliced into the opening sequence of every episode. Just over 1.5 metres tall, she has an age-defying energy and a take-no-prisoners attitude.

Julie Andrew's house looked down on Lynette and Chris Dawson's house in Bayview, and from her backyard she witnessed Chris Dawson abusing Lynette in the months before she disappeared. Her evidence was explosive, her manner impassioned.

Julie told the court that within a few months of Lynette disappearing, she had formed the view that Chris Dawson had murdered Lynette and she had observed this distressing scene only a few months before Lynette disappeared. But she didn't go to the police or reach out to Lynette's family. Until the early to mid-1980s, the home was regarded as a private place. What went on behind closed doors was often not seen, or if it was seen, the thing to do was to pretend it hadn't been seen. Julie Andrew is such a forceful individual that doing nothing seemed completely out of character, but she told the court that in 1982, she was a different person, living in different times.

Julie's involvement in *The Teacher's Pet* was an issue. Audio of her chatting on the phone to Hedley Thomas was played in court. They sounded chummy and light-hearted.

Julie Andrew was the first witness involved in *The Teacher's Pet* to give evidence. Hedley Thomas was worried that her evidence wouldn't be accepted; I was worried too.

Justice Harrison told us that he had no trouble accepting what she said. In his judgment he stated: 'In my opinion, Ms Andrew's evidence about the trampoline incident and her subsequent conversation with Lynette Dawson about it is entirely believable.'[33]

The Crown's key witness

Wednesday 18 May 2022 was a warm, late autumn day. Outside the Supreme Court building, a large media contingent chatted and drank coffee. Suddenly, as if a secret signal was sent around, cameras and microphones were shoved into action and journalists swarmed in a pack around JC as she crossed Queen's Square, heading towards the Supreme Court building. Some were almost jogging to keep up with her wide strides, and in front of her, cameramen and photographers moved swiftly and dangerously backwards, clicking their cameras furiously. The schoolgirl was now fifty-eight years old and was dressed in her trademark black – trousers, jacket, handbag, sunglasses – and a pale blue COVID mask. She kept her head down. In news reports and coverage, they pixellated her face but they couldn't pixellate her distinctive walk.

In a criminal trial, the prosecution, also referred to as the Crown, has the burden of proof. In this trial that meant the Crown had to prove beyond reasonable doubt that Chris Dawson had murdered Lynette, and in attempting to do this JC was the Crown's key witness. Her evidence provided the timeline and the motive that told the story of Lynette's disappearance. There were other important witnesses, but it was hard to see how the prosecution could make their case if JC wasn't believed.

Evidence-in-chief is the evidence led by the party who called the witness. Questions to the witness by the opposing side is the cross-examination. The Crown led JC through her evidence-in-chief, beginning with how she met Chris Dawson. 'He told me he had seen me in the playground the year before when I was 15 and decided that he would like to get to know me better because I was attractive to him.'[34]

This part of the story was reduced to one word. Playground. Justice Harrison said, 'I found that JC's insistence during her evidence that she was at the time only a child to be an evocative description of her predicament.'[35]

A Christmas card and other cards from Chris Dawson to JC had been projected onto a large screen in the courtroom. From a thirty-six-year-old Chris Dawson to a schoolgirl, they were unmistakable evidence of grooming. Some cards were signed 'GOD'.

'He wanted to disguise who he was,' JC told the court. 'It was 1980 and I was sixteen and that's what he called himself.'[36] The cards were artifacts that Chris Dawson could not disown – he could only quibble about their dates.

Justice Harrison found 'that the notes and cards that are in evidence were written by him and presented to her when JC was still at school, or shortly after she left, as she said in her evidence. The words written by Mr Dawson bespeak, even at that relatively early stage, an infatuation of significant strength.'[37]

When they separated in 1990, Chris Dawson asked JC to destroy the cards. In one of her first acts of independence, she refused. Did she understand their significance? Or was it his request that signalled their importance? Justice Harrison accepted the cards as evidence.

The date that JC moved back into the Bayview house after Lynette disappeared was somewhat elastic. JC had given slightly different accounts, as had Chris Dawson. In her 1999 statement, she said that Chris Dawson collected her on 15 January, but in subsequent statements she said that was a mistake, and she corrected the date to 'on or about 10, 11 or 12 January 1982'.

My apprehension that this made JC's evidence vulnerable was swept away when Justice Harrison took a sensible view of the exact date. 'As with much else in this case, the fact that Mr Dawson drove to South West Rocks to collect JC at some time between 10 January and 16 January 1982 is not in dispute.'[38] Perhaps the exact date wasn't critical given that Chris Dawson agreed to the fact that he did collect her. Nonetheless, when considered with the evidence of MC, the schoolfriend of JC's who was also at South West Rocks, Justice Harrison was able to be more specific. 'However, when account is taken of the independent evidence of MC, I am satisfied beyond reasonable doubt that Mr Dawson collected JC from South West Rocks before MC's eighteenth birthday on 12 January 1982.'[39]

And in quite brutal language Justice Harrison said that the dates were not important. What was important was that Lynette was out of the way:

> It puts an incredible strain on human experience to accept, as a reasonable possibility, that Mr Dawson's evident desire to instal [sic] his teenage lover as his de facto wife and the mother to his children was fulfilled by the completely fortuitous and cost-free disappearance of the wife that he loathed.[40]

A cross-examiner's purpose is to punch holes in a witness's evidence by punching holes in the witness. A witness who is defensive under attack, or confused, or brought to tears or anger, can cast doubt on their own testimony, or it can provoke them to say something that is helpful to the other side's argument. Being cross-examined can be bruising, but I was pretty confident that JC would manage it well. When she gave evidence at the inquest, she told me that it was 'stressful but also easy' and I understood that meant that she just told the truth.

The evidence JC gave in court were the same stories she had told me.

She was mostly composed and articulate, and under cross-examination she even rattled Pauline David. When David depicted JC as on a 'mission to destroy' Chris Dawson, for example, JC fired straight back: 'I'm not going to destroy him. He'll destroy himself for what he's done to people.'[41]

Still, a clever barrister can elevate an inconsistency to doubt – it was a murder trial after all. Under cross-examination, JC acknowledged the inconsistency in the hit-man story but denied that she had made it up. 'That's ridiculous. No. I didn't make up this story. It's true.'[42] Justice Harrison dismissed the hit-man story completely.

JC could also be distressed or teary. When Pauline David cross-examined JC about why she moved back into the Dawson family home when she returned from South West Rocks, she was clearly distressed and confused. Even so, JC didn't present as David hoped she would.

JC expressed two kinds of distress. One was the pressure of cross-examination and the other was the visceral distress of a child. It was difficult to hear this without wishing that an adult could have intervened in 1982 when JC needed help. And I wondered how Chris Dawson felt as he sat listening. Did he feel guilty? Was it the first time that he understood what he had done to her? Was it the first time he understood that she had been a child? Over the years, he had dismissed his damaging role in her life – we heard some of that in the intercepted telephone calls. But courtrooms confront human intention, and I wondered if, behind his blue COVID-19 mask, he accepted the damage he had caused this woman. He is the father of three women. It's unlikely he would have wanted a predatory teacher pursuing them when they were schoolgirls.

Pauline David attacked JC's evidence that when she moved back into the house, she had to learn to cook and clean, 'To be a substitute housekeeper, sex slave, stepmother, babysitter. Slave. Just a slave.'[43] JC rejected David's suggestion that her claims of being a 'sex slave' were made up to include in the book I was writing.

PD: It's pretty sensational stuff for a book, isn't it, to say that you're a sex slave? It is a more recent construction by you, isn't it?

JC: I think it's the most accurate construction I can give.

PD: I suggest to you that you have reinvented your life with Mr Dawson with the intent of destroying him most unfairly.

JC: No.

PD: You have characterised this man in a way that is completely untrue.

JC: No . . . I don't make up stories about Mr Dawson.[44]

The truth is that JC did endure many of the features of slavery. Chris Dawson had controlled JC while she was at school and continued to exert control over her after she left school. He needed her in the house. He viewed her as his chattel; Lynette too.

At the 2003 inquest into Lynette's disappearance, the coroner concluded that JC was a reliable witness. In 2022, Judge Harrison came to the same conclusion. Justice Harrison mentioned JC, 570 times in his judgment, and only found fault with one piece of her evidence: the hit man allegation.

JC told Greg and Merilyn the hit-man story when she first met them in 1990. The first time I interviewed Greg and Merilyn, they recounted JC telling them about it at their first meeting on the Central Coast in 1990. But when Merilyn gave evidence in the trial, Justice Harrison noted, 'It was curiously not until she was cross-examined that Merilyn Simms made any reference to it.'[45] She only mentioned it after she was prompted.

It's perplexing why Greg and Merilyn didn't offer the hit-man evidence freely. Afterwards, they were perplexed as well.

The evidence of another witness, KL, a high school friend of JC's, included an additional detail. 'He told her to stay in the car, and he took something out of the glove box and she said she felt it was money to pay someone to kill Lyn, or who had killed Lyn.'[46]

JC had never mentioned the glovebox to me or to Greg and Merilyn. She may never have mentioned it to KL either. Some stories attract filaments.

Justice Harrison rejected all evidence about the hit man but he made a point of saying that he believed everything else that JC said.

> I am not satisfied that Mr Dawson ever said to JC that he had contemplated hiring a hitman to kill Lynette Dawson but that he had changed his mind.
>
> It seems to me to be difficult legitimately to reason to a conclusion that giving voice to a proposal that is simultaneously rejected can be probative of anything at all.
>
> I am not able to be satisfied that any such conversation occurred.
>
> I am, however, satisfied that JC's evidence is otherwise truthful and reliable.[47]

Greg and Merilyn Simms

In a cabinet in Greg and Merilyn Simms's home near Newcastle is a vast trove of documents and correspondence that Greg has collected during the forty-year fight to find out what happened to Lynette. As a life's work, it had been everything and not enough. When Greg and Merilyn gave evidence, all of the documents were put aside, and they told the court in their own words, what they had seen and heard when Lynette disappeared.

Not long before Lynette disappeared, Greg recalled being with his mother and Chris Dawson in Helena's kitchen at Clovelly. Talk turned to Lynette and Chris Dawson said with distaste, 'She can get in the bloody kitchen where she belongs.' Pauline David pressed Greg to accept that Chris Dawson had said it in a joking way. 'No, that's incorrect,' he said. 'It wasn't said as a joke.'[48]

Greg also told the court that approximately ten months after Lynette disappeared, he was visiting his mother when Chris Dawson delivered Lynette's belongings to Helena in 'big green plastic bags'.[49] Greg's garbage bag evidence corroborated JC's account that not long after she moved back into the house, she packed Lynette's clothes into garbage bags. She stayed in the car when Chris Dawson gave them to Lynette's mother. I imagine that as Chris Dawson listened to this in court, he must have regretted his lackadaisical behaviour and his assumption that others were as indifferent to Lynette's disappearance as he was. It's easier to get rid of someone after you've dehumanised them. The journalist David Murray reported that Greg was 'trying to contain his emotions'.[50]

Greg told the court that Lynette's contact lenses and her nursing badge were in the garbage bags. It would be hard for her to find work without them. Justice Harrison enumerated other searches that failed to turn up signs of life: that Lynette has never been seen since she disappeared; she has not contacted anyone; she has not used her passport; she is not registered with Medicare or the Australian Tax Office; she doesn't have a driver's licence in any state or territory; no human remains have been identified as her; she is not enrolled to vote; and she is not registered with Centrelink. And *The Teacher's Pet* had generated so much publicity that anyone who knew her in the years since her disappearance would have come forward.

Merilyn Simms is softly spoken with pale skin and rosy cheeks, but the sum of those features concealed her hard resolve. When the decades-long search for Lynette threatened to overwhelm Greg, necessity demanded that she share the ever-increasing demands. She responded with intelligence and poise.

Merilyn told the court that in one of her last conversations with Lynette, Lynette confided that her sexual relationship with Chris Dawson had stopped; that there would be no more children; and she was worried about Chris Dawson moving JC into the house. As a chain of thought, Lynette had identified the problems but not the cause.

Merilyn also told the court about a telephone conversation she overheard between Helena Simms and Chris Dawson. Merilyn said that Chris Dawson was very agitated and he accused Helena of secretly taking the girls to visit Lynette. 'You've taken the girls away, you've kept them away, you're taking them to see Lyn secretly, you know where she is.'[51]

To establish a narrative that Lynette was still alive, Chris Dawson implicated Lynette's daughters in a lie to Lynette's mother. Helena then handed the phone to Merilyn, who told the court of the conversation that followed: 'He said that he wanted Lyn to come back, he wanted to see her walk in the door and that he missed her.'[52]

It was only when she was prompted that Merilyn said that JC had told her and Greg the hit-man story when they first met her in 1990.

Justice Harrison was impressed by Greg Simms and Merilyn as witnesses.

> I observed Mr Simms very closely in the witness box as he gave his evidence. Mr Simms presented as a quiet and gentle man. He was not easily ruffled. In the final analysis, his evidence of significance is limited to his recollections of Mr Dawson's venomous comments about Lynette Dawson and the occasion when Lynette Dawson's belongings were returned to her family home in Clovelly. Despite his involvement with Hedley Thomas and his podcast, Mr Simms' measured responses to all questions asked of him convince me that his evidence is truthful.[53]

And of Merilyn:

> Alike with her husband, Ms Simms was quiet and measured. She was not cross-examined to the point where, in my view, any of her evidence became doubtful. I consider that Ms Simms' evidence can be accepted without qualification, especially her evidence that informed the nature of the relationship between Mr Dawson and his wife.[54]

Sightings of Lynette

Six days after Chris Dawson was charged with murder, Ross Hutcheon sent an email to his brother-in-law, Peter Dawson. In the email, he told Peter that three to six months after Lynette disappeared he had seen her standing on the side of Victoria Road in Gladesville.

In 2019 he gave a statement to the police. During that interview, Ross Hutcheon said that he had previously mentioned the sighting to two police officers who came to his home in 1999 and spoke to him and to his wife Lynette, who is Chris Dawson's sister. One of the police officers' notes from that visit read: 'Neither Lynette Hutcheon or Ross Hutcheon have ever had any contact with the Missing Person, Lynette Dawson since her disappearance.'[55] Mr Hutcheon was shown that note. 'That's wrong. That's absolutely wrong,' he said.[56]

Ross Hutcheon was dead by the time of the trial. However, his statement to the police in 2019 was video-recorded and he had given evidence at Chris Dawson's committal hearing in 2020. Justice Harrison formed a strong view about him.

> I appreciate and am mindful of the fact that Mr Hutcheon is dead, and so is unable to defend himself against the Crown contention that his version is a lie. However, the judicial process is not always gentle or polite. I am satisfied that Mr Hutcheon's version of sighting Lynette Dawson at Gladesville is a fabrication.[57]

After the police interviewed Lynette Hutcheon and her husband Ross in 1999, she rang Chris Dawson. That telephone call was intercepted by the police and the recording was played for Lynette Hutcheon at the trial. She was asked why she didn't mention to Chris Dawson that her husband had just told the police that he had seen Lynette on the side of the road a few months after she disappeared.

She answered, 'Well it . . . and you heard the conversation. It didn't come up. I didn't tell him everything else that was in the . . . in the conversation. I . . . it . . . as I said, you know, if I'd known it was going to come up now I would have . . . I would have listed everything that we said but I . . . it wasn't important. We still thought that she would come . . . come home or she would be, you know, be around. It wasn't . . . it wasn't important to me to tell him at that stage. I was more concerned about the girls and my parents.'[58]

Justice Harrison said of Lynette Hutcheon's evidence on this matter:

> Mrs Hutcheon told her brother that she had just had a visit from the police who were checking up on Lynette Dawson's disappearance and were interviewing all her relations 'to make sure she is still missing'. Despite this, Mrs Hutcheon does not mention the sighting to her brother at all. Mrs Hutcheon even relates telling the police that the last thing she heard of her sister-in-law's whereabouts was that she was on a hippy commune somewhere in Byron Bay.[59]

Lynette Hutcheon was also asked why she hadn't told Chris Dawson about her husband's sighting of Lynette in 2018, when *The Teacher's Pet* podcast was accusing him of murder. She said, 'The fact that Ross saw her didn't . . . I didn't realise it was going to be that important . . . I didn't think it was important enough for me to ring and say . . . I don't know what was in *Teacher's Pet*, I don't know who wrote it, I don't know anything about it, I just don't know.'[60]

Justice Harrison said of this and other evidence given by Lynette Hutcheon:

> Even aside from Mrs Hutcheon's failure to tell the police about the sighting in 1999, the Crown maintains that her explanation for not telling her brother about the Gladesville sighting after the allegations in the podcast had become so public and notorious, is equally unconvincing. By that time, Mrs Hutcheon knew that

> Chris Dawson, a brother she held in high esteem, was being routinely accused of murdering his wife and yet she did not think her information was sufficiently important to tell him about it. The Crown submitted that this is inherently unbelievable.[61]
>
> I have regrettably formed the same view concerning Mrs Hutcheon's evidence that she heard her husband tell the police in 1999 about the Gladesville sighting. I appreciate that at the date she gave her evidence, Mr Hutcheon had only recently died. However, I am entirely unable to accept that Mrs Hutcheon would not have told her brother that her husband had just that very day informed the police that he had seen Lynette Dawson alive and well at Gladesville if, and in my view when, she was or must have been aware of its significance to the inquiring police at the time.[62]

The police work, and the threading of evidence by the Crown, were a warning to anyone tempted to come to court and not tell the truth.

The defence's only witness

Paul Cooper was the one witness the defence called. He was a late addition to their list and he came forward to say that he'd met Lynette very shortly after she disappeared.

Paul Cooper is a small man in his sixties, with a kindly and weathered face, and it was no surprise to learn that his life had been a hard one. In 2018, he saw an image of Lynette on *A Current Affair* and he got in touch with Chris Dawson's solicitor, Greg Walsh. He did not contact the police. He told the court that in 1982 he had a drink with a woman in a pub in Warners Bay, 150 kilometres north of Sydney, on the northern end of Lake Macquarie. He recalled for the court that over a drink she told him that her husband was unfaithful and controlling and she was leaving the marriage and her children for good.

'She had money because she sold something and she'd been planning it for a couple of weeks.

'She was waiting to get a passport from somebody who was going to meet her in a couple of weeks, she had to wait two weeks to get a passport . . . She was going to go to Bali and then head off to another country overseas.

'I said to her they're going to think he knocked ya. And I got the impression that was the whole process of it, leaving everything behind. I was taken aback by it.'[63]

Getting a passport from 'somebody' might have been easy for Mr Cooper but for Lynette it was improbable. His belief that Lynette was framing Chris Dawson with her murder was fanciful. Craig Everson made short work dismantling Mr Cooper's credibility.

Q. What was preventing you from working?

A. Ah, spinal injury.

Q. Anything else apart from a spinal injury?

A. No, I dunno what you mean as to what?

Q. Did you go away anywhere?

A. Oh yeah I've been to jail, yeah.

Q. What for?

A. Lots of things.

Q. Tell His Honour what that was, please.

A. Oh drugs, break and enter and all sorts of things.

Q. Armed robbery?

A. Yeah, yeah.

Q. And plenty of offences of dishonesty?

A. Um theft and that, yeah.

Q. False pretences?

A. Yep.

Q. When are you going to put your hand up to claim the reward for information leading to the resolving of the disappearance of Lynette Dawson?

A. I didn't know there was a reward.[64]

Despite his familiarity with the criminal justice system, Paul Cooper thought he could quarantine his criminal record. The defence would have known that it would come out during cross-examination: they knew that Paul Cooper wasn't a very good witness, but it seemed that he was all they had.

Still, the anti-hero had the court's sympathy. 'I watched my father murder my mother as a child, which caused me to end up using drugs and crime and everything.' No one doubted that was the truth. He was adamant that drug use had not affected his memories of his chance meeting with Lynette Dawson in a pub forty years ago. 'You don't forget something like that. No, it was her, 100 per cent. I'll give you 200 per cent,' he said.[65]

Justice Harrison responded with compassion to Paul Cooper's evidence.

I pause to observe that I am not particularly attracted to the general proposition that heavy illicit drug use necessarily leads to a diminution in a person's memory, even if it can occasionally be seen to be a convenient assumption. Nor was Mr Cooper demonstrably influenced by any fixed view he could be said to have about

> the outcome of these proceedings. It is not possible to say that Mr Cooper's version of what he described is a lie . . . however . . . I do not accept it as establishing that the woman he spoke to was Lynette Dawson.[66]

One by one, Justice Harrison gave detailed reasons for dismissing all of the alleged sightings of Lynette Dawson.

Two schoolboys

PS was a sixteen-year-old school student at Manly Boys High School when he met JC. They both had a part-time job at Coles and he wanted to ask her out to 'see if she wanted to go to the local disco'.[67] In 2014 he gave a statement to police. He also appeared on *The Teacher's Pet*, but Justice Harrison emphasised, 'His statement to the police . . . was four years before Hedley Thomas' *Teacher's Pet* podcast was released'.[68]

PS told the court that at work one day he was asked to collect shopping trolleys from the underground car park and return them to the bays at the entrance to Coles. While he was in the car park, Chris Dawson approached him. PS told the court about that meeting.

> A. He shoved me against the concrete ramp that went on an angle up to the store and he sort of backed me into that concrete structure and, you know, held me against the structure.
> Q. Who was it that did that to you?
> A. Chris Dawson.
> Q. Were there any words exchanged between you and he before that happened?

A. Apart from him saying 'Hey you' or words to that effect, no.
Q. After he did what you described, were there any words exchanged between you and him?
A. Well, my memory is that Mr Dawson said words to the effect of, 'I just want you to stay away from her. Don't go near her or else,' or words to that effect.
Q. Was anything else said by him at about that time?
A. Well, I think probably the next thing that occurred was me saying, 'I don't know what you're talking about.' I was very scared. I was sixteen years old and very small, and he was a very large man, and I can recall just being shocked by what was going on and I think I said something like, 'Who are you talking about? I don't know what you're talking about.'
Q. Was there a reply?
A. Yes, well, that's when he said, '[JC]'.[69]

Justice Harrison noted, 'PS did not thereafter ask JC out on a date again.'[70]

There were no witnesses to the incident in the Coles car park. However, on 30 November 2018 a telephone call between Chris Dawson and one of his daughters was intercepted by the police and Pauline David referred to it in court. 'Your Honour has heard in one of the telecommunication intercepts, that's at exhibit 35 at call 5949, Mr Dawson denies having committed the act as described by [PS], although he said 'I may have touched him on the' . . . he accepts he may have touched him on the chest in relation to . . . in response to what he perceived as the pestering of [JC]. But he doesn't have . . . he indicated he doesn't have a lot of recollection about it.'[71]

Chris Dawson's muffled admission that he confronted a sixteen-year-old schoolboy in a car park begs the question, why? Were it not for the intercepted telephone call, Chris Dawson might have denied that the incident ever occurred. Pauline David told the court that Chris Dawson 'doesn't have a lot of recollection about it'. Justice Harrison concluded:

> The Crown maintains that this incident is wholly consistent with Mr Dawson's controlling and possessive, if not obsessive, concern that no one should come between him and JC. The Crown maintains that this obsession was still operative on 8 and 9 January 1982 and also inspired Mr Dawson's journey to South West Rocks some days later.[72]

That telephone call was intercepted on 30 November 2018. Five days later, on 5 December 2018, Chris Dawson was charged with murder. Was it this admission by Chris Dawson that gave the police the confidence to charge him with murder?

PS came across as a thoroughly decent person. As a young man, he represented choices JC should have had were she not controlled by Chris Dawson.

Another schoolboy also gave evidence about Chris Dawson warning him off any interest in JC. RH went to Cromer High School and Chris Dawson was his PE teacher and rugby league coach. RH felt close to Chris Dawson and confided that he liked JC and would like to ask her out. Chris Dawson hatched a strange plan. He said that he would be at JC's home one morning and he told RH to come over; when RH arrived, Chris Dawson would leave, providing RH with the opportunity to ask JC out.

But RH told the court that when he got to JC's house, the plan changed.

> Q. What was it that happened that prompts you to say that the plan had changed?
> A. I was expecting, being [JC's] house, for [JC] to greet me at the front door, but instead Chris greeted me at the front door and said, you know, the plan . . . words to the effect of, you know, plan's aborted.
> Q. What did you do?
> A. I could see through his shoulder, over his shoulder that [JC] was there. I left in confusion, rode off.[73]

Chris Dawson set this young man up. The plan hadn't changed, it worked just as Chris Dawson intended. In cross-examination Pauline David did not suggest to RH that Chris Dawson had not been at JC's that day; instead, she suggested that Chris Dawson had a follow-up conversation with RH and explained that there had been a violent incident at JC's house that day and that was why he was there. RH could not recollect any follow up conversation with Chris Dawson.

Women at the childcare centre

Apart from Chris Dawson, the women who worked at the childcare centre with Lynette were the last people to see her. They knew that Lynette was having marriage difficulties and they had also heard the gossip that Chris Dawson was involved with one of his students.

Barbara Cruise was the director of the childcare centre, and she recalled that Chris Dawson rang her on Monday 11 January 1982 to tell her that Lynette had decided to go away for a few days. After the first call from Chris Dawson, Barbara told the court that there were others. 'I would ring him and say, "Have you heard from Lyn?" And I think Chris did ring me another couple of times after the first time to say that Lyn still needed more time out, is my memory, but no indication of when she would be returning. Or he had no indication.'[74]

A to-and-fro of telephone calls between Barbara and Chris Dawson suggests a mutual concern for Lynette's whereabouts. Justice Harrison didn't see it that way:

> Apart from Robyn Warren, none of Lynette Dawson's girlfriends or work colleagues said that Mr Dawson had contacted them asking whether they had heard from Lynette Dawson or whether they might know where she was. That includes Barbara Cruise who Mr Dawson contacted for the purpose of telling her something, rather than asking her something, as her evidence reveals.[75]

Sue Strath also worked with Lynette at the childcare centre. Lynette had told Sue about Chris Dawson's abusive and escalating behaviour at home in the twelve months before she disappeared, and Sue had heard the local gossip that Chris Dawson was involved with a student. This alarmed Sue so much that she did what Julie Andrew told the court she regretted not doing – she went to the police. When the police showed little interest, she made her complaint to the ombudsman. The ombudsman directed the police to conduct a review of their investigation. Nothing came of it.

Sue's evidence was uncontroversial but important. She spoke of Lynette's love for her children and her husband. 'She loved her husband and she loved her children. And they were everything to her.'[76] Her voice was one of many that Justice Harrison laid on top of each other to build a clear picture of Lynette Dawson as a person who would not have left her children.

Sue Strath is the person we all hope we would be in similar circumstances. She didn't get the result she was after but she did everything she could for her friend.

Anna Grantham also worked with Lynette at the childcare centre. When I visited her at home on the escarpment that looked down on the Northern Beaches, her lips had trembled when she told me about a violent incident between Lynette and Chris Dawson. She told the court the same story. 'She said he grabbed her by the back of her hair and he pressed it on the floor on the mud with her face . . . I said, "Oh my god. He could have easily killed you." They are the words . . . She said, "Yes, he could easily have killed me."'[77]

When Pauline David cross-examined Anna, she said that she didn't suggest to Lynette that she should go to the police because Lynette was 'very secretive about her private life'. Women living with domestic violence rarely go to the police.

But Justice Harrison didn't like what Anna had to say.

> [I]t does seem entirely unusual that Lynette Dawson, a woman described by Ms Grantham as a person who did not confide about her personal life, would have related a story as dramatic as the incident appears to be. The evidence from Ms Grantham, and others, is that Lynette Dawson adored her husband. I have

some doubt that Lynette Dawson would have related anything to Ms Grantham that was so explicitly critical of him.[78]

I was a bit surprised by Justice Harrison's seemingly curt dismissal of Anna Grantham's evidence. Did he discount her evidence because she had not suggested to Lynette that she should go to police? It was clear to Anna that Lynette remained hopeful that she and Chris could work things out. Going to the police would have ended their marriage. When a woman is living with domestic violence, friends and family need to tread lightly or they too will be perceived as a threat and pushed away. There is no safe place for a person who is looking at the world through the lens of domestic violence.

I will never forget the hot day that Hedley Thomas and I visited Annette Leary in her home. Recording equipment is sensitive, so we had to shut the window against the deafening singing of cicadas. A noisy fan in the room had to be turned off. It was 38 degrees outside and in Annette's dining room the temperature kept climbing. Hedley had sweat running down his face. Annette was visibly unwell but she was determined to tell us about her friend.

Annette had worked at the childcare centre the day before Lynette disappeared, and she saw Lynette and Chris Dawson after they had seen the marriage counsellor. Lynette told Annette that when they were in the lift on the way to the appointment, Chris had choked her and said that if the marriage counselling session didn't work, he was going to get rid of her. Annette said there were bruises on Lynette's throat. Like the other women from the childcare centre,

Annette had given statements to the police and had been telling this story for forty years. But, as with Anna Grantham, Justice Harrison didn't accept what Annette Leary had to say:

> I am unable to accept that the version given by Ms Leary of the incident in the lift is reliable. First, the timing of the visit to the marriage counsellor does not fit with Ms Leary's recollection that the incident was somewhere between 10 am and lunchtime. Secondly, but in a related sense, even if the incident could notionally be placed at 2 pm, the likelihood that bruising would have developed in such a short space of time is small. Thirdly, Ms Leary agrees that she has been influenced by the accounts given by others. Fourthly, Ms Leary was also spoken to by Hedley Thomas, a fact that carries a risk that she has been influenced by her dealings with him. Fifthly, the happy demeanour described by others of Lynette Dawson returning from marriage counselling holding her husband's hand is fundamentally inconsistent with her having been physically assaulted in a violent way and verbally threatened as well. Finally, and hypothetically having regard to my view about Ms Leary's evidence, if Lynette Dawson did not herself appear to consider what is said to have occurred as serious, it is a dangerous step to move to a conclusion that the incident, if it occurred, tells me anything useful about Mr Dawson in any event.
>
> In the circumstances, I am unable to have any confidence in the suggestion that the incident as described by Ms Leary ever occurred.[79]

This was a disappointing finding because it legitimised one of the persistent myths about domestic violence, that 'it can't be that bad if she can cover it up'. Justice Harrison accepted evidence elsewhere that Lynette was living with Chris Dawson's abusive behaviours: Julie Andrew witnessed Chris Dawson assaulting Lynette; JC was moved into her home against her wishes; JC witnessed a verbal fight between Lynette and Chris after Lynette saw JC sitting on his lap while they played with the girls; Chris left Lynette and their two young daughters stranded without a lift home; he left Lynette a note just before Christmas saying he had left her and he made no mention of how she and the girls would manage financially but he did ask Lynette not to 'paint too dark a picture' of him to the girls and Lynette did as he asked. Lynette pulled herself up after each blow. She hid most of Chris's abusive behaviour from her siblings, parents and friends; Lynette was practised at pretending that everything was okay.

Equally perplexing was Justice Harrison's conclusion that 'The evidence does not also enable me to make any findings or draw any conclusions about whether Mr Dawson engaged in non-physical domestic violence and I put it aside completely for present purposes.'[80]

Intimate partner violence is still not well understood.

The Dawsons: Peter, Paul and Marilyn

Over the years, much has been made of the closeness between Chris Dawson and his twin brother Paul, but it was their older brother Peter who was with him at every court mention and every day of the murder trial.

Pauline David asked Peter Dawson what his reaction was to the news that his sister-in-law had disappeared. 'Because of other factors, it struck me as not all that unusual,' he said. These 'other factors' were that when Peter Dawson's first wife, Lynelle, was ten years old, her mother abandoned the family. She never saw her mother again although she was later found to be living in New Zealand. Justice Harrison observed:

> Mr Dawson relied upon the disappearance of the mother of Peter Dawson's first wife when she was only ten years old, who walked out never to be seen alive by the family again, as supportive of the reasonableness of the possibility that Lynette Dawson did the same. However, the evidence relating to that incident only supports, if support were needed, that it is not beyond the realm of human experience that men and women may choose simply to disappear.[81]

In other words, the court was only interested in what Lynette Dawson would have done. Justice Harrison continued: 'That Lynette Dawson, a sane, intelligent and determined woman, would step from her husband's car on a Saturday morning with little but the clothes that she wore, somehow having rationally chosen to evaporate forever, seeping invisibly and unnoticed into an uncertain future with nothing and no one . . . To paraphrase the Crown's submission, the proposition is ludicrous.'[82]

Justice Harrison noted, 'With the exception of Peter Dawson, who was prepared only to describe her as a "competent" mother, Lynette Dawson was the subject of otherwise unanimous commendation for her parenting skills and the love of her daughters.'[83]

Paul Dawson gave evidence by audiovisual link from the police station at Tweed Heads. Tweed Heads is the last town before crossing the border from New South Wales into Queensland and it is only a half-hour drive from where Chris and JC and Paul and his wife, Marilyn, moved when they left Bayview. At seventy-three years of age, this was the first time the twins were confronted with real separation. In court, Chris Dawson looked up at his twin brother on the television monitor fixed high on the wall.

Paul Dawson also adverted to the strength of the relationship between Lynette Dawson and his brother in the context of being asked about his surprise and disappointment that Mr Dawson did not spend Christmas with the family in 1981. He said this:

'Q. Mr Dawson, just take it slowly. Can you just indicate what you recall you said to Lyn and what she said to you, just do your best if you could?

A. Well, I was visibly upset, and Lyn asked me why, or Lyn would have known why, and I told her it was the first Christmas I had ever spent in my life without Chris being there, and she said, she basically calmed me down and told me not to worry, and I said I was worried about their marriage and where they were going, and she said, 'Don't worry,' you know, 'we will work it out'. She basically calmed me down and acted, comforted me that everything would be all right.

Q. All right. Were you surprised about her reaction?

A. Well, we had, we had, we didn't have that sort of close relationship where we opened our hearts up to each other, so I was surprised with the reaction as far as comforting me, and very pleased that she was confident they were going to be working things out over time.'[84]

Justice Harrison commented:

> The conversation with Paul Dawson, for example, was in the contemporaneous shadow of Mr Dawson's absence from the family Christmas because he was at that time spending time with JC at Paul and Marilyn Dawson's home, although Lynette Dawson was at that time unaware of that fact.[85]

During cross-examination, Paul Dawson also said that Lynette Dawson had said of herself, 'She never felt that her children needed her because Chris did a lot of mummying and looking after them anyway, but the children that she looked after as a nurse and in the child care, they needed her more, so I think that was a bit of a source of perhaps disappointment to her, I don't know, but she was certainly a good mother.'[86]

Paul Dawson's wife, Marilyn, gave the same honest responses in court that she had given Damian Loone when he interviewed her in 1999. Unlike her husband, she described Lynette as 'very happy to be a mum' and some of her evidence corroborated parts of JC's evidence.

Craig Everson asked Marilyn about the holiday that she and Paul and their children had on the Central Coast, when Lynette disappeared. When did they decide to take the holiday? Did she know where South West Rocks was? How close were they to the highway to South West Rocks? Did she remember any visitors while they were there? 'Not that I recall, no,' Marilyn said.

Justice Harrison stated towards the very end of his judgment:

> Nothing is known about what Mr Dawson did that day [of 9 January 1982]. No one has given evidence of seeing or speaking to Mr Dawson on that day or of being told anything by him about what he was doing on the night of 9 January 1982. No person has given any evidence about seeing him later that day or night. JC was by now in South West Rocks. Paul and Marilyn Dawson were in Lake Munmorah on their one and only holiday in Aunt Audrey's caravan.[87]
>
> The evidence does not reveal how Mr Dawson killed Lynette Dawson. It does not reveal whether he did so with the assistance of anyone else or by himself.[88]

Lynette Dawson should not be assessed as 'as a member of a class', Justice Harrison warned. He was interested in Lynette, the person:

> It is important in this context to observe that no general, gender-based assumptions should be made about Lynette Dawson. Simply because Lynette Dawson was a mother does not thereby produce some unambiguously logical conclusion that weighs in favour of the argument that she did not leave voluntarily. Women and mothers are already burdened with more than enough vicarious emotional baggage without further adding to the weight of unfair expectations that are imposed upon them. Men seem not to be regularly stereotyped for making arguably irrational or selfish decisions, whereas women are somehow expected to abide by a higher standard. In forming any opinion or making any finding based upon the fact that Lynette Dawson was a mother, it is advisable to

> bear in mind that she is entitled to be assessed as Lynette Dawson and not as a member of a class with immutable characteristics. If the contention that Lynette Dawson did not abandon her home is to be inferentially supported by reference to her motherhood or her relationship to her children, as the Crown contends, it must be based upon what is known about Lynette Dawson in particular and not upon what is thought to be known about women or mothers in general.[89]

Women who had tuned in to hear the judgment gave a silent fist pump.

Lynette emerged from evidence of friends and family as a woman who adored her daughters. Pat told the court that her sister 'absolutely adored' her daughters.[90] Barbara Cruise said that Lynette's girls 'were her world'.[91] Annette Leary said that Lynette loved her daughters, 'she was such a good mother'.[92] Ros McLoughlin said, 'She absolutely adored them. They were the light like, she really doted on her children and loved them very much and they were her priority in her life.'[93] Virginia Raisin said that as a mother, 'Lyn could not have been more loving. I mean she was so desperate for children. Absolutely desperate. And she showered all the love that she had.'[94]

Marilyn Dawson said, 'She was a loving mum. She was attentive. She did work when the children were very young, did go back to work, but she was, um, very happy to be a mum.'[95] Marilyn knew Lynette intimately – she was married to Chris Dawson's twin brother Paul and they lived only a few houses away. When she was asked how often Lynette had gone away without her daughters, she said, 'I don't think there were any times.'[96] Merilyn Simms said that Lynette 'was overjoyed' to be a mother. 'She was thrilled to bits.'[97]

The only dissenters were Peter Dawson, who described Lynette as a 'competent' mother,[98] and Paul Dawson, who allowed that she was 'a good mother'[99] but 'her children didn't need her as much as the children she cared for, she looked after'. Asked how he knew that, he said, 'Well, she told us.'[100]

Apart from the Dawson brothers, every other witness said that Lynette would never leave her children – or her husband for that matter. In an intercepted telephone call, Chris Dawson told his brother Gary that Lynette didn't think about the children at all when she disappeared. 'I don't see why I've got to have all the answers as to why she did this or why she did that. Okay, our marriage broke up, she took off.'[101]

Detective Sergeant Damian Loone

Four weeks into the trial, retired Detective Sergeant Damian Loone made his way into the Supreme Court. His strawberry blond hair was greying and his thinning shoulders didn't fill his black suit as they used to. It had been twenty-four years since he first opened Lynette Dawson's file.

Damian was one of the main planks of Chris Dawson's defence. The defence argued that from the beginning of his investigation, Damian had a fixed view that Chris Dawson had murdered Lynette and he ignored any evidence that didn't support his case theory. Pauline David put this allegation to him.

> Q. Do you agree that it is important to consider evidence even if it is inconsistent with your case theory?
>
> A. Yes.

Q. And your case theory in this case was that Lynette Dawson was dead, do you agree?

A. Yes.

Q. And your case theory was also that Christopher Dawson had killed her?

A. Yes.

Q. You were incapable, weren't you, officer, of looking or considering any evidence outside of that?

A. I disagree.

Q. Just coming to the issue of your capacity to look beyond your own case theory, do you agree that in your opinion you put no credence or . . . sorry, I withdraw 'opinion', that you put no credence on any suggestion that Mrs Dawson had been seen after 8 January 1982?

A. That's correct.

Q. So, again, you were incapable, weren't you, of looking beyond your own case theory?

A. No.[102]

Phillip Day and Helena Simms were the chief antagonist of the defence's attack on Damian. They had both died years before Chris Dawson was charged with murder. Nonetheless, they were two of the loudest voices in the trial.

Helena Simms and Phillip Day had separately told Damian that on 9 January 1982 they witnessed Chris Dawson being called to the Northbridge Baths office to take a telephone call. When he returned, he told them that the telephone call was from Lynette, who said she was going away for a few days. Damian took notes when he spoke to Helena Simms and Phillip Day but he didn't take a statement. Pauline David argued that Damian didn't take a statement from them because they corroborated Chris Dawson's version of events. But the context of Phillip and Helena being at Northbridge Baths was equally important.

Chris Dawson had asked Phillip to come to Northbridge Baths to talk about his marriage problems. On Friday afternoon, Phillip phoned Chris to confirm the plan to meet at Northbridge Baths the next day. Lynette answered the phone and she happily confirmed the plan. In one of the most disturbing details, when Lynette confirmed the plan with Phillip, she was, in fact, helping Chris dispose of her body.

Justice Harrison got to the heart of Phillip Day's important yet unwitting role.

> Phillip Day had been asked by Mr Dawson to be at the Northbridge Baths so that he could talk to him about his marital difficulties. It might in those circumstances have been expected that Phillip Day would recount that Mr Dawson told him that he had been in a sexual relationship with the babysitter which had caused some tension in his marriage; that he and the babysitter had left to go to Queensland; that they had come back but not attended Christmas with his wife and their children, instead staying in bed at his brother's place with JC; that he did not spend time with his wife and children on New Year's Eve, instead preferring the company of that same teenage girl and that these were the problems that he had.
>
> On the contrary, Mr Day said that he did not learn about JC until sometime later. On the Crown case, this supports the contention that Mr Day's presence at the pool was to facilitate

> Mr Dawson's opportunity to be free of his parental responsibilities on the evening of 9 January 1982.[103]

Justice Harrison also noted that in leaving Northbridge Baths with Helena and the girls, Phillip was the last person to see Chris Dawson that day.

> Apart from the evidence to suggest that Mr Dawson took Lynette Dawson to Mona Vale on the morning of 9 January 1982, which I reject, nothing is known about what Mr Dawson did that day. No one has given evidence of seeing or speaking to Mr Dawson on the night of 9 January 1982. No person has given evidence about seeing him later that day or night.[104]

Phillip Day was such an integral part of Chris Dawson's plan that I have often wondered what he would have done if Phillip had become sick overnight and had to cancel the plan to come to Northbridge Baths. Or if he had an accident on the way. Did Chris Dawson have a plan b?

Damian Loone's failure to take a statement from Helena Simms was largely rectified by her diaries and, to a lesser degree, by the follow-up profile that the police requested. Helena asked Lynette's sister, Pat Jenkins, to destroy her diaries after she died. Pat herself is a letter writer and, faithful to the potential of words, she saw the capacity for Helena's diaries to be something bigger, if Chris Dawson was ever charged with Lynette's murder.

With the restraint of her generation, Helena's diaries charted her confusion and heartache for her lost daughter. In short no-fuss entries, Helena meticulously logged the dates and each piece of 'news' that Chris Dawson gave her about Lynette.

Justice Harrison was riveted by Helena's diaries as powerful documentary evidence.

> Helena Simms was also never interviewed but her contribution has been somewhat extraordinarily documented in her prolific diaries and letters that give what might be characterised as a real-time commentary on events as she perceived them at the time. These have been received as evidence in this trial as well.[105]

Helena recorded that the night before she disappeared, Lynette was angry with the children, and she speculated that this uncharacteristic breakdown could explain why she left the next day. The defence wanted to rely on Mrs Simms's diary note to corroborate Lynette's breakdown, which by inference, could explain why Lynette left. Justice Harrison rejected Helena's dairy note as corroborative because 'the only source of that evidence is Mr Dawson, who would appear to have passed it on to Mrs Simms'.[106]

Several months after Lynette disappeared, the police requested that Helena Simms and Chris Dawson provide a follow-up missing person's profile. Helena's handwritten profile, dated 21 August 1982, put the problems with the 'babysitter' front and centre. Towards the end of her profile, she wrote: 'Until recently I have held my son in law in high esteem + got along well with him but my faith has been shaken when for all his talk of wanting me to look after his 2 little girls, Lyn "goes" + he has introduced the teenager back into the home as early as Feb 6, that I heard of it.'[107]

Helena's updated profile tells a different story to the one Chris Dawson was telling about his wife who had deserted him.

Damian Loone convened two coronial inquests into Lynette's disappearance. The coroner at each inquest referred the matter to the DPP with a recommendation that charges should be laid. The DPP refused on both occasions. Justice Harrison concluded:

> Even accepting Mr Dawson's contention that Detective Loone had formed a view that Mr Dawson had killed his wife, and consciously went out of his way to ignore evidence that may have assisted him, the assembling of only inculpatory material was not considered sufficient to charge Mr Dawson before the brief left Detective Loone's supervision or for some years thereafter.[108]

Detective Senior Constable Daniel Poole

On the day that Chris Dawson was arrested, then New South Wales Police Commissioner Mick Fuller held a press conference and praised Detective Senior Constable Daniel Poole, who had taken charge of Lynette's file in 2015: 'Over the next three years, Detective Dan Poole has worked tirelessly gathering evidence, preparing a brief of evidence.'[109] In April 2018, the brief was submitted to the DPP, and in December 2018, Chris Dawson was charged with murder.

As a witness, Daniel Poole was even-tempered and, if not reticent, economic with his answers. Pauline David queried the reliability of witnesses: *The Teacher's Pet* touched everyone. Daniel had advised Greg, Merilyn and Pat that he would prefer that they didn't participate in *The Teacher's Pet*. Hedley Thomas had also contacted him, and he declined to be involved in the podcast. However, he did take advantage of the podcast to intercept Dawson family telephone conversations that might have been stimulated by issues raised in the podcast. This was done without the cooperation or knowledge of Hedley Thomas. He agreed that he had concerns about witnesses who spoke to Hedley Thomas, or appeared on *The Teacher's Pet*. He also had concerns that witnesses who heard or read about the evidence of other witnesses were susceptible to 'unconscious bias' and 'contamination'.

The real test of witness bias or contamination was to test their evidence in court. And Craig Everson told the court that most of the witnesses had given statements many years before *The Teacher's Pet*.

In 2015, Daniel Poole located Chris Dawson's 17 August 1982 handwritten profile, which he had headed 'antecedent report'. The 'antecedent report' is the companion to Helena's profile dated 21 August 1982. It was a critical piece of evidence.

In Chris Dawson's 1991 police interview, he told the detectives that he was being advised by friends and acquaintances who were police officers, and Damian's view is that one of them mentioned the term 'antecedent report', which Chris Dawson adopted to throw suspicions off him by speaking in terms that the police would readily accept. The antecedent report had been referred to in other documents over the years but the report itself was lost before Damian Loone began his investigation. Chris Dawson's antecedent report told a different story to the missing-person report he made six weeks after Lynette disappeared and was different again to the video-recorded interview he gave to detectives in 1991.

There had been few challenges to Chris Dawson's version of events in the days and months after Lynette disappeared, so when he was invited to the police station for an interview, perhaps he thought that he could give the detectives ho-hum answers that would go unchallenged. And in a way he was right. After the interview nothing happened, despite the detectives putting the allegation of murder to him directly. Twenty-one years later, that interview was played in court.

On the wall-mounted television monitor, a much younger Chris Dawson was beamed into court and gave life to the listless seventy-three-year-old man who shuffled into court each day. In 1991, he was still athletically slim, with a head of thick blond hair; he was forty-four-years-old but looked ten years younger. In a bare police interview room, Chris Dawson was slumped in a plastic chair, his long legs stretched out in front of him. It was a posture of boredom that changed as the interview progressed. Detectives queried some of the dates he gave them which conflicted with the dates he'd given in his missing person report on 18 February 1982 and in his handwritten 'antecedent report' six months later. He was circling around, trying to patch up holes. They also confronted him with some of the allegations that JC had made in the statement she gave to the police in 1990, a few months after she left him.

Although Chris Dawson wasn't cautioned until question 124, Justice Harrison noted, 'Mr Dawson was legally represented.' A curious aspect of the 1991 interview was that until the interview was wrapping up, Chris Dawson's solicitor sat quietly next to him. In the transcript of the interview, his solicitor was recorded as 'Pauline Davey' and also 'Pauline Davies'. It was now apparent that these were typos and his solicitor was Pauline David, who was now a barrister and representing him in Court 9D at his murder trial.

CHAPTER TWENTY-ONE

The day's long verdict

THE TECHNICAL LEGAL LANGUAGE OF THE JUDGMENT WAS NOT always easy to understand, and the circular consideration of the evidence was not always easy to follow. By late afternoon, Greg and Merilyn's nerves were raw.

Not far into the judgment, Justice Harrison considered Peter Breese's evidence that he saw Lynette working as a nurse at Rockcastle Hospital, where Mr Breese had a surgical procedure, two and a half years after Lynette disappeared. Justice Harrison observed that, 'The Breeses' evidence must also be assessed by reference to the general unreliability of identification evidence and to the other circumstantial material in this case that supports an inference that Lynette Dawson was dead by no later than 9 January 1982.'[110]

There was a long way to go, but from that moment I knew Justice Harrison had found Chris Dawson guilty.

Justice Harrison catalogued the lies Chris Dawson told during the 1991 police interview:

> In answer to question 10, Mr Dawson told the police that he travelled north for a few days for 'time away from home' but failed to mention that he did so in the company of JC. However, that omission is corrected in his answer to question 17. He told the police that 'after marriage guidance for a few days Lyn seemed . . . disturbed by the results of that'. The reference to 'a few days' is not correct as Lynette Dawson disappeared the following day . . . I have already found that Mr Dawson did not receive a phone call from Lynette Dawson at the Northbridge Baths or at any time thereafter, contrary to his representations to the police. Mr Dawson was also not 'for the remaining period after twelve months . . . constantly in touch with . . . people . . . to try and find and locate where Lyn was'.[111]
>
> Mr Dawson said in answer to question 14 that he received a phone call from his wife 'several days after the first phone calls'. I have found that Mr Dawson did not receive such calls.[112]
>
> In answer to question 19, Mr Dawson said that on his return from Queensland with JC, he did not go to his brother Paul's place but 'went to [his] place'. That is not correct.[113]
>
> In answer to question 21, Mr Dawson said that JC telephoned him from South West Rocks 'and asked [him] if she, would she like to come back, more or less I think she wanted to get away from South West Rocks and all'. Question and answer 196 was to a similar effect:
>
> 'Q196. And ah tell me this, whose instigation was it for you to give [*sic*] up to South West Rocks and pick [JC] up?

A. [JC's] instigation. There was no way I could have contacted. She, she contacted me and asked if I could come, and, I, I drove up through the night and met her the following morning.'

I consider those answers to be untruthful.[114]

Mr Dawson said in answer to question 23 that he drove to South West Rocks to collect JC 'probably about a week or so after'. In answer to question 24, Mr Dawson curiously gives the unsolicited answer that 'I doubt very much it wasn't the day after'. In answer to question 28, Mr Dawson said that it 'would probably be correct' to say that he drove up on Saturday 16 January 1982. I have found that that is not correct.[115]

Mr Dawson's answer to question 31 was as follows:

'Um, the first phone call. And then after that I was in contact with [Mrs Simms], telling her . . . well I, I rang her to see if she had heard from Lyn and we were in contact for a while. Then when [JC] moved in to live with me, obviously her mother for family reasons um, obviously she stopped contacting me for further information and was um, naturally feeling antagonistic towards me . . . marriage breakdown.'

To the extent that Mr Dawson's answer indicates, as I consider it does, that JC did not immediately move in to live with him at Gilwinga Drive upon their return from South West Rocks, it is incorrect.[116]

Mr Dawson said . . . that he 'was very anxious for Lyn to come back to us to work things out'.[117]

In answer to question 88, Mr Dawson said that he had received 'several phone calls' from Lynette Dawson. I have already rejected that evidence as a lie.[118]

Finally, the following questions should also be noted:

'Q197. How um, at that time how often ah, were you in phone contact with her?
A. With [JC]?
Q198. Ah hmm.
A. Um, that was probably the first phone call from South West Rocks . . . so, probably I hadn't heard from [JC] for a week or so.
Q199. So what, you didn't have daily contact?
A. Not by memory, no.
Q200. [JC] alleges that at the time that you were speaking together on the phone every single day.
A. Was I ringing her?
Q201. Well, she says that you were phoning. But ah, regardless of who was doing the phoning, did you have phone contact?
A. Not by memory, no. As I said, I might have had one phone call four or five days prior to her starting her holiday but I think the only phone call prior to that was the fact that I obviously, [JC] was going to have time up with her sister and father and I assume she was coming, whenever she did return she was going back to the family home and as far as we were both concerned, our relationship had finished. And at the next phone call I had was when she asked me if I could come and bring her back down because she wanted to come back sooner.'

I do not accept that Mr Dawson considered that the relationship 'had finished'.[119]

By 4.45 pm, normal sitting hours had passed and outside it was getting dark. Justice Harrison asked the court staff if they could stay on. Who could refuse a man who had worked so hard and was delivering a decision that would grant someone his liberty or see him die in jail?

Throughout the reading, Justice Harrison leaned forward on his red-robed forearms, which he pressed together by a hand above each elbow. In the final moments his grip tightened, his eyes darted towards Chris Dawson. Two sheriffs entered the court. Peter Dawson placed a hand on his brother's shoulder.

> The circumstantial evidence in this case, considered as a whole, is persuasive and compelling. None of the circumstances considered alone can establish Mr Dawson's guilt but when regard is had to their combined force I am left in no doubt.
>
> I am satisfied beyond reasonable doubt that the only rational inference that the circumstances enable me to draw is that Lynette Dawson died on or about 8 January 1982 as the result of a conscious and voluntary act committed by Mr Dawson with the intention of causing her death.
>
> I am satisfied beyond reasonable doubt that the Crown has proved the single count in the indictment.
>
> Christopher Michael Dawson, on the charge that on or about 8 January 1982 at Bayview or elsewhere in the State of New South Wales you did murder Lynette Joy Dawson, I find you guilty.[120]

Chris Dawson was handcuffed as Justice Harrison pronounced his guilt. At the same moment cheers erupted from Banco Court, where the overflow of the public watched proceedings on the live feed.

The sun was setting as Lynette's family and friends emerged from court. Greg and Merilyn faced the media from the top of the Supreme Court steps. For Lynette, Greg wore a pink shirt, while

Merilyn, family and friends wore pink ribbons. Greg held back tears as he read from notes to the waiting media.

'I'm a little bit emotional. After forty years my sister's been vindicated.

'Chris Dawson took the life of our beloved Lyn back in 1982.

'Our journey is not complete. She is still missing. We still need to bring her home. We would ask Chris Dawson to find it in himself, to finally do the decent thing and allow us to bring Lyn home to a peaceful rest.

'From now on, we would like her to be known as Lynette Joy Simms.

'We can now go back to try and live our own lives.'

Merilyn also spoke. Their daughter Renee stepped in, too. She smiled and fielded media questions calmly, even giving a cheeky reply. She looked up at Greg often, her rosy cheeks and gentle smile reassuring her father, who was rigid and, I thought, visibly withdrawing.

CHAPTER TWENTY-TWO

The sentence

ON THE MORNING OF THE SENTENCING SUBMISSIONS, I MET GREG and Merilyn at the Radisson Hotel in the city for a coffee. It had been three months since the verdict and I looked forward to seeing a more relaxed Greg, the one that I knew before the trial. But as he drank his coffee, the effort to speak or keep up the final push seemed almost too much.

We walked to court together, and as we stepped out of the lift Greg Walsh thrust his hand at Greg Simms, and gave him a vigorous shake and congratulations, as if they had just contested a rugby match. Later, Greg told me that he didn't want to shake the hand of the man who had defended Chris Dawson.

A lot of familiar faces were in court. Damian Loone, Daniel Poole, Pat's son David, journalists, Lynette's friends. Chris Dawson's eldest daughter arrived and was seated with a friend at the bar table.

At 12.05 pm Chris Dawson arrived through a side door, wearing a thick green tracksuit. A convicted murderer, he sat inside a glass-encased dock. He was in the right place now, yet it was still confronting. Justice Harrison arrived. He warned that these were 'solemn and serious' proceedings and he would not tolerate inappropriate behaviour. Justice Harrison did not want a repeat of the cheers that had erupted from the Banco Court when he pronounced Chris Dawson guilty three months earlier.

There are statutory sentencing guidelines to consider. Did the prisoner make a guilty plea? Was the victim a child? Did the murder occur in a domestic setting? The Crown and Greg Walsh addressed these in their written submissions. Having defended Dawson's innocence for four years, Greg Walsh now had to accept the verdict.

Written submissions were handed up to the judge.

Greg Simms had written a victim impact statement and requested that, as is permissible, a support person read it for him.

'You were accepted into our family unconditionally when you married Lyn. You were accepted as a new son for my parents and a brother for Phil, Pat and me. We considered you an equal in all respects. You repaid us by committing the ultimate betrayal.

'The absence of Lyn in our lives has left a huge hole that can never be replaced. The heartache, tears, anxiety and emptiness has been constant since you carried out your foul deed by committing your foul deed.

'I am anxious, lost my confidence, find it difficult to breathe, I question everything I do and think it's not good enough . . . I used to be a good sleeper but am now restless . . .

'Our brother Phil died and was not able to be a part of these proceedings . . . unable to finally hear that you were convicted.

'You kept my mother thinking Lyn was going to ring, you denied her contact with her two grandchildren . . . it was the lowest of low.'[121]

Chris Dawson's eldest daughter stepped forward to make her statement. She bolstered herself with a few audible breaths. Chris Dawson looked at her briefly: his stern features suddenly lost composure. But he quickly recovered and looked down and didn't look up at her again.

'All these years there were always parts of me looking for her in communes, consulting psychics, registering with the Salvation Army, haunted by regular thoughts of "Why did she leave, where is she, when will she return?"

'Until the day I realised she wasn't going to.

'You took that away and so much more and you had NO RIGHT to. YOU ARE NOT GOD.'

Still Chris Dawson did not look up, even as she sat looking at him for a long and uncomfortable moment, willing him to look at her.

On 2 December 2022, three weeks after the sentencing submissions, Justice Harrison handed down the sentence. Walking up Phillip Street, I crossed the driveway where Chris Dawson would be delivered from Silverwater Correctional Complex securely into the court complex. In Queen's Square, Greg Walsh and Peter Dawson sat drinking a coffee in front of St James's Church. The media hovered in the square.

Upstairs in Court 13A, the seats filled quickly. Damian Loone arrived and we chatted. I noticed Sue Strath come in and sit at the end of the row.

Greg and Merilyn arrived and moved with ease in a place that had once been foreign. Greg and I raised a hand to each other, and Merilyn leaned over and gave me a kiss.

At 11.58 am, the door behind the dock opened and Chris Dawson took his place. He looked over to his brother Peter sitting at the bar table with Greg Walsh and gave him a feeble, close-mouthed smile. Every time Chris Dawson entered the court, the stakes went up. Having eluded accountability for so long, he looked disbelieving of his fate. I too had moments of disbelief. It was impossible to watch him on this precipice and not try to guess at his state of mind. My guess was that he'd be asking questions. *What is the point of sending me to jail now? What difference is it going to make to anyone now?*

At 12 pm, the judge's associate announced: 'The King and Christopher Michael Dawson.' Justice Harrison began.

From the dock, Chris Dawson kept a weak but steady gaze on the judge. Deprivation of liberty is the only appropriate sanction for murder, but it is still a brutal end of the justice system.

Justice Harrison told the court that Chris Dawson's state of mind when he murdered Lynette would be reflected in the sentence: that Chris Dawson intended to kill Lynette Dawson; it wasn't spontaneous; he concealed the location of Lynette's body; he killed her in a domestic setting, in her home; he continued to maintain his innocence; and he continued to show no signs of remorse.

Justice Harrison noted that the victim impact statements reflected the 'painful uncertainty' of not knowing what happened to Lynette. His sentence would be the same without them. Justice Harrison said that the defence submissions indicated that Chris Dawson suffered depression and some cognitive impairment, which a brain scan showed was most likely early-stage dementia, and that the publicity from *The Teacher's Pet* podcast had resulted in vilification in jail. But Justice Harrison was not moved.

> Mr Dawson is not old by contemporary standards but the reality is that he will not live to reach the end of his non-parole period or by reason of his deteriorating cognitive condition and physical capacity, become seriously disabled well before then even if he does . . . I recognise the unavoidable prospect is that Mr Dawson will probably die in gaol.
>
> Please stand, Mr Dawson.
>
> Christopher Michael Dawson, for the murder of Lynette Dawson on or about 8 January 1982, I sentence you to imprisonment for 24 years commencing 30 August 2022 and expiring on 29 August 2046 with a non-parole period of 18 years expiring of 29 August 2040. The first day upon which you will become eligible for parole is therefore 30 August 2040.[122]

After a word of advice to Chris Dawson about his rights as a high-risk offender, Justice Harrison told him to leave with the corrective services officers. Chris Dawson turned quickly and put his hand on the doorhandle at the back of the dock. My blood pressure shot up because I knew that he was no longer free to decide when to open a door and feared that he was going to be physically subdued, but the corrective services officers quickly stepped in and told him to take his hand away.

Justice Harrison left the courtroom.

Almost four years to the day since Chris Dawson was charged with murder, the trial was over.

There were smiles, hugs, and congratulations. Greg Walsh interrupted my conversation with Greg Simms to give him another vigorous one-sided handshake. I wondered if Greg Walsh's compulsion to shake his hand was meant to convey that it was the right verdict. Or perhaps I read too much into it. By the end of the trial, Greg Walsh looked intermittently exhausted and angry; he had represented Chris Dawson with distinction for four years. A few weeks before the trial finished, Pauline David was sworn in as a District Court judge; she didn't attend the sentencing hearings.

Daniel Poole put his detective hat aside and joined the bonhomie. Danny Doherty, the New South Wales homicide squad commander had come to court along with Detective John Lehmann, who I'd spoken to some years earlier. And Damian Loone accepted a stream of congratulations.

Half an hour after court finished, the remaining group showed no signs of leaving the courtroom, and a court attendant eventually herded us outside. The group began to drift away. I gave Greg and Merilyn and Damian a kiss goodbye and I got the lift down to the ground floor of the Supreme Court building for the last time.

CHAPTER TWENTY-THREE

All over

IN THE MONTHS AFTER THE TRIAL FINISHED, GREG'S EXHAUSTION stayed with me. I worried about his recovery and what lay beyond fighting for Lynette.

Damian Loone had retired to the North Coast of New South Wales, and I flew up to see him. We ate lunch in a restaurant by the river and Damian's wife, Rachel, joined us. They hadn't been married very long – another happiness in his life.

Not long after the trial finished, Damian Loone and others, particularly Bev McNally who had been a babysitter for the Dawson's and who gave evidence at the trial, successfully lobbied for 'No Body, No Parole' legislation, informally referred to as 'Lyn's Law'.

'I wanted to do the no-body, no-parole stuff for a while,' Damian said. 'I got in touch with someone who put me through to someone at the A-G. It was debated in Parliament,' he said, his eyes widening at the speed with which the legislation was passed. 'Couldn't believe it! I could have more impact now that I'm outside the system!'

We talked about the trial – what had been proven, the things that were discounted, the things about Chris Dawson that still made us squirm. When we came to something we didn't agree with or that wasn't resolved, we narrowed our eyes at each other, as if we could communicate telepathically. Hedley and I do the same thing. It's hard to put it away.

'It was all there, already,' Damian said.

'It was all there,' I said, opening my hands towards him as if to say, you told them. 'He could have been convicted in 1982. But maybe the world wasn't ready then? You know, before "#MeToo", before domestic violence was fully recognised.'

'Na,' Damian said, his frustration still there. 'It could have been done.'

'Well, it certainly should have been done when you got two inquests, two referrals to the DPP.'

'It's not about me,' he said, but I cut him off.

'Damian, you fought for Lynette Dawson for *years*, and you were right. How is it that others who should have seen it, didn't? Why did the DPP knock it back twice?' I asked him rhetorically, imploring him to acknowledge that any failures were not his.

'I hope he doesn't get off on appeal,' he said.

'Kerry Whelan, Keli Lane didn't,' I said, naming the other big circumstantial murder convictions. 'I think Harrison made sure his judgment is watertight.'

'I hope so,' he said.

Hedley and I met for lunch at Icebergs at Bondi Beach, where our work and friendship had begun. We had a table by the window with a mesmerising view out to sea. When we'd started out, we'd had similar worries about our kids but we now happily reported that they were all doing well. We riled each other over politics for a bit but we spent most of the five-hour lunch raking over the trial, the evidence, and the gaps that would most likely never be known. And we went over our beginning – the podcast, the people we met, the good and tough and sometimes chaotic times, the improbability of it all.

'I couldn't have done it without you, Hazel,' he said warmly. 'I mean it.'

If Hedley opens his long arms to you, it's a warm embrace. Lynette Dawson had brought us together in this very place. Now, just a few kilometres south of where we were having lunch, Chris Dawson was in Long Bay jail on the headland above Little Bay.

On the way home, I thought about all of the lives upended. Chris Dawson couldn't conceive of other lives and other needs, not even his own daughters. Or JC. Forty years on, his grandchildren are reckoning with a grandfather jailed because he murdered their grandmother. On and on.

In the course of writing this book I learned a lot about Lynette's life and her marriage, I got to know her family. Lynette loved her husband, and she loved her daughters who brought her a joy she never thought she'd have. She held her family together, her parents, brothers and sister, their partners and their children. It was at her house that they gathered for barbeques and birthdays; the Dawsons too. She was generous and joyful, and she wanted everyone to share her almost perfect life. Every day, she told her colleagues something new about her daughters. Every week, she and the girls would meet up with her mother. And they would speak on the phone more often than that. I learned that Lynette would not have walked away.

Each year, more than 35,000 people go missing in Australia – one every fifteen minutes. At last count, mid-2023, 2500 people are missing long term, that is, for more than three months. On average, one woman a week is murdered by her current or former partner.

When I got home after lunch with Hedley, I sent Detective Poole an email: 'I just checked the National Missing Persons Register and Lynette's name is still there. Would it be the family or the police who make the notification that Lynette's status has changed?'

Postscript

On 28 June 2023, after Chris Dawson faced a judge-alone trial in the New South Wales District Court, where he pleaded not guilty to one count of carnal knowledge of a girl aged between ten and seventeen, he was found guilty of the historical sex offence of carnal knowledge.

Notes

Quotes from the inquest have been reproduced from the transcript of the *inquest into the death of Lynette Joy Dawson*, V5795 40/03 RC–A1, 24–28 February 2003.

1 'Shocked neighbours plan Christmas get-together after deaths of reclusive couple', *Sydney Morning Herald*, 18 December 2012.
2 Margaret Harrison, Australian Institute of Family Studies, Australian Family Briefings No. 2, *Family Law and Marriage Breakdown in Australia*, 1993.
3 'Inquest told of teacher twins' sex with pupils', *Courier-Mail*, 26 February 2003.
4 'Relentless cop's DNA quest in cardigan killer case', *Daily Telegraph*, 23 May 2009.
5 'DNA link found in missing persons case of mother Lynette Dawson', *Daily Telegraph*, 26 July 2010.
6 'Teachers deny seducing students', *Courier-Mail*, 10 March 2001.
7 'Teacher Peter Wayne Scott sentenced to jail for sexually abusing teenage boys', *Sydney Morning Herald*, 2 May 2014.

8 'Why three women made the tough decision to leave their children', *Sydney Morning Herald*, 17 March 2018.

9 Monika Henderson, Peter Henderson and Carol Kiernan, 'Missing persons: incidence, issues and impacts', *Trends & issues in crime and criminal justice*, no. 144, Canberra: Australian Institute of Criminology, aic.gov.au/publications/tandi/tandi144, 2000.

10 Lyn Richards, 'Suburbia: domestic dreaming' in Johnson, Louise (ed.), *Suburban Dreaming: An Interdisciplinary Approach to Australian Cities*, Deakin University Press, 1994.

11 '"Body in Bush" tip: Body in bush, says medium', *Manly Daily*, 11 October 2003.

12 'Dead men do tell tales after all, says clairvoyant Debbie Malone', *Daily Telegraph*, 30 May 2009.

13 'Lynette Dawson – Painting a picture of a woman murdered', *Daily Telegraph*, 24 April 2013.

14 FAQ: Family and Friends of Missing Persons Unit (FFMPU), missingpersons.justice.nsw.gov.au/Pages/missingpersons/ffmpu_faq.aspx

15 'Murder probe starts almost 50 years after Judith Bartlett disappeared', *Australian*, 27 May 2013.

16 *The Teacher's Pet*: Chris Dawson arrives in Sydney as it's revealed former student love to be key witness, *Australian*, 6 December 2018.

17 AAP video, 6 December 2018.

18 '*The Teacher's Pet* podcast may have "contaminated" evidence in Dawson trial', 14 February 2019, *Sydney Morning Herald*.

19 'Diary "critical" to helping Chris Dawson beat murder charge, says lawyer', ABC News, 14 February 2019.

20 *R v Dawson* [2020] NSWSC 1221 [443].

21 Ibid [444].

22 *R v Dawson* [2022] NSWSC 552 [46].

23 Ibid [33].

24 *R v Dawson* [2022] NSWSC 555 [10].

25 Ibid [11].

26 'Chris Dawson murder trial: Dawson proceedings "all over the shop"', *Australian*, 7 July 2022.

27 'Chris Dawson trial: Dawson "could have loved two women at the same time": Defence', *Australian*, 8 July 2022.

28 'Chris Dawson murder trial: Dawson proceedings "all over the shop"', *Australian*, 7 July 2022.

29 'And so it ends, not with a bang but a flu-ridden cough', *Australian*, 11 July 2022.
30 *R v Dawson* [2022] NSWSC 1131 [1].
31 Ibid [18].
32 Ibid [13].
33 Ibid [480].
34 AAP, 18 May 2022.
35 *R v Dawson* [2022] NSWSC 1131 [233]
36 'Dawson "wanted to disguise who he was: babysitter begins evidence"', *Australian*, 18 May 2022.
37 *R v Dawson* [2022] NSWSC 1131 [737].
38 Ibid [430].
39 Ibid [432].
40 Ibid [727].
41 '"He'll destroy himself . . . I'm telling the truth": defence accuses JC of lying', *Australian*, 19 May 2022.
42 Ibid.
43 'Housekeeper, sex slave, stepmother, babysitter: JC's life after Lyn disappeared', *Australian*, 19 May 2022.
44 'Chris Dawson's former student tells court she wanted his missing wife to come back', *Guardian*, 20 May 2022.
45 *R v Dawson* [2020] NSWSC 1221 [409].
46 Ibid [413].
47 Ibid [416–7].
48 'Dawson spoke with 'venom' about Lyn: brother', *Australian*, 18 May 2022.
49 '"Black eyes flashing": Lynette Dawson spoke of Chris' rage', sister says, *Sydney Morning Herald*, 17 May 2022.
50 'Chris Dawson murder trial live updates', *Australian*, 17 May 2022.
51 *R v Dawson* [2022] NSWSC 1131 [499].
52 Ibid.
53 Ibid [494].
54 Ibid [501].
55 Ibid [89].
56 Ibid [94].
57 Ibid [106].
58 Ibid [97].
59 Ibid [101].

60 Ibid [99].
61 Ibid [100].
62 Ibid [108].
63 'Surprise witness at Chris Dawson trial claims he saw Lynette alive in 1982', Nine news online, 4 July 2022.
64 '"Oh yeah I've been to jail": Dawson witness', *Australian*, 4 July 2022.
65 '"It was her, 100 per cent": Bombshell witnesses tell of Lynette Dawson sighting', news.com.au, 4 July, 2022'
66 *R v Dawson* [2022] NSWSC 1131 [140].
67 Ibid [372].
68 Ibid [374].
69 Ibid [374].
70 Ibid [375].
71 Ibid [381].
72 Ibid [383].
73 Ibid [387].
74 Ibid [576].
75 Ibid.
76 Ibid [291].
77 Ibid [450].
78 Ibid [454].
79 Ibid [468–469].
80 Ibid [545].
81 Ibid [326].
82 Ibid.
83 Ibid [252].
84 Ibid [295].
85 Ibid [296].
86 Ibid [314].
87 Ibid [736].
88 Ibid [756].
89 Ibid [240].
90 Ibid [267].
91 Ibid. [269].
92 Ibid [270].
93 Ibid [271].
94 Ibid [272].

95 Ibid [275].
96 Ibid.
97 Ibid [276].
98 Ibid [252].
99 Ibid.
100 Ibid [314].
101 Ibid [726]
102 Ibid [649].
103 Ibid [735].
104 Ibid [736].
105 Ibid [635].
106 Ibid [317].
107 Ibid [704].
108 Ibid [658].
109 'How Senior Constable Daniel Poole's work uncovered new leads which led to Chris Dawson's sensational arrest', news.com.au, 8 December 2018.
110 *R v Dawson* [2022] NSWSC 1131 [126].
111 Ibid [608].
112 Ibid [610].
113 Ibid [611].
114 Ibid [612]–[613].
115 Ibid [615].
116 Ibid [616]–[617].
117 Ibid [618].
118 Ibid [623].
119 Ibid [625]–[626].
120 Ibid [756]–[759].
121 Victim impact statements from Lyn Dawson's family, *Australian*, 10 November 2022.
122 *R v Dawson* [2022] NSWSC 1632 [37]–[38].

Acknowledgements

My heartfelt thanks and admiration go to JC, Greg and Merilyn Simms, Damian Loone, Pat Jenkins, Carl Milovanovich. I also thank the many people who generously spoke to me.

Thank you to Meredith Curnow, Genevieve Buzo, Emma Schwarz and Alison Arnold.

My affection and thanks go to Malcolm Knox, Anna Funder, Wenona Byrne, Julian Short, Teresa Hazel, Gus Hazel, Mandy Chambers and Peter Rozen. And special thanks to Hedley Thomas.

Above all, I thank Harry, Max, Greta and Seb.

Resources

If anything in this book has raised concerns for you, you can contact the helplines below or visit these websites:

1800RESPECT
Confidential information, counselling and support for domestic, family and sexual violence
1800respect.org.au
1800 737 732

Bravehearts
An Australian child protection organisation dedicated to the prevention and treatment of child sexual abuse
bravehearts.org.au
1800 272 831

Family Advocacy and Support Services
Legal advice at court for domestic and family violence
24/7 crisis line 180 737 732
familyviolencelaw.gov.au

GriefLine

Support for anyone experiencing grief

griefline.org.au

1300 845 745

NSW Domestic Violence Line

For counselling and referrals if you are experiencing or fleeing domestic violence

1800 65 64 63

Relationships Australia

Relationship support services for individuals, families and communities

relationships.org.au

1300 364 277

Salvation Army

Offers advice to anyone enduring family and domestic violence on how to get help and support

Salvationarmy.org.au/need-help/family-and-domestic-violence

Women's Domestic Violence Court Advocacy Service

Advice in local courts for Apprehended Domestic Violence Orders, family and financial law, and referrals

1800 888 529

legalaid.[state]gov.au